Free Software, Free Society:
Selected Essays of Richard M. Stallman

Happy Hacking

Richard Stallman

Introduction by Lawrence Lessig

Edited by Joshua Gay

GNU Press
www.gnupress.org
Free Software Foundation
Boston, MA USA

First printing, first edition.
Copyright © 2002 Free Software Foundation, Inc.

ISBN 1-882114-98-1
Published by the Free Software Foundation
59 Temple Place
Boston, MA Tel: 1-617-542-5942
Fax: 1-617-542-2652
Email: gnu@gnu.org
Web: www.gnu.org

GNU Press is an imprint of the FSF.
Email: press@gnu.org
Web: www.gnupress.org
Please contact the GNU Press for information regarding bulk purchases for class-room or user group use, reselling, or any other questions or comments.

Original artwork by Etienne Suvasa. Cover design by Jonathan Richard.

Table of Contents

Editor's Note

The waning days of the 20th century seemed like an Orwellian nightmare: laws preventing publication of scientific research on software; laws preventing sharing software; an overabundance of software patents preventing development; and end-user license agreements that strip the user of all freedoms—including ownership, privacy, sharing, and understanding how their software works. This collection of essays and speeches by Richard M. Stallman addresses many of these issues. Above all, Stallman discusses the philosophy underlying the free software movement. This movement combats the oppression of federal laws and evil end-user license agreements in hopes of spreading the idea of software freedom.

With the force of hundreds of thousands of developers working to create GNU software and the GNU/Linux operating system, free software has secured a spot on the servers that control the Internet, and—as it moves into the desktop computer market—is a threat to Microsoft and other proprietary software companies.

These essays cater to a wide audience; you do not need a computer science background to understand the philosophy and ideas herein. However, there is a "Note on Software," to help the less technically inclined reader become familiar with some common computer science jargon and concepts, as well as footnotes throughout.

Many of these essays have been updated and revised from their originally published version. Each essay carries permission to redistribute verbatim copies.

The ordering of the essays is fairly arbitrary, in that there is no required order to read the essays in, for they were written independently of each other over a period of 18 years. The first section, "The GNU Project and Free Software," is intended to familiarize you with the history and philosophy of free software and the GNU project. Furthermore, it provides a road map for developers, educators, and business people to pragmatically incorporate free software into society, business, and life. The second section, "Copyright, Copyleft, and Patents," discusses the philosophical and political groundings of the copyright and patent system and how it has changed over the past couple of hundred years. Also, it discusses how the current laws and regulations for patents and copyrights are not in the best interest of the consumer and end user of software, music, movies, and other media. Instead, this section discusses how laws are geared towards helping business and government crush your freedoms. The third section, "Freedom, Society, and Software" continues the discussion of freedom and rights, and how they are being threatened by proprietary software, copyright law, globalization, "trusted computing," and other socially harmful rules, regulations, and policies. One way that industry and government are attempting to persuade people to give up certain rights and freedoms is by using terminology that implies that sharing information, ideas, and software is bad; therefore, we have included an essay explaining certain words that are confusing and should probably be avoided. The fourth section, "The Licenses," contains the GNU General Public License, the GNU Lesser General Public License, and the GNU Free Documentation License; the cornerstones of the GNU project.

If you wish to purchase this book for yourself, for classroom use, or for distribution, please write to the Free Software Foundation (FSF) at sales@fsf.org or visit http://order.fsf.org/. If you wish to help further the cause of software freedom, please considering donating to the FSF by visiting http://donate.fsf.org (or write to donations@fsf.org for more details). You can also contact the FSF by phone at +1-617-542-5942.

There are perhaps thousands of people who should be thanked for their contributions to the GNU Project; however, their names will never fit on any single list. Therefore, I wish to extend my thanks to all of those nameless hackers, as well as people who have helped promote, create, and spread free software around the world.

For helping make this book possible, I would like to thank:

Julie Sussman, P.P.A., for editing multiple copies at various stages of development, for writing the "Topic Guide," and for giving her insights into everything from commas to the ordering of the chapters;

Lisa (Opus) Goldstein and Bradley M. Kuhn for their help in organizing, proofreading, and generally making this collection possible;

Claire H. Avitabile, Richard Buckman, Tom Chenelle, and (especially) Stephen Compall for their careful proofreading of the entire collection;

Karl Berry, Bob Chassell, Michael Mounteney, and M. Ramakrishnan for their expertise in the helping to format and edit this collection in TEXinfo, (http://www.texinfo.org);

Mats Bengtsson for his help in formatting the Free Software Song in Lilypond (http://www.gnu.org/software/lilypond/);

Etienne Suvasa for the images that begin each section, and for all the art he has contributed to the Free Software Foundation over the years;

and Melanie Flanagan and Jason Polan for making helpful suggestions for the everyday reader. A special thanks to Bob Tocchio, from Paul's Transmission Repair, for his insight on automobile transmissions.

Also, I wish to thank my mother and father, Wayne and Jo-Ann Gay, for teaching me that one should live by the ideals that one stands for, and for introducing me, my two brothers, and three sisters to the importance of sharing.

Lastly and most importantly, I would like to extend my gratitude to Richard M. Stallman for the GNU philosophy, the wonderful software, and the literature that he has shared with the world.

Joshua Gay
josh@gnu.org

A Note on Software

This section is intended for people who have little or no knowledge of the technical aspects of computer science. It is not necessary to read this section to understand the essays and speeches presented in this book; however, it may be helpful to those readers not familar with some of the jargon that comes with programming and computer science.

A computer *programmer* writes software, or computer programs. A program is more or less a recipe with *commands* to tell the computer what to do in order to carry out certain tasks. You are more than likely familiar with many different programs: your Web browser, your word processor, your email client, and the like.

A program usually starts out as *source code*. This higher-level set of commands is written in a *programming language* such as C or Java. After that, a tool known as a *compiler* translates this to a lower-level language known as *assembly language*. Another tool known as an *assembler* breaks the assembly code down to the final stage of *machine language*—the lowest level—which the computer understands *natively*.

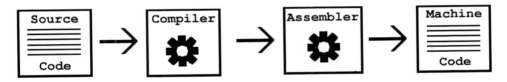

For example, consider the "hello world" program, a common first program for people learning C, which (when compiled and executed) prints "Hello World!" on the screen.[1]

```
int main(){
    printf(''Hello World!'');
    return 0;
}
```

In the Java programming language the same program would be written like this:

```
public class hello {
    public static void main(String args[]) {
        System.out.println(''Hello World!'');
    }
}
```

---

[1] In other programming languages, such as Scheme, the *Hello World* program is usually not your first program. In Scheme you often start with a program like this:

```
(define (factorial n)
   (if (= n 0)
      1
      (* n (factorial (- n 1)))))
```

This computes the factorial of a number; that is, running (factorial 5) would output 120, which is computed by doing 5 * 4 * 3 * 2 * 1 * 1.

However, in machine language, a small section of it may look similar to this:

```
110001111011101010010100100100101010101110
011010101001100000111100101101010101111101
010011111111111001011011000000010100100
0100100001100101011011000110110001101111
0010000001010111011011110111001001101100
0110010000100001010000100110111101101111
```

The above form of machine language is the most basic representation known as binary. All data in computers is made up of a series of 0-or-1 values, but a person would have much difficulty understanding the data. To make a simple change to the binary, one would have to have an intimate knowledge of how a particular computer interprets the machine language. This could be feasible for small programs like the above examples, but any interesting program would involve an exhausting effort to make simple changes.

As an example, imagine that we wanted to make a change to our "Hello World" program written in C so that instead of printing "Hello World" in English it prints it in French. The change would be simple; here is the new program:

```
int main() {
    printf(''Bonjour, monde!'');
    return 0;
}
```

It is safe to say that one can easily infer how to change the program written in the Java programming language in the same way. However, even many programmers would not know where to begin if they wanted to change the binary representation. When we say "source code," we do not mean machine language that only computers can understand—we are speaking of higher-level languages such as C and Java. A few other popular programming languages are C++, Perl, and Python. Some are harder than others to understand and program in, but they are all much easier to work with compared to the intricate machine language they get turned into after the programs are compiled and assembled.

Another important concept is understanding what an *operating system* is. An operating system is the software that handles input and output, memory allocation, and task scheduling. Generally one considers common or useful programs such as the *Graphical User Interface* (GUI) to be a part of the operating system. The GNU/Linux operating system contains a both GNU and non-GNU software, and a *kernel* called *Linux*. The kernel handles low-level tasks that applications depend upon such as input/output and task scheduling. The GNU software comprises much of the rest of the operating system, including GCC, a general-purpose compiler for many languages; GNU Emacs, an extensible text editor with many, many features; GNOME, the GNU desktop; GNU libc, a library that all programs other than the kernel must use in order to communicate with the kernel; and Bash, the GNU command interpreter that reads your command lines. Many of these programs were pioneered by Richard Stallman early on in the GNU Project and come with any modern GNU/Linux operating system.

It is important to understand that even if *you* cannot change the source code for a given program, or directly use all these tools, it is relatively easy to find someone who can. Therefore, by having the source code to a program you are usually given the power to change, fix, customize, and learn about a program—this is a power that you do not have if you are not given the source code. Source code is one of the requirements that makes a piece of software *free*. The other requirements will be found along with the philosophy and ideas behind them in this collection. Enjoy!

Richard E. Buckman
Joshua Gay

Topic Guide

Since the essays and speeches in this book were addressed to different audiences at different times, there is a considerable amount of overlap, with some issues being discussed in more than one place. Because of this, and because we did not have the opportunity to make an index for this book, it could be hard to go back to something you read about unless its location is obvious from a chapter title.

We hope that this short guide, though sketchy and incomplete (it does not cover all topics or all discussions of a given topic), will help you find some of the ideas and explanations you are interested in.

–Julie Sussman, P.P.A.

Overview

Chapter 1 gives an overview of just about all the software-related topics in this book. Chapter 20 is also an overview.

For the non-software topics, see Privacy and Personal Freedom, Intellectual Property, and Copyright, below.

GNU Project

For the history of the GNU project, see Chapters 1 and 20

For a delightful explanation of the origin and pronunciation of the recursive acronym GNU (GNU's Not Unix, pronounced guh-NEW), see Chapter 20.

The "manifesto" that launched the GNU Project is included here as Chapter 2.

See also the Linux, GNU/Linux topic below.

Free Software Foundation

You can read about the history and function of the Free Software Foundation in Chapters 1 and 20, and under "Funding Free Software" in Chapter 18.

Free software

We will not attempt to direct you to all discussions of free software in this book, since every chapter *except* 11, 12, 13, 16, 17, and 19 deals with free software.

For a history of free software—from free software to proprietary software and back again—see Chapter 1.

Free Software is defined, and the definition discussed, in Chapter 3. The definition is repeated in several other chapters.

For a discussion of the ambiguity of the word "free" and why we still use it to mean "free" as in "free speech," not as in "free beer," see "Free as in Freedom" in Chapter 1 and "Ambiguity" in chapter 6.

See also Source Code, Open Source, and Copyleft, below.

Free software is translated into 21 languages in Chapter 21.

Source Code, Source

Source code is mentioned throughout the discussions of free software. If you're not sure what that is, read "A Note on Software."

Linux, GNU/Linux

For the origin of Linux, and the distinction between Linux (the operating-system kernel) and GNU/Linux (a full operating system), see the short mention under "Linux and GNU/Linux" in Chapter 1 and the full story in Chapter 20.

For reasons to say *GNU/Linux* when referring to that operating system rather than abbreviating it to *Linux* see Chapters 5 and 20.

Privacy and Personal Freedom

For some warnings about the loss of personal freedom, privacy, and access to written material that we have long taken for granted, see Chapters 11, 13, and 17. All of these are geared to a general audience.

Open Source

For the difference between the Open Source movement and the Free Software movement, see Chapter 6. This is also discussed in Chapter 1 (under "Open Source") and Chapter 20.

Intellectual Property

For an explanation of why the term "intellectual property" is both misleading and a barrier to addressing so-called "intellectual property" issues, see Chapter 21 and the beginning of Chapter 16.

For particular types of "intellectual property" see the Copyright and Patents topics, below.

Copyright

Note: Most of these copyright references are *not* about software.

For the history, purpose, implementation, and effects of copyright, as well as recommendations for copyright policy, see Chapters 12 and 19. Topics critical in our digital age, such as e-books and the Digital Millennium Copyright Act (DMCA), are addressed here.

For the difference between patents and copyrights, see Chapter 16.

For the use of copyright in promoting free software and free documentation, see Copyleft, just below.

Copyleft

For an explanation of copyleft and how it uses the copyright system to promote free software, see Chapter 1 (under "Copyleft and the GNU GPL"), Chapter 14, and Chapter 20. See also Licenses, below.

For an argument that copyleft is practical and effective as well as idealistic, see Chapter 15.

Chapter 9 argues for free manuals to accompany free software.

Licenses

The GNU licenses, which can be used to copyleft software or manuals, are introduced in Chapter 14 and given in full in Section Four.

Patents

See Chapter 16 for the difference between patents and copyrights and for arguments against patenting software and why it is different from other patentable things. Software-patent policy in other countries is also discussed.

Hacker versus **Cracker**

For the proper use of these terms see the beginning of Chapter 1.

Introduction

Every generation has its philosopher—a writer or an artist who captures the imagination of a time. Sometimes these philosophers are recognized as such; often it takes generations before the connection is made real. But recognized or not, a time gets marked by the people who speak its ideals, whether in the whisper of a poem, or the blast of a political movement.

Our generation has a philosopher. He is not an artist, or a professional writer. He is a programmer. Richard Stallman began his work in the labs of MIT, as a programmer and architect building operating system software. He has built his career on a stage of public life, as a programmer and an architect founding a movement for freedom in a world increasingly defined by "code."

"Code" is the technology that makes computers run. Whether inscribed in software or burned in hardware, it is the collection of instructions, first written in words, that directs the functionality of machines. These machines—computers—increasingly define and control our life. They determine how phones connect, and what runs on TV. They decide whether video can be streamed across a broadband link to a computer. They control what a computer reports back to its manufacturer. These machines run us. Code runs these machines.

What control should we have over this code? What understanding? What freedom should there be to match the control it enables? What power?

These questions have been the challenge of Stallman's life. Through his works and his words, he has pushed us to see the importance of keeping code "free." Not free in the sense that code writers don't get paid, but free in the sense that the control coders build be transparent to all, and that anyone have the right to take that control, and modify it as he or she sees fit. This is "free software"; "free software" is one answer to a world built in code.

"Free." Stallman laments the ambiguity in his own term. There's nothing to lament. Puzzles force people to think, and this term "free" does this puzzling work quite well. To modern American ears, "free software" sounds utopian, impossible. Nothing, not even lunch, is free. How could the most important words running the most critical machines running the world be "free." How could a sane society aspire to such an ideal?

Yet the odd clink of the word "free" is a function of us, not of the term. "Free" has different senses, only one of which refers to "price." A much more fundamental sense of "free" is the "free," Stallman says, in the term "free speech," or perhaps better in the term "free labor." Not free as in costless, but free as in limited in its control by others. Free software is control that is transparent, and open to change, just as free laws, or the laws of a "free society," are free when they make their control knowable, and open to change. The aim of Stallman's "free software movement" is to make as much code as it can transparent, and subject to change, by rendering it "free."

The mechanism of this rendering is an extraordinarily clever device called "copyleft" implemented through a license called GPL. Using the power of copyright law, "free software" not only assures that it remains open, and subject to change, but that other software that takes and uses "free software" (and that technically counts as a "derivative work") must also itself be free. If you use and adapt a free software program, and then release that adapted version to the public, the released version must be as free as the version it was adapted from. It must, or the law of copyright will be violated.

"Free software," like free societies, has its enemies. Microsoft has waged a war against the GPL, warning whoever will listen that the GPL is a "dangerous" license. The dangers it names, however, are largely illusory. Others object to the "coercion" in GPL's insistence that modified versions are also free. But a condition is not coercion. If it is not coercion for Microsoft to refuse to permit users to distribute modified versions of its product Office without paying it (presumably) millions, then it is not coercion when the GPL insists that modified versions of free software be free too.

And then there are those who call Stallman's message too extreme. But extreme it is not. Indeed, in an obvious sense, Stallman's work is a simple translation of the freedoms that our tradition crafted in the world before code. "Free software" would assure that the world governed by code is as "free" as our tradition that built the world before code.

For example: A "free society" is regulated by law. But there are limits that any free society places on this regulation through law: No society that kept its laws secret could ever be called free. No government that hid its regulations from the regulated could ever stand in our tradition. Law controls. But it does so justly only when visibly. And law is visible only when its terms are knowable and controllable by those it regulates, or by the agents of those it regulates (lawyers, legislatures).

This condition on law extends beyond the work of a legislature. Think about the practice of law in American courts. Lawyers are hired by their clients to advance their clients' interests. Sometimes that interest is advanced through litigation. In the course of this litigation, lawyers write briefs. These briefs in turn affect opinions written by judges. These opinions decide who wins a particular case, or whether a certain law can stand consistently with a constitution.

All the material in this process is free in the sense that Stallman means. Legal briefs are open and free for others to use. The arguments are transparent (which is different from saying they are good) and the reasoning can be taken without the permission of the original lawyers. The opinions they produce can be quoted in later briefs. They can be copied and integrated into another brief or opinion. The "source code" for American law is by design, and by principle, open and free for anyone to take. And take lawyers do—for it is a measure of a great brief that it achieves its creativity through the reuse of what happened before. The source is free; creativity and an economy is built upon it.

This economy of free code (and here I mean free legal code) doesn't starve lawyers. Law firms have enough incentive to produce great briefs even though the stuff they build can be taken and copied by anyone else. The lawyer is a craftsman; his or her product is public. Yet the crafting is not charity. Lawyers get paid; the public doesn't demand such work without price. Instead this economy flourishes, with later work added to the earlier.

We could imagine a legal practice that was different—briefs and arguments that were kept secret; rulings that announced a result but not the reasoning. Laws that were kept by the police but published to no one else. Regulation that operated without explaining its rule.

We could imagine this society, but we could not imagine calling it "free." Whether or not the incentives in such a society would be better or more efficiently allocated, such a society could not be known as free. The ideals of freedom, of life within a free society, demand more than efficient application. Instead, openness and transparency are the constraints within which a legal system gets built, not options to be added if convenient to the leaders. Life governed by software code should be no less.

Code writing is not litigation. It is better, richer, more productive. But the law is an obvious instance of how creativity and incentives do not depend upon perfect control over the products created. Like jazz, or novels, or architecture, the law gets built upon the work that went before. This adding and changing is what creativity always is. And a free society is one that assures that its most important resources remain free in just this sense.

For the first time, this book collects the writing and lectures of Richard Stallman in a manner that will make their subtlety and power clear. The essays span a wide range, from copyright to the history of the free software movement. They include many arguments not well known, and among these, an especially insightful account of the changed circumstances that render copyright in the digital world suspect. They will serve as a resource for those who seek to understand the thought of this most powerful man—powerful in his ideas, his passion, and his integrity, even if powerless in every other way. They will inspire others who would take these ideas, and build upon them.

I don't know Stallman well. I know him well enough to know he is a hard man to like. He is driven, often impatient. His anger can flare at friend as easily as foe. He is uncompromising and persistent; patient in both.

Yet when our world finally comes to understand the power and danger of code— when it finally sees that code, like laws, or like government, must be transparent to be free—then we will look back at this uncompromising and persistent programmer and recognize the vision he has fought to make real: the vision of a world where freedom and knowledge survives the compiler. And we will come to see that no man, through his deeds or words, has done as much to make possible the freedom that this next society could have.

We have not earned that freedom yet. We may well fail in securing it. But whether we succeed or fail, in these essays is a picture of what that freedom could be. And in the life that produced these words and works, there is inspiration for anyone who would, like Stallman, fight to create this freedom.

Lawrence Lessig
Professor of Law, Stanford Law School.

Section One

The GNU Project
and Free Software

1 The GNU Project

The First Software-Sharing Community

When I started working at the MIT Artificial Intelligence Lab in 1971, I became part of a software-sharing community that had existed for many years. Sharing of software was not limited to our particular community; it is as old as computers, just as sharing of recipes is as old as cooking. But we did it more than most.

The AI Lab used a timesharing operating system called ITS (the Incompatible Timesharing System) that the lab's staff hackers had designed and written in assembler language for the Digital PDP-10, one of the large computers of the era. As a member of this community, an AI lab staff system hacker, my job was to improve this system.

We did not call our software "free software," because that term did not yet exist; but that is what it was. Whenever people from another university or a company wanted to port and use a program, we gladly let them. If you saw someone using an unfamiliar and interesting program, you could always ask to see the source code, so that you could read it, change it, or cannibalize parts of it to make a new program.

The use of "hacker" to mean "security breaker" is a confusion on the part of the mass media. We hackers refuse to recognize that meaning, and continue using the word to mean, "Someone who loves to program and enjoys being clever about it."[1]

The Collapse of the Community

The situation changed drastically in the early 1980s, with the collapse of the AI Lab hacker community followed by the discontinuation of the PDP-10 computer.

In 1981, the spin-off company Symbolics hired away nearly all of the hackers from the AI Lab, and the depopulated community was unable to maintain itself. (The book *Hackers*, by Steven Levy, describes these events, as well as giving a

---

[1] It is hard to write a simple definition of something as varied as hacking, but I think what most "hacks" have in common is playfulness, cleverness, and exploration. Thus, hacking means exploring the limits of what is possible, in a spirit of playful cleverness. Activities that display playful cleverness have "hack value." You can help correct the misunderstanding simply by making a distinction between security breaking and hacking—by using the term "cracking" for security breaking. The people who do it are "crackers." Some of them may also be hackers, just as some of them may be chess players or golfers; most of them are not ("On Hacking," RMS; 2002).

Originally published in the book *Open Sources: Voices from the Open Source Revolution*; O'Reilly, 1999. This version is part of *Free Software, Free Society: Selected Essays of Richard M. Stallman*, 2002, GNU Press (http://www.gnupress.org); ISBN 1-882114-98-1.

clear picture of this community in its prime.) When the AI Lab bought a new PDP-10 in 1982, its administrators decided to use Digital's non-free timesharing system instead of ITS on the new machine.

Not long afterwards, Digital discontinued the PDP-10 series. Its architecture, elegant and powerful in the 60s, could not extend naturally to the larger address spaces that were becoming feasible in the 80s. This meant that nearly all of the programs composing ITS were obsolete. That put the last nail in the coffin of ITS; 15 years of work went up in smoke.

The modern computers of the era, such as the VAX or the 68020, had their own operating systems, but none of them were free software: you had to sign a nondisclosure agreement even to get an executable copy.

This meant that the first step in using a computer was to promise not to help your neighbor. A cooperating community was forbidden. The rule made by the owners of proprietary software was, "If you share with your neighbor, you are a pirate. If you want any changes, beg us to make them."

The idea that the proprietary-software social system—the system that says you are not allowed to share or change software—is antisocial, that it is unethical, that it is simply wrong, may come as a surprise to some readers. But what else could we say about a system based on dividing the public and keeping users helpless? Readers who find the idea surprising may have taken this proprietary-software social system as given, or judged it on the terms suggested by proprietarysoftware businesses. Software publishers have worked long and hard to convince people that there is only one way to look at the issue.

When software publishers talk about "enforcing" their "rights" or "stopping piracy," what they actually "say" is secondary. The real message of these statements is in the unstated assumptions they take for granted; the public is supposed to accept them uncritically. So let's examine them.

One assumption is that software companies have an unquestionable natural right to own software and thus have power over all its users. (If this were a natural right, then no matter how much harm it does to the public, we could not object.) Interestingly, the U.S. Constitution and legal tradition reject this view; copyright is not a natural right, but an artificial government-imposed monopoly that limits the users' natural right to copy.

Another unstated assumption is that the only important thing about software is what jobs it allows you to do—that we computer users should not care what kind of society we are allowed to have.

A third assumption is that we would have no usable software (or would never have a program to do this or that particular job) if we did not offer a company power over the users of the program. This assumption may have seemed plausible before the free software movement demonstrated that we can make plenty of useful software without putting chains on it.

If we decline to accept these assumptions, and judge these issues based on ordinary common-sense morality while placing the users first, we arrive at very different conclusions. Computer users should be free to modify programs to fit their needs, and free to share software, because helping other people is the basis of society.

A Stark Moral Choice

With my community gone, to continue as before was impossible. Instead, I faced a stark moral choice.

The easy choice was to join the proprietary software world, signing nondisclosure agreements and promising not to help my fellow hacker. Most likely I would also be developing software that was released under nondisclosure agreements, thus adding to the pressure on other people to betray their fellows too.

I could have made money this way, and perhaps amused myself writing code. But I knew that at the end of my career, I would look back on years of building walls to divide people, and feel I had spent my life making the world a worse place.

I had already experienced being on the receiving end of a nondisclosure agreement, when someone refused to give me and the MIT AI Lab the source code for the control program for our printer. (The lack of certain features in this program made use of the printer extremely frustrating.) So I could not tell myself that nondisclosure agreements were innocent. I was very angry when he refused to share with us; I could not turn around and do the same thing to everyone else.

Another choice, straightforward but unpleasant, was to leave the computer field. That way my skills would not be misused, but they would still be wasted. I would not be culpable for dividing and restricting computer users, but it would happen nonetheless.

So I looked for a way that a programmer could do something for the good. I asked myself, was there a program or programs that I could write, so as to make a community possible once again?

The answer was clear: what was needed first was an operating system. That is the crucial software for starting to use a computer. With an operating system, you can do many things; without one, you cannot run the computer at all. With a free operating system, we could again have a community of cooperating hackers—and invite anyone to join. And anyone would be able to use a computer without starting out by conspiring to deprive his or her friends.

As an operating system developer, I had the right skills for this job. So even though I could not take success for granted, I realized that I was elected to do the job. I chose to make the system compatible with Unix so that it would be portable, and so that Unix users could easily switch to it. The name GNU was chosen following a hacker tradition, as a recursive acronym for "GNU's Not Unix."

An operating system does not mean just a kernel, barely enough to run other programs. In the 1970s, every operating system worthy of the name included command processors, assemblers, compilers, interpreters, debuggers, text editors, mailers, and much more. ITS had them, Multics had them, VMS had them, and Unix had them. The GNU operating system would include them too.

Later I heard these words, attributed to Hillel:

"If I am not for myself, who will be for me? If I am only for myself, what am I? If not now, when?"

The decision to start the GNU project was based on a similar spirit.

As an atheist, I don't follow any religious leaders, but I sometimes find I admire something one of them has said.

Free as in Freedom

The term "free software" is sometimes misunderstood—it has nothing to do with price. It is about freedom. Here, therefore, is the definition of free software: a program is free software, for you, a particular user, if:

- You have the freedom to run the program, for any purpose.
- You have the freedom to modify the program to suit your needs. (To make this freedom effective in practice, you must have access to the source code, since making changes in a program without having the source code is exceedingly difficult.)
- You have the freedom to redistribute copies, either gratis or for a fee.
- You have the freedom to distribute modified versions of the program, so that the community can benefit from your improvements.

Since "free" refers to freedom, not to price, there is no contradiction between selling copies and free software. In fact, the freedom to sell copies is crucial: collections of free software sold on CD-ROMs are important for the community, and selling them is an important way to raise funds for free software development. Therefore, a program that people are not free to include on these collections is not free software.

Because of the ambiguity of "free," people have long looked for alternatives, but no one has found a suitable alternative. The English Language has more words and nuances than any other, but it lacks a simple, unambiguous word that means "free," as in freedom—"unfettered" being the word that comes closest in meaning. Such alternatives as "liberated," "freedom," and "open" have either the wrong meaning or some other disadvantage.

GNU Software and the GNU System

Developing a whole system is a very large project. To bring it into reach, I decided to adapt and use existing pieces of free software wherever that was possible. For example, I decided at the very beginning to use TeX as the principal text formatter; a few years later, I decided to use the X Window System rather than writing another window system for GNU.

Because of this decision, the GNU system is not the same as the collection of all GNU software. The GNU system includes programs that are not GNU software, programs that were developed by other people and projects for their own purposes, but that we can use because they are free software.

Commencing the Project

In January 1984 I quit my job at MIT and began writing GNU software. Leaving MIT was necessary so that MIT would not be able to interfere with distributing GNU as free software. If I had remained on the staff, MIT could have claimed to own the work, and could have imposed their own distribution terms, or even turned the work into a proprietary software package. I had no intention of doing a large amount of work only to see it become useless for its intended purpose: creating a new software-sharing community.

However, Professor Winston, then the head of the MIT AI Lab, kindly invited me to keep using the lab's facilities.

The First Steps

Shortly before beginning the GNU project, I heard about the Free University Compiler Kit, also known as VUCK. (The Dutch word for "free" is written with a V.) This was a compiler designed to handle multiple languages, including C and Pascal, and to support multiple target machines. I wrote to its author asking if GNU could use it.

He responded derisively, stating that the university was free but the compiler was not. I therefore decided that my first program for the GNU project would be a multi-language, multi-platform compiler.

Hoping to avoid the need to write the whole compiler myself, I obtained the source code for the Pastel compiler, which was a multi-platform compiler developed at Lawrence Livermore Lab. It supported, and was written in, an extended version of Pascal, designed to be a system-programming language. I added a C front end, and began porting it to the Motorola 68000 computer. But I had to give that up when I discovered that the compiler needed many megabytes of stack space, and the available 68000 Unix system would only allow 64k.

I then realized that the Pastel compiler functioned by parsing the entire input file into a syntax tree, converting the whole syntax tree into a chain of "instructions," and then generating the whole output file, without ever freeing any storage. At this point, I concluded I would have to write a new compiler from scratch. That new compiler is now known as GCC; none of the Pastel compiler is used in it, but I managed to adapt and use the C front end that I had written. But that was some years later; first, I worked on GNU Emacs.

GNU Emacs

I began work on GNU Emacs in September 1984, and in early 1985 it was beginning to be usable. This enabled me to begin using Unix systems to do editing; having no interest in learning to use vi or ed, I had done my editing on other kinds of machines until then.

At this point, people began wanting to use GNU Emacs, which raised the question of how to distribute it. Of course, I put it on the anonymous ftp server on the MIT computer that I used. (This computer, prep.ai.mit.edu, thus became the principal GNU ftp distribution site; when it was decommissioned a few years later, we transferred the name to our new ftp server.) But at that time, many of the interested people were not on the Internet and could not get a copy by ftp. So the question was, what would I say to them?

I could have said, "Find a friend who is on the net and who will make a copy for you." Or I could have done what I did with the original PDP-10 Emacs: tell them, "Mail me a tape and a SASE, and I will mail it back with Emacs on it." But I had no job, and I was looking for ways to make money from free software. So I announced that I would mail a tape to whoever wanted one, for a fee of $150. In this way, I started a free software distribution business, the precursor of the companies that today distribute entire Linux-based GNU systems.

Is a program free for every user?

If a program is free software when it leaves the hands of its author, this does not necessarily mean it will be free software for everyone who has a copy of it. For example, public domain software (software that is not copyrighted) is free software; but anyone can make a proprietary modified version of it. Likewise, many free programs are copyrighted but distributed under simple permissive licenses that allow proprietary modified versions.

The paradigmatic example of this problem is the X Window System. Developed at MIT, and released as free software with a permissive license, it was soon adopted by various computer companies. They added X to their proprietary Unix systems, in binary form only, and covered by the same nondisclosure agreement. These copies of X were no more free software than Unix was.

The developers of the X Window System did not consider this a problem—they expected and intended this to happen. Their goal was not freedom, just "success," defined as "having many users." They did not care whether these users had freedom, only that they should be numerous.

This lead to a paradoxical situation where two different ways of counting the amount of freedom gave different answers to the question, "Is this program free?" If you judged based on the freedom provided by the distribution terms of the MIT release, you would say that X was free software. But if you measured the freedom of the average user of X, you would have to say it was proprietary software. Most X users were running the proprietary versions that came with Unix systems, not the free version.

Copyleft and the GNU GPL

The goal of GNU was to give users freedom, not just to be popular. So we needed to use distribution terms that would prevent GNU software from being turned into proprietary software. The method we use is called *copyleft*.

Copyleft uses copyright law, but flips it over to serve the opposite of its usual purpose: instead of a means of privatizing software, it becomes a means of keeping software free.

The central idea of copyleft is that we give everyone permission to run the program, copy the program, modify the program, and distribute modified versions—but not permission to add restrictions of their own. Thus, the crucial freedoms that define "free software" are guaranteed to everyone who has a copy; they become inalienable rights.

For an effective copyleft, modified versions must also be free. This ensures that work based on ours becomes available to our community if it is published. When programmers who have jobs as programmers volunteer to improve GNU software, it is copyleft that prevents their employers from saying, "You can't share those changes, because we are going to use them to make our proprietary version of the program."

The requirement that changes must be free is essential if we want to ensure freedom for every user of the program. The companies that privatized the X Window System usually made some changes to port it to their systems and hardware. These changes were small compared with the great extent of X, but they were not trivial. If making changes were an excuse to deny the users freedom, it would be easy for anyone to take advantage of the excuse.

A related issue concerns combining a free program with non-free code. Such a combination would inevitably be non-free; whichever freedoms are lacking for the non-free part would be lacking for the whole as well. To permit such combinations would open a hole big enough to sink a ship. Therefore, a crucial requirement for copyleft is to plug this hole: anything added to or combined with a copylefted program must be such that the larger combined version is also free and copylefted.

The specific implementation of copyleft that we use for most GNU software is the GNU General Public License, or GNU GPL for short. We have other kinds of copyleft that are used in specific circumstances. GNU manuals are copylefted also, but use a much simpler kind of copyleft, because the complexity of the GNU GPL is not necessary for manuals.

In 1984 or 1985, Don Hopkins (a very imaginative fellow) mailed me a letter. On the envelope he had written several amusing sayings, including this one: "Copyleft—all rights reversed." I used the word "copyleft" to name the distribution concept I was developing at the time.

The Free Software Foundation

As interest in using Emacs was growing, other people became involved in the GNU project, and we decided that it was time to seek funding once again. So in 1985 we created the Free Software Foundation, a tax-exempt charity for free software development. The FSF also took over the Emacs tape distribution business; later it extended this by adding other free software (both GNU and non-GNU) to the tape, and by selling free manuals as well.

The FSF accepts donations, but most of its income has always come from sales— of copies of free software, and of other related services. Today it sells CD-ROMs of source code, CD-ROMs with binaries, nicely printed manuals (all with freedom to redistribute and modify), and Deluxe Distributions (where we build the whole collection of software for your choice of platform).

Free Software Foundation employees have written and maintained a number of GNU software packages. Two notable ones are the C library and the shell. The GNU C library is what every program running on a GNU/Linux system uses to communicate with Linux. It was developed by a member of the Free Software Foundation staff, Roland McGrath. The shell used on most GNU/Linux systems is BASH, the Bourne Again Shell, which was developed by FSF employee Brian Fox.

We funded development of these programs because the GNU project was not just about tools or a development environment. Our goal was a complete operating system, and these programs were needed for that goal.

"Bourne again Shell" is a joke on the name "Bourne Shell," which was the usual shell on Unix.

Free Software Support

The free software philosophy rejects a specific widespread business practice, but it is not against business. When businesses respect the users' freedom, we wish them success.

Selling copies of Emacs demonstrates one kind of free software business. When the FSF took over that business, I needed another way to make a living. I found it in selling services relating to the free software I had developed. This included teaching, for subjects such as how to program GNU Emacs and how to customize GCC, and software development, mostly porting GCC to new platforms.

Today each of these kinds of free software business is practiced by a number of corporations. Some distribute free software collections on CD-ROM; others sell support at various levels ranging from answering user questions, to fixing bugs, to adding major new features. We are even beginning to see free software companies based on launching new free software products.

Watch out, though—a number of companies that associate themselves with the term "open source" actually base their business on non-free software that works with free software. These are not free software companies, they are proprietary software companies whose products tempt users away from freedom. They call these "value added," which reflects the values they would like us to adopt: convenience above freedom. If we value freedom more, we should call them "freedom subtracted" products.

Technical goals

The principal goal of GNU was to be free software. Even if GNU had no technical advantage over Unix, it would have a social advantage, allowing users to cooperate, and an ethical advantage, respecting the user's freedom.

But it was natural to apply the known standards of good practice to the work—for example, dynamically allocating data structures to avoid arbitrary fixed size limits, and handling all the possible 8-bit codes wherever that made sense.

In addition, we rejected the Unix focus on small memory size, by deciding not to support 16-bit machines (it was clear that 32-bit machines would be the norm by the time the GNU system was finished), and to make no effort to reduce memory usage unless it exceeded a megabyte. In programs for which handling very large files was not crucial, we encouraged programmers to read an entire input file into core, then scan its contents without having to worry about I/O.

These decisions enabled many GNU programs to surpass their Unix counterparts in reliability and speed.

Donated Computers

As the GNU project's reputation grew, people began offering to donate machines running Unix to the project. These were very useful, because the easiest way to develop components of GNU was to do it on a Unix system, and replace the components of that system one by one. But they raised an ethical issue: whether it was right for us to have a copy of Unix at all.

Unix was (and is) proprietary software, and the GNU project's philosophy said that we should not use proprietary software. But, applying the same reasoning that leads to the conclusion that violence in self defense is justified, I concluded that it was legitimate to use a proprietary package when that was crucial for developing a free replacement that would help others stop using the proprietary package.

But, even if this was a justifiable evil, it was still an evil. Today we no longer have any copies of Unix, because we have replaced them with free operating systems. If we could not replace a machine's operating system with a free one, we replaced the machine instead.

The GNU Task List

As the GNU project proceeded, and increasing numbers of system components were found or developed, eventually it became useful to make a list of the remaining gaps. We used it to recruit developers to write the missing pieces. This list became known as the GNU task list. In addition to missing Unix components, we listed various other useful software and documentation projects that, we thought, a truly complete system ought to have.

Today, hardly any Unix components are left in the GNU task list—those jobs have been done, aside from a few inessential ones. But the list is full of projects that some might call "applications." Any program that appeals to more than a narrow class of users would be a useful thing to add to an operating system.

Even games are included in the task list—and have been since the beginning. Unix included games, so naturally GNU should too. But compatibility was not an issue for games, so we did not follow the list of games that Unix had. Instead, we listed a spectrum of different kinds of games that users might like.

The GNU Library GPL

The GNU C library uses a special kind of copyleft called the GNU Library General Public License, which gives permission to link proprietary software with the library. Why make this exception?

It is not a matter of principle; there is no principle that says proprietary software products are entitled to include our code. (Why contribute to a project predicated on refusing to share with us?) Using the LGPL for the C library, or for any library, is a matter of strategy.

The C library does a generic job; every proprietary system or compiler comes with a C library. Therefore, to make our C library available only to free software would not have given free software any advantage—it would only have discouraged use of our library.

One system is an exception to this: on the GNU system (and this includes GNU/Linux), the GNU C library is the only C library. So the distribution terms of the GNU C library determine whether it is possible to compile a proprietary program for the GNU system. There is no ethical reason to allow proprietary applications on the GNU system, but strategically it seems that disallowing them would do more to discourage use of the GNU system than to encourage development of free applications.

That is why using the Library GPL is a good strategy for the C library. For other libraries, the strategic decision needs to be considered on a case-by-case basis. When a library does a special job that can help write certain kinds of programs, then releasing it under the GPL, limiting it to free programs only, is a way of helping other free software developers, giving them an advantage against proprietary software.

Consider GNU Readline,[2] a library that was developed to provide command-line editing for BASH. Readline is released under the ordinary GNU GPL, not the Library GPL. This probably does reduce the amount Readline is used, but that is no loss for us. Meanwhile, at least one useful application has been made free software specifically so it could use Readline, and that is a real gain for the community.

Proprietary software developers have the advantages money provides; free software developers need to make advantages for each other. I hope some day we will have a large collection of GPL-covered libraries that have no parallel available to proprietary software, providing useful modules to serve as building blocks in new free software, and adding up to a major advantage for further free software development.

Scratching an itch?

Eric Raymond says that "Every good work of software starts by scratching a developer's personal itch." Maybe that happens sometimes, but many essential pieces of GNU software were developed in order to have a complete free operating system. They come from a vision and a plan, not from impulse.

For example, we developed the GNU C library because a Unix-like system needs a C library, the Bourne Again Shell (BASH) because a Unix-like system needs a shell, and GNU tar because a Unix-like system needs a tar program. The same is true for my own programs—the GNU C compiler, GNU Emacs, GDB and GNU Make.

Some GNU programs were developed to cope with specific threats to our freedom. Thus, we developed gzip to replace the Compress program, which had been lost to the community because of the LZW[3] patents. We found people to develop LessTif, and more recently started GNOME and Harmony, to address the problems

---

[2] The GNU Readline library provides a set of functions for use by applications that allow users to edit command lines as they are typed in.

[3] The Lempel-Ziv-Welch algorithm is used for compressing data.

caused by certain proprietary libraries (see "Non-Free Libraries" below). We are developing the GNU Privacy Guard to replace popular non-free encryption software, because users should not have to choose between privacy and freedom.

Of course, the people writing these programs became interested in the work, and many features were added to them by various people for the sake of their own needs and interests. But that is not why the programs exist.

Unexpected developments

At the beginning of the GNU project, I imagined that we would develop the whole GNU system, then release it as a whole. That is not how it happened.

Since each component of the GNU system was implemented on a Unix system, each component could run on Unix systems, long before a complete GNU system existed. Some of these programs became popular, and users began extending them and porting them—to the various incompatible versions of Unix, and sometimes to other systems as well.

The process made these programs much more powerful, and attracted both funds and contributors to the GNU project. But it probably also delayed completion of a minimal working system by several years, as GNU developers' time was put into maintaining these ports and adding features to the existing components, rather than moving on to write one missing component after another.

The GNU Hurd

By 1990, the GNU system was almost complete; the only major missing component was the kernel. We had decided to implement our kernel as a collection of server processes running on top of Mach. Mach is a microkernel developed at Carnegie Mellon University and then at the University of Utah; the GNU Hurd is a collection of servers (or "herd of gnus") that run on top of Mach, and do the various jobs of the Unix kernel. The start of development was delayed as we waited for Mach to be released as free software, as had been promised.

One reason for choosing this design was to avoid what seemed to be the hardest part of the job: debugging a kernel program without a source-level debugger to do it with. This part of the job had been done already, in Mach, and we expected to debug the Hurd servers as user programs, with GDB. But it took a long time to make that possible, and the multi-threaded servers that send messages to each other have turned out to be very hard to debug. Making the Hurd work solidly has stretched on for many years.

Alix

The GNU kernel was not originally supposed to be called the Hurd. Its original name was Alix—named after the woman who was my sweetheart at the time. She, a Unix system administrator, had pointed out how her name would fit a common naming pattern for Unix system versions; as a joke, she told her friends, "Someone should name a kernel after me." I said nothing, but decided to surprise her with a kernel named Alix.

It did not stay that way. Michael Bushnell (now Thomas), the main developer of the kernel, preferred the name Hurd, and redefined Alix to refer to a certain part of the kernel—the part that would trap system calls and handle them by sending messages to Hurd servers.

Ultimately, Alix and I broke up, and she changed her name; independently, the Hurd design was changed so that the C library would send messages directly to servers, and this made the Alix component disappear from the design.

But before these things happened, a friend of hers came across the name Alix in the Hurd source code, and mentioned the name to her. So the name did its job.

Linux and GNU/Linux

The GNU Hurd is not ready for production use. Fortunately, another kernel is available. In 1991, Linus Torvalds developed a Unix-compatible kernel and called it Linux. Around 1992, combining Linux with the not-quite-complete GNU system resulted in a complete free operating system. (Combining them was a substantial job in itself, of course.) It is due to Linux that we can actually run a version of the GNU system today.

We call this system version GNU/Linux, to express its composition as a combination of the GNU system with Linux as the kernel.

Challenges in Our Future

We have proved our ability to develop a broad spectrum of free software. This does not mean we are invincible and unstoppable. Several challenges make the future of free software uncertain; meeting them will require steadfast effort and endurance, sometimes lasting for years. It will require the kind of determination that people display when they value their freedom and will not let anyone take it away.

The following four sections discuss these challenges.

Secret Hardware

Hardware manufactures increasingly tend to keep hardware specifications secret. This makes it difficult to write free drivers so that Linux and XFree86[4] can support new hardware. We have complete free systems today, but we will not have them tomorrow if we cannot support tomorrow's computers.

There are two ways to cope with this problem. Programmers can do reverse engineering to figure out how to support the hardware. The rest of us can choose the hardware that is supported by free software; as our numbers increase, secrecy of specifications will become a self-defeating policy.

---

[4] XFree86 is a program that provides a desktop environment that interfaces with your display hardware (mouse, keyboard, etc). It runs on many different platforms.

Reverse engineering is a big job; will we have programmers with sufficient determination to undertake it? Yes—if we have built up a strong feeling that free software is a matter of principle, and non-free drivers are intolerable. And will large numbers of us spend extra money, or even a little extra time, so we can use free drivers? Yes, if the determination to have freedom is widespread.

Non-Free Libraries

A non-free library that runs on free operating systems acts as a trap for free software developers. The library's attractive features are the bait; if you use the library, you fall into the trap, because your program cannot usefully be part of a free operating system. (Strictly speaking, we could include your program, but it won't run with the library missing.) Even worse, if a program that uses the proprietary library becomes popular, it can lure other unsuspecting programmers into the trap.

The first instance of this problem was the Motif[5] toolkit, back in the 80s. Although there were as yet no free operating systems, it was clear what problem Motif would cause for them later on. The GNU Project responded in two ways: by asking individual free software projects to support the free X toolkit widgets as well as Motif, and by asking for someone to write a free replacement for Motif. The job took many years; LessTif, developed by the Hungry Programmers, became powerful enough to support most Motif applications only in 1997.

Between 1996 and 1998, another non-free Graphical User Interface (GUI) toolkit library, called Qt, was used in a substantial collection of free software, the desktop KDE.

Free GNU/Linux systems were unable to use KDE, because we could not use the library. However, some commercial distributors of GNU/Linux systems who were not strict about sticking with free software added KDE to their systems—producing a system with more capabilities, but less freedom. The KDE group was actively encouraging more programmers to use Qt, and millions of new "Linux users" had never been exposed to the idea that there was a problem in this. The situation appeared grim.

The free software community responded to the problem in two ways: GNOME and Harmony.

GNOME, the GNU Network Object Model Environment, is GNU's desktop project. Started in 1997 by Miguel de Icaza, and developed with the support of Red Hat Software, GNOME set out to provide similar desktop facilities, but using free software exclusively. It has technical advantages as well, such as supporting a variety of languages, not just C++. But its main purpose was freedom: not to require the use of any non-free software.

Harmony is a compatible replacement library, designed to make it possible to run KDE software without using Qt.

In November 1998, the developers of Qt announced a change of license which, when carried out, should make Qt free software. There is no way to be sure, but I think that this was partly due to the community's firm response to the problem that

---

[5] Motif is a graphical interface and window manager that runs on top of X Windows.

Qt posed when it was non-free. (The new license is inconvenient and inequitable, so it remains desirable to avoid using Qt.)[6]

How will we respond to the next tempting non-free library? Will the whole community understand the need to stay out of the trap? Or will many of us give up freedom for convenience, and produce a major problem? Our future depends on our philosophy.

Software Patents

The worst threat we face comes from software patents, which can put algorithms and features off limits to free software for up to twenty years. The LZW compression algorithm patents were applied for in 1983, and we still cannot release free software to produce proper compressed GIFs. In 1998, a free program to produce MP3 compressed audio was removed from distribution under threat of a patent suit.

There are ways to cope with patents: we can search for evidence that a patent is invalid, and we can look for alternative ways to do a job. But each of these methods works only sometimes; when both fail, a patent may force all free software to lack some feature that users want. What will we do when this happens?

Those of us who value free software for freedom's sake will stay with free software anyway. We will manage to get work done without the patented features. But those who value free software because they expect it to be techically superior are likely to call it a failure when a patent holds it back. Thus, while it is useful to talk about the practical effectiveness of the "cathedral" model of development,[7] and the reliability and power of some free software, we must not stop there. We must talk about freedom and principle.

Free Documentation

The biggest deficiency in our free operating systems is not in the software—it is the lack of good free manuals that we can include in our systems. Documentation is an essential part of any software package; when an important free software package does not come with a good free manual, that is a major gap. We have many such gaps today.

Free documentation, like free software, is a matter of freedom, not price. The criterion for a free manual is pretty much the same as for free software: it is a matter of giving all users certain freedoms. Redistribution (including commercial sale) must be permitted, on-line and on paper, so that the manual can accompany every copy of the program.

Permission for modification is crucial too. As a general rule, I don't believe that it is essential for people to have permission to modify all sorts of articles and books. For example, I don't think you or I are obliged to give permission to modify articles like this one, which describe our actions and our views.

---

[6] In September 2000, Qt was rereleased under the GNU GPL, which essentially solved this problem.

[7] I probably meant to write "of the 'bazaar' model," since that was the alternative that was new and initially controversial.

But there is a particular reason why the freedom to modify is crucial for documentation for free software. When people exercise their right to modify the software, and add or change its features, if they are conscientious they will change the manual too—so they can provide accurate and usable documentation with the modified program. A manual that does not allow programmers to be conscientious and finish the job, does not fill our community's needs.

Some kinds of limits on how modifications are done pose no problem. For example, requirements to preserve the original author's copyright notice, the distribution terms, or the list of authors, are ok. It is also no problem to require modified versions to include notice that they were modified, even to have entire sections that may not be deleted or changed, as long as these sections deal with nontechnical topics. These kinds of restrictions are not a problem because they don't stop the conscientious programmer from adapting the manual to fit the modified program. In other words, they don't block the free software community from making full use of the manual.

However, it must be possible to modify all the "technical" content of the manual, and then distribute the result in all the usual media, through all the usual channels; otherwise, the restrictions do obstruct the community, the manual is not free, and we need another manual.

Will free software developers have the awareness and determination to produce a full spectrum of free manuals? Once again, our future depends on philosophy.

We Must Talk About Freedom

Estimates today are that there are ten million users of GNU/Linux systems such as Debian GNU/Linux and Red Hat Linux. Free software has developed such practical advantages that users are flocking to it for purely practical reasons.

The good consequences of this are evident: more interest in developing free software, more customers for free software businesses, and more ability to encourage companies to develop commercial free software instead of proprietary software products.

But interest in the software is growing faster than awareness of the philosophy it is based on, and this leads to trouble. Our ability to meet the challenges and threats described above depends on the will to stand firm for freedom. To make sure our community has this will, we need to spread the idea to the new users as they come into the community.

But we are failing to do so: the efforts to attract new users into our community are far outstripping the efforts to teach them the civics of our community. We need to do both, and we need to keep the two efforts in balance.

"Open Source"

Teaching new users about freedom became more difficult in 1998, when a part of the community decided to stop using the term "free software" and say "open source software" instead.

Some who favored this term aimed to avoid the confusion of "free" with "gratis"—a valid goal. Others, however, aimed to set aside the spirit of principle that had motivated the free software movement and the GNU project, and to appeal instead to executives and business users, many of whom hold an ideology that places profit above freedom, above community, above principle. Thus, the rhetoric of "open source" focuses on the potential to make high-quality, powerful software, but shuns the ideas of freedom, community, and principle.

The "Linux" magazines are a clear example of this—they are filled with advertisements for proprietary software that works with GNU/Linux. When the next Motif or Qt appears, will these magazines warn programmers to stay away from it, or will they run ads for it?

The support of business can contribute to the community in many ways; all else being equal, it is useful. But winning their support by speaking even less about freedom and principle can be disastrous; it makes the previous imbalance between outreach and civics education even worse.

"Free software" and "open source" describe the same category of software, more or less, but say different things about the software, and about values. The GNU Project continues to use the term "free software," to express the idea that freedom, not just technology, is important.

Try!

Yoda's philosophy ("There is no 'try'") sounds neat, but it doesn't work for me. I have done most of my work while anxious about whether I could do the job, and unsure that it would be enough to achieve the goal if I did. But I tried anyway, because there was no one but me between the enemy and my city. Surprising myself, I have sometimes succeeded.

Sometimes I failed; some of my cities have fallen. Then I found another threatened city, and got ready for another battle. Over time, I've learned to look for threats and put myself between them and my city, calling on other hackers to come and join me.

Nowadays, often I'm not the only one. It is a relief and a joy when I see a regiment of hackers digging in to hold the line, and I realize, this city may survive—for now. But the dangers are greater each year, and now Microsoft has explicitly targeted our community. We can't take the future of freedom for granted. Don't take it for granted! If you want to keep your freedom, you must be prepared to defend it.

2 The GNU Manifesto

The GNU Manifesto was written at the beginning of the GNU Project, to ask for participation and support. For the first few years, it was updated in minor ways to account for developments, but now it seems best to leave it unchanged as most people have seen it. Since that time, we have learned about certain common misunderstandings that different wording could help avoid, and footnotes have been added over the years to explain these misunderstandings.

What's GNU? Gnu's Not Unix!

GNU, which stands for Gnu's Not Unix, is the name for the complete Unix-compatible software system which I am writing so that I can give it away free to everyone who can use it.[1] Several other volunteers are helping me. Contributions of time, money, programs and equipment are greatly needed.

So far we have an Emacs text editor with Lisp for writing editor commands, a source-level debugger, a yacc-compatible parser generator, a linker, and around 35 utilities. A shell (command interpreter) is nearly completed. A new portable optimizing C compiler has compiled itself and may be released this year. An initial kernel exists but many more features are needed to emulate Unix. When the kernel and compiler are finished, it will be possible to distribute a GNU system suitable for program development. We will use TEX as our text formatter, but an nroff is being worked on. We will use the free, portable X window system as well. After this we will add a portable Common Lisp, an Empire game, a spreadsheet, and hundreds of other things, plus on-line documentation. We hope to supply, eventually, everything useful that normally comes with a Unix system, and more.

GNU will be able to run Unix programs, but will not be identical to Unix. We will make all improvements that are convenient, based on our experience with other operating systems. In particular, we plan to have longer file names, file version numbers, a crashproof file system, file name completion perhaps, terminal-

---

[1] The wording here was careless. The intention was that nobody would have to pay for *permission* to use the GNU system. But the words do not make this clear, and people often interpret them as saying that copies of GNU should always be distributed at little or no charge. That was never the intent; later on, the manifesto mentions the possibility of companies providing the service of distribution for a profit. Subsequently I have learned to distinguish carefully between "free" in the sense of freedom and "free" in the sense of price. Free software is software that users have the freedom to distribute and change. Some users may obtain copies at no charge, while others pay to obtain copies—and if the funds help support improving the software, so much the better. The important thing is that everyone who has a copy has the freedom to cooperate with others in using it.

Originally written in 1984, this version is part of *Free Software, Free Society: Selected Essays of Richard M. Stallman*, 2002, GNU Press (http://www.gnupress.org); ISBN 1-882114-98-1.

independent display support, and perhaps eventually a Lisp-based window system through which several Lisp programs and ordinary Unix programs can share a screen. Both C and Lisp will be available as system programming languages. We will try to support UUCP, MIT Chaosnet, and Internet protocols for communication.

GNU is aimed initially at machines in the 68000/16000 class with virtual memory, because they are the easiest machines to make it run on. The extra effort to make it run on smaller machines will be left to someone who wants to use it on them.

To avoid horrible confusion, please pronounce the 'G' in the word 'GNU' when it is the name of this project.

Why I Must Write GNU

I consider that the golden rule requires that if I like a program I must share it with other people who like it. Software sellers want to divide the users and conquer them, making each user agree not to share with others. I refuse to break solidarity with other users in this way. I cannot in good conscience sign a nondisclosure agreement or a software license agreement. For years I worked within the Artificial Intelligence Lab to resist such tendencies and other inhospitalities, but eventually they had gone too far: I could not remain in an institution where such things are done for me against my will.

So that I can continue to use computers without dishonor, I have decided to put together a sufficient body of free software so that I will be able to get along without any software that is not free. I have resigned from the AI lab to deny MIT any legal excuse to prevent me from giving GNU away.

Why GNU Will Be Compatible with Unix

Unix is not my ideal system, but it is not too bad. The essential features of Unix seem to be good ones, and I think I can fill in what Unix lacks without spoiling them. And a system compatible with Unix would be convenient for many other people to adopt.

How GNU Will Be Available

GNU is not in the public domain. Everyone will be permitted to modify and redistribute GNU, but no distributor will be allowed to restrict its further redistribution. That is to say, proprietary modifications will not be allowed. I want to make sure that all versions of GNU remain free.

Why Many Other Programmers Want to Help

I have found many other programmers who are excited about GNU and want to help.

Many programmers are unhappy about the commercialization of system software. It may enable them to make more money, but it requires them to feel in conflict with other programmers in general rather than feel as comrades. The fundamental act of friendship among programmers is the sharing of programs; marketing arrangements now typically used essentially forbid programmers to treat others as friends. The purchaser of software must choose between friendship and obeying the law. Naturally, many decide that friendship is more important. But those who believe in law often do not feel at ease with either choice. They become cynical and think that programming is just a way of making money.

By working on and using GNU rather than proprietary programs, we can be hospitable to everyone and obey the law. In addition, GNU serves as an example to inspire and a banner to rally others to join us in sharing. This can give us a feeling of harmony which is impossible if we use software that is not free. For about half the programmers I talk to, this is an important happiness that money cannot replace.

How You Can Contribute

I am asking computer manufacturers for donations of machines and money. I'm asking individuals for donations of programs and work.

One consequence you can expect if you donate machines is that GNU will run on them at an early date. The machines should be complete, ready to use systems, approved for use in a residential area, and not in need of sophisticated cooling or power.

I have found very many programmers eager to contribute part-time work for GNU. For most projects, such part-time distributed work would be very hard to coordinate; the independently-written parts would not work together. But for the particular task of replacing Unix, this problem is absent. A complete Unix system contains hundreds of utility programs, each of which is documented separately. Most interface specifications are fixed by Unix compatibility. If each contributor can write a compatible replacement for a single Unix utility, and make it work properly in place of the original on a Unix system, then these utilities will work right when put together. Even allowing for Murphy[2] to create a few unexpected problems, assembling these components will be a feasible task. (The kernel will require closer communication and will be worked on by a small, tight group.)

If I get donations of money, I may be able to hire a few people full or part time. The salary won't be high by programmers' standards, but I'm looking for people for whom building community spirit is as important as making money. I view this as a way of enabling dedicated people to devote their full energies to working on GNU by sparing them the need to make a living in another way.

---

[2] This is a reference to "Murphy's Law," a humorous law that states, if anything can possibly go wrong, it will go wrong.

Why All Computer Users Will Benefit

Once GNU is written, everyone will be able to obtain good system software free, just like air.[3]

This means much more than just saving everyone the price of a Unix license. It means that much wasteful duplication of system programming effort will be avoided. This effort can go instead into advancing the state of the art.

Complete system sources will be available to everyone. As a result, a user who needs changes in the system will always be free to make them himself, or hire any available programmer or company to make them for him. Users will no longer be at the mercy of one programmer or company which owns the sources and is in sole position to make changes.

Schools will be able to provide a much more educational environment by encouraging all students to study and improve the system code. Harvard's computer lab used to have the policy that no program could be installed on the system if its sources were not on public display, and upheld it by actually refusing to install certain programs. I was very much inspired by this.

Finally, the overhead of considering who owns the system software and what one is or is not entitled to do with it will be lifted.

Arrangements to make people pay for using a program, including licensing of copies, always incur a tremendous cost to society through the cumbersome mechanisms necessary to figure out how much (that is, which programs) a person must pay for. And only a police state can force everyone to obey them. Consider a space station where air must be manufactured at great cost: charging each breather per liter of air may be fair, but wearing the metered gas mask all day and all night is intolerable even if everyone can afford to pay the air bill. And the TV cameras everywhere to see if you ever take the mask off are outrageous. It's better to support the air plant with a head tax and chuck the masks.

Copying all or parts of a program is as natural to a programmer as breathing, and as productive. It ought to be as free.

Some easily rebutted objections to GNU's goals:

> "Nobody will use it if it is free, because that means they can't rely on any support."

> "You have to charge for the program to pay for providing the support."

If people would rather pay for GNU plus service than get GNU free without service, a company to provide just service to people who have obtained GNU free ought to be profitable.

We must distinguish between support in the form of real programming work and mere hand-holding. The former is something one cannot rely on from a software vendor. If your problem is not shared by enough people, the vendor will tell you to get lost.

---

[3] This is another place I failed to distinguish carefully between the two different meanings of "free." The statement as it stands is not false—you can get copies of GNU software at no charge, from your friends or over the Internet. But it does suggest the wrong idea.

If your business needs to be able to rely on support, the only way is to have all the necessary sources and tools. Then you can hire any available person to fix your problem; you are not at the mercy of any individual. With Unix, the price of sources puts this out of consideration for most businesses. With GNU this will be easy. It is still possible for there to be no available competent person, but this problem cannot be blamed on distribution arrangements. GNU does not eliminate all the world's problems, only some of them.

Meanwhile, the users who know nothing about computers need hand-holding: doing things for them which they could easily do themselves but don't know how.

Such services could be provided by companies that sell just hand-holding and repair service. If it is true that users would rather spend money and get a product with service, they will also be willing to buy the service having got the product for free. The service companies will compete in quality and price; users will not be tied to any particular one. Meanwhile, those of us who don't need the service should be able to use the program without paying for the service.

> "You cannot reach many people without advertising, and you must charge for the program to support that."

> "It's no use advertising a program people can get free."

There are various forms of free or very cheap publicity that can be used to inform numbers of computer users about something like GNU. But it may be true that one can reach more microcomputer users with advertising. If this is really so, a business which advertises the service of copying and mailing GNU for a fee ought to be successful enough to pay for its advertising and more. This way, only the users who benefit from the advertising pay for it.

On the other hand, if many people get GNU from their friends, and such companies don't succeed, this will show that advertising was not really necessary to spread GNU. Why is it that free market advocates don't want to let the free market decide this[4]?

> "My company needs a proprietary operating system to get a competitive edge."

GNU will remove operating system software from the realm of competition. You will not be able to get an edge in this area, but neither will your competitors be able to get an edge over you. You and they will compete in other areas, while benefiting mutually in this one. If your business is selling an operating system, you will not like GNU, but that's tough on you. If your business is something else, GNU can save you from being pushed into the expensive business of selling operating systems.

---

[4] The Free Software Foundation raises most of its funds from a distribution service, although it is a charity rather than a company. If **no one** chooses to obtain copies by ordering them from the FSF, it will be unable to do its work. But this does not mean that proprietary restrictions are justified to force every user to pay. If a small fraction of all the users order copies from the FSF, that is sufficient to keep the FSF afloat. So we ask users to choose to support us in this way. Have you done your part?

I would like to see GNU development supported by gifts from many manufacturers and users, reducing the cost to each.[5]

"Don't programmers deserve a reward for their creativity?"

If anything deserves a reward, it is social contribution. Creativity can be a social contribution, but only in so far as society is free to use the results. If programmers deserve to be rewarded for creating innovative programs, by the same token they deserve to be punished if they restrict the use of these programs.

"Shouldn't a programmer be able to ask for a reward for his creativity?"

There is nothing wrong with wanting pay for work, or seeking to maximize one's income, as long as one does not use means that are destructive. But the means customary in the field of software today are based on destruction.

Extracting money from users of a program by restricting their use of it is destructive because the restrictions reduce the amount and the ways that the program can be used. This reduces the amount of wealth that humanity derives from the program. When there is a deliberate choice to restrict, the harmful consequences are deliberate destruction.

The reason a good citizen does not use such destructive means to become wealthier is that, if everyone did so, we would all become poorer from the mutual destructiveness. This is Kantian ethics; or, the Golden Rule. Since I do not like the consequences that result if everyone hoards information, I am required to consider it wrong for one to do so. Specifically, the desire to be rewarded for one's creativity does not justify depriving the world in general of all or part of that creativity.

"Won't programmers starve?"

I could answer that nobody is forced to be a programmer. Most of us cannot manage to get any money for standing on the street and making faces. But we are not, as a result, condemned to spend our lives standing on the street making faces, and starving. We do something else.

But that is the wrong answer because it accepts the questioner's implicit assumption: that without ownership of software, programmers cannot possibly be paid a cent. Supposedly it is all or nothing.

The real reason programmers will not starve is that it will still be possible for them to get paid for programming; just not paid as much as now.

Restricting copying is not the only basis for business in software. It is the most common basis because it brings in the most money. If it were prohibited, or rejected by the customer, software business would move to other bases of organization which are now used less often. There are always numerous ways to organize any kind of business.

Probably programming will not be as lucrative on the new basis as it is now. But that is not an argument against the change. It is not considered an injustice that sales clerks make the salaries that they now do. If programmers made the same, that would not be an injustice either. (In practice they would still make considerably more than that.)

---

[5] A group of computer companies recently pooled funds to support maintenance of the GNU C Compiler.

"Don't people have a right to control how their creativity is used?"

"Control over the use of one's ideas" really constitutes control over other people's lives; and it is usually used to make their lives more difficult.

People who have studied the issue of intellectual property rights carefully (such as lawyers) say that there is no intrinsic right to intellectual property. The kinds of supposed intellectual property rights that the government recognizes were created by specific acts of legislation for specific purposes.

For example, the patent system was established to encourage inventors to disclose the details of their inventions. Its purpose was to help society rather than to help inventors. At the time, the life span of 17 years for a patent was short compared with the rate of advance of the state of the art. Since patents are an issue only among manufacturers, for whom the cost and effort of a license agreement are small compared with setting up production, the patents often do not do much harm. They do not obstruct most individuals who use patented products.

The idea of copyright did not exist in ancient times, when authors frequently copied other authors at length in works of non-fiction. This practice was useful, and is the only way many authors' works have survived even in part. The copyright system was created expressly for the purpose of encouraging authorship. In the domain for which it was invented—books, which could be copied economically only on a printing press—it did little harm, and did not obstruct most of the individuals who read the books.

All intellectual property rights are just licenses granted by society because it was thought, rightly or wrongly, that society as a whole would benefit by granting them. But in any particular situation, we have to ask: are we really better off granting such license? What kind of act are we licensing a person to do?

The case of programs today is very different from that of books a hundred years ago. The fact that the easiest way to copy a program is from one neighbor to another, the fact that a program has both source code and object code which are distinct, and the fact that a program is used rather than read and enjoyed, combine to create a situation in which a person who enforces a copyright is harming society as a whole both materially and spiritually; in which a person should not do so regardless of whether the law enables him to.

"Competition makes things get done better."

The paradigm of competition is a race: by rewarding the winner, we encourage everyone to run faster. When capitalism really works this way, it does a good job; but its defenders are wrong in assuming it always works this way. If the runners forget why the reward is offered and become intent on winning, no matter how, they may find other strategies—such as, attacking other runners. If the runners get into a fist fight, they will all finish late.

Proprietary and secret software is the moral equivalent of runners in a fist fight. Sad to say, the only referee we've got does not seem to object to fights; he just regulates them ("For every ten yards you run, you can fire one shot"). He really ought to break them up, and penalize runners for even trying to fight.

"Won't everyone stop programming without a monetary incentive?"

Actually, many people will program with absolutely no monetary incentive. Programming has an irresistible fascination for some people, usually the people who are best at it. There is no shortage of professional musicians who keep at it even though they have no hope of making a living that way.

But really this question, though commonly asked, is not appropriate to the situation. Pay for programmers will not disappear, only become less. So the right question is, will anyone program with a reduced monetary incentive? My experience shows that they will.

For more than ten years, many of the world's best programmers worked at the Artificial Intelligence Lab for far less money than they could have had anywhere else. They got many kinds of non-monetary rewards: fame and appreciation, for example. And creativity is also fun, a reward in itself.

Then most of them left when offered a chance to do the same interesting work for a lot of money.

What the facts show is that people will program for reasons other than riches; but if given a chance to make a lot of money as well, they will come to expect and demand it. Low-paying organizations do poorly in competition with high-paying ones, but they do not have to do badly if the high-paying ones are banned.

> "We need the programmers desperately. If they demand that we stop helping our neighbors, we have to obey."

You're never so desperate that you have to obey this sort of demand. Remember: millions for defense, but not a cent for tribute!

> "Programmers need to make a living somehow."

In the short run, this is true. However, there are plenty of ways that programmers could make a living without selling the right to use a program. This way is customary now because it brings programmers and businessmen the most money, not because it is the only way to make a living. It is easy to find other ways if you want to find them.

Here are a number of examples:

- A manufacturer introducing a new computer will pay for the porting of operating systems onto the new hardware.

- The sale of teaching, hand-holding and maintenance services could also employ programmers.

- People with new ideas could distribute programs as freeware, asking for donations from satisfied users, or selling hand-holding services. I have met people who are already working this way successfully.

- Users with related needs can form users' groups, and pay dues. A group would contract with programming companies to write programs that the group's members would like to use.

All sorts of development can be funded with a Software Tax:

- Suppose everyone who buys a computer has to pay x percent of the price as a software tax. The government gives this to an agency like the NSF to spend on software development.

- But if the computer buyer makes a donation to software development himself, he can take a credit against the tax. He can donate to the project of his own choosing—often, chosen because he hopes to use the results when it is done. He can take a credit for any amount of donation up to the total tax he had to pay.
- The total tax rate could be decided by a vote of the payers of the tax, weighted according to the amount they will be taxed on.

The consequences:

- The computer-using community supports software development.
- This community decides what level of support is needed.
- Users who care which projects their share is spent on can choose this for themselves.

In the long run, making programs free is a step toward the post-scarcity world, where nobody will have to work very hard just to make a living. People will be free to devote themselves to activities that are fun, such as programming, after spending the necessary ten hours a week on required tasks such as legislation, family counseling, robot repair, and asteroid prospecting. There will be no need to be able to make a living from programming.

We have already greatly reduced the amount of work that the whole society must do for its actual productivity, but only a little of this has translated itself into leisure for workers because much nonproductive activity is required to accompany productive activity. The main causes of this are bureaucracy and isometric struggles against competition. Free software will greatly reduce these drains in the area of software production. We must do this, in order for technical gains in productivity to translate into less work for us.

3 Free Software Definition

We maintain this free software definition to show clearly what must be true about a particular software program for it to be considered free software.

"Free software" is a matter of liberty, not price. To understand the concept, you should think of "free" as in "free speech," not as in "free beer."

Free software is a matter of the users' freedom to run, copy, distribute, study, change, and improve the software. More precisely, it refers to four kinds of freedom, for the users of the software:

- Freedom 0: The freedom to run the program, for any purpose.

- Freedom 1: The freedom to study how the program works, and adapt it to your needs. (Access to the source code is a precondition for this.)

- Freedom 2: The freedom to redistribute copies so you can help your neighbor.

- Freedom 3: The freedom to improve the program, and release your improvements to the public, so that the whole community benefits. (Access to the source code is a precondition for this.)

A program is free software if users have all of these freedoms. Thus, you should be free to redistribute copies, either with or without modifications, either gratis or charging a fee for distribution, to anyone anywhere. Being free to do these things means (among other things) that you do not have to ask or pay for permission.

You should also have the freedom to make modifications and use them privately in your own work or play, without even mentioning that they exist. If you do publish your changes, you should not be required to notify anyone in particular, or in any particular way.

The freedom to use a program means the freedom for any kind of person or organization to use it on any kind of computer system, for any kind of overall job, and without being required to communicate subsequently with the developer or any other specific entity.

The freedom to redistribute copies must include binary or executable forms of the program, as well as source code, for both modified and unmodified versions. (Distributing programs in runnable form is necessary for conveniently installable free operating systems.) It is OK if there is no way to produce a binary or executable form, but people must have the freedom to redistribute such forms should they find a way to make them.

In order for freedoms 1 and 3 (the freedom to make changes and the freedom to publish improved versions) to be meaningful, one must have access to the source code of the program. Therefore, accessibility of source code is a necessary condition for free software.

Originally written in 1996, this version is part of *Free Software, Free Society: Selected Essays of Richard M. Stallman*, 2002, GNU Press (http://www.gnupress.org); ISBN 1-882114-98-1.

In order for these freedoms to be real, they must be irrevocable as long as you do nothing wrong; if the developer of the software has the power to revoke the license, without your doing anything to give cause, the software is not free.

However, certain kinds of rules about the manner of distributing free software are acceptable, when they don't conflict with the central freedoms. For example, copyleft (very simply stated) is the rule that when redistributing the program, you cannot add restrictions to deny other people the central freedoms. This rule does not conflict with the central freedoms; rather it protects them.

Thus, you may have paid money to get copies of free software, or you may have obtained copies at no charge. But regardless of how you got your copies, you always have the freedom to copy and change the software, even to sell copies.

"Free software" does not mean "non-commercial." A free program must be available for commercial use, commercial development, and commercial distribution. Commercial development of free software is no longer unusual; such free commercial software is very important.

Rules about how to package a modified version are acceptable, if they do not effectively block your freedom to release modified versions. Rules that "if you make the program available in this way, you must make it available in that way also" can be acceptable too, on the same condition. (Note that such a rule still leaves you the choice of whether to publish the program or not.) It is also acceptable for the license to require that, if you have distributed a modified version and a previous developer asks for a copy of it, you must send one.

In the GNU project, we use "copyleft" to protect these freedoms legally for everyone. But non-copylefted free software also exists. We believe there are important reasons why it is better to use copyleft, but if your program is non-copylefted free software, we can still use it.

Sometimes government export control regulations and trade sanctions can constrain your freedom to distribute copies of programs internationally. Software developers do not have the power to eliminate or override these restrictions, but what they can and must do is refuse to impose them as conditions of use of the program. In this way, the restrictions will not affect activities and people outside the jurisdictions of these governments.

When talking about free software, it is best to avoid using terms like "give away" or "for free," because those terms imply that the issue is about price, not freedom. Some common terms such as "piracy" embody opinions we hope you won't endorse. See "Words to Avoid" in this book for a discussion of these terms. We also have a list of translations of "free software" into various languages.

Finally, note that criteria such as those stated in this free software definition require careful thought for their interpretation. To decide whether a specific software license qualifies as a free software license, we judge it based on these criteria to determine whether it fits their spirit as well as the precise words. If a license includes unconscionable restrictions, we reject it, even if we did not anticipate the issue in these criteria. Sometimes a license requirement raises an issue that calls for extensive thought, including discussions with a lawyer, before we can decide if the requirement is acceptable. When we reach a conclusion about a new issue, we often update these criteria to make it easier to see why certain licenses do or don't qualify.

If you are interested in whether a specific license qualifies as a free software license, see our list of licenses, http://www.gnu.org/licenses/license-list.html. If the license you are concerned with is not listed there, you can ask us about it by sending us email at licensing@gnu.org.

4 Why Software Should Not Have Owners

Digital information technology contributes to the world by making it easier to copy and modify information. Computers promise to make this easier for all of us.

Not everyone wants it to be easier. The system of copyright gives software programs "owners," most of whom aim to withhold software's potential benefit from the rest of the public. They would like to be the only ones who can copy and modify the software that we use.

The copyright system grew up with printing—a technology for mass production copying. Copyright fit in well with this technology because it restricted only the mass producers of copies. It did not take freedom away from readers of books. An ordinary reader, who did not own a printing press, could copy books only with pen and ink, and few readers were sued for that.

Digital technology is more flexible than the printing press: when information has digital form, you can easily copy it to share it with others. This very flexibility makes a bad fit with a system like copyright. That's the reason for the increasingly nasty and draconian measures now used to enforce software copyright. Consider these four practices of the Software Publishers Association (SPA):

- Massive propaganda saying it is wrong to disobey the owners to help your friend.

- Solicitation for stool pigeons to inform on their coworkers and colleagues.

- Raids (with police help) on offices and schools, in which people are told they must prove they are innocent of illegal copying.

- Prosecution (by the U.S. government, at the SPA's request) of people such as MIT's David LaMacchia,[1] not for copying software (he is not accused of copying any), but merely for leaving copying facilities unguarded and failing to censor their use.

All four practices resemble those used in the former Soviet Union, where every copying machine had a guard to prevent forbidden copying, and where individuals had to copy information secretly and pass it from hand to hand as *samizdat*. There is of course a difference: the motive for information control in the Soviet Union was political; in the U.S. the motive is profit. But it is the actions that affect us, not the motive. Any attempt to block the sharing of information, no matter why, leads to the same methods and the same harshness.

Owners make several kinds of arguments for giving them the power to control how we use information:

---

[1] On January 27th, 1995, David LaMacchia's case was dismissed and has not yet been appealed.

Originally written in 1994, this version is part of *Free Software, Free Society: Selected Essays of Richard M. Stallman*, 2002, GNU Press (http://www.gnupress.org); ISBN 1-882114-98-1.

Name Calling

Owners use smear words such as "piracy" and "theft," as well as expert terminology such as "intellectual property" and "damage," to suggest a certain line of thinking to the public—a simplistic analogy between programs and physical objects.

Our ideas and intuitions about property for material objects are about whether it is right to take an object away from someone else. They don't directly apply to making a copy of something. But the owners ask us to apply them anyway.

Exaggeration

Owners say that they suffer "harm" or "economic loss" when users copy programs themselves. But the copying has no direct effect on the owner, and it harms no one. The owner can lose only if the person who made the copy would otherwise have paid for one from the owner.

A little thought shows that most such people would not have bought copies. Yet the owners compute their "losses" as if each and every one would have bought a copy. That is exaggeration—to put it kindly.

The Law

Owners often describe the current state of the law, and the harsh penalties they can threaten us with. Implicit in this approach is the suggestion that today's law reflects an unquestionable view of morality—yet at the same time, we are urged to regard these penalties as facts of nature that can't be blamed on anyone.

This line of persuasion isn't designed to stand up to critical thinking; it's intended to reinforce a habitual mental pathway.

It's elementary that laws don't decide right and wrong. Every American should know that, forty years ago, it was against the law in many states for a black person to sit in the front of a bus; but only racists would say sitting there was wrong.

Natural Rights

Authors often claim a special connection with programs they have written, and go on to assert that, as a result, their desires and interests concerning the program simply outweigh those of anyone else—or even those of the whole rest of the world. (Typically companies, not authors, hold the copyrights on software, but we are expected to ignore this discrepancy.)

To those who propose this as an ethical axiom—the author is more important than you—I can only say that I, a notable software author myself, call it bunk.

But people in general are only likely to feel any sympathy with the natural rights claims for two reasons.

One reason is an over-stretched analogy with material objects. When I cook spaghetti, I do object if someone else eats it, because then I cannot eat it. His action hurts me exactly as much as it benefits him; only one of us can eat the spaghetti, so the question is, which? The smallest distinction between us is enough to tip the ethical balance.

But whether you run or change a program I wrote affects you directly and me only indirectly. Whether you give a copy to your friend affects you and your friend much more than it affects me. I shouldn't have the power to tell you not to do these things. No one should.

The second reason is that people have been told that natural rights for authors is the accepted and unquestioned tradition of our society.

As a matter of history, the opposite is true. The idea of natural rights of authors was proposed and decisively rejected when the U.S. Constitution was drawn up. That's why the Constitution only permits a system of copyright and does not require one; that's why it says that copyright must be temporary. It also states that the purpose of copyright is to promote progress—not to reward authors. Copyright does reward authors somewhat, and publishers more, but that is intended as a means of modifying their behavior.

The real established tradition of our society is that copyright cuts into the natural rights of the public—and that this can only be justified for the public's sake.

Economics

The final argument made for having owners of software is that this leads to production of more software.

Unlike the others, this argument at least takes a legitimate approach to the subject. It is based on a valid goal—satisfying the users of software. And it is empirically clear that people will produce more of something if they are well paid for doing so.

But the economic argument has a flaw: it is based on the assumption that the difference is only a matter of how much money we have to pay. It assumes that "production of software" is what we want, whether the software has owners or not.

People readily accept this assumption because it accords with our experiences with material objects. Consider a sandwich, for instance. You might well be able to get an equivalent sandwich either free or for a price. If so, the amount you pay is the only difference. Whether or not you have to buy it, the sandwich has the same taste, the same nutritional value, and in either case you can only eat it once. Whether you get the sandwich from an owner or not cannot directly affect anything but the amount of money you have afterwards.

This is true for any kind of material object—whether or not it has an owner does not directly affect what it is, or what you can do with it if you acquire it.

But if a program has an owner, this very much affects what it is, and what you can do with a copy if you buy one. The difference is not just a matter of money. The system of owners of software encourages software owners to produce something—but not what society really needs. And it causes intangible ethical pollution that affects us all.

What does society need? It needs information that is truly available to its citizens—for example, programs that people can read, fix, adapt, and improve, not just operate. But what software owners typically deliver is a black box that we can't study or change.

Society also needs freedom. When a program has an owner, the users lose freedom to control part of their own lives.

And above all society needs to encourage the spirit of voluntary cooperation in its citizens. When software owners tell us that helping our neighbors in a natural way is "piracy," they pollute our society's civic spirit.

This is why we say that free software is a matter of freedom, not price.

The economic argument for owners is erroneous, but the economic issue is real. Some people write useful software for the pleasure of writing it or for admiration and love; but if we want more software than those people write, we need to raise funds.

For ten years now, free software developers have tried various methods of finding funds, with some success. There's no need to make anyone rich; the median U.S. family income, around $35k, proves to be enough incentive for many jobs that are less satisfying than programming.

For years, until a fellowship made it unnecessary, I made a living from custom enhancements of the free software I had written. Each enhancement was added to the standard released version and thus eventually became available to the general public. Clients paid me so that I would work on the enhancements they wanted, rather than on the features I would otherwise have considered highest priority.

The Free Software Foundation (FSF), a tax-exempt charity for free software development, raises funds by selling GNU CD-ROMs, T-shirts, manuals, and deluxe distributions, (all of which users are free to copy and change) as well as from donations. It now has a staff of five programmers, plus three employees who handle mail orders.

Some free software developers make money by selling support services. Cygnus Support,[2] with around 50 employees [when this article was written, in 1994], estimates that about 15 per cent of its staff activity is free software development—a respectable percentage for a software company.

A number of companies have funded the continued development of the free GNU compiler for the language C. Meanwhile, the GNU compiler for the Ada language is being funded by the U.S. Air Force, which believes this is the most cost-effective way to get a high quality compiler [Air Force funding ended some time ago; the GNU Ada Compiler is now in service, and its maintenance is funded commercially].

All these examples are small; the free software movement is still small, and still young. But the example of listener-supported radio in the U.S. shows it's possible to support a large activity without forcing each user to pay.

As a computer user today, you may find yourself using a proprietary program. If your friend asks to make a copy, it would be wrong to refuse. Cooperation is more important than copyright. But underground, closet cooperation does not make for a

---

[2] Cygnus Support continued to be successful, but then it accepted outside investment, got greedy, and began developing non-free software. Then it was acquired by Red Hat, which has rereleased most of those programs as free software.

good society. A person should aspire to live an upright life openly with pride, and this means saying "No" to proprietary software.

You deserve to be able to cooperate openly and freely with other people who use software. You deserve to be able to learn how the software works, and to teach your students with it. You deserve to be able to hire your favorite programmer to fix it when it breaks.

You deserve free software.

5 What's in a Name?

Names convey meanings; our choice of names determines the meaning of what we say. An inappropriate name gives people the wrong idea. A rose by any name would smell as sweet—but if you call it a pen, people will be rather disappointed when they try to write with it. And if you call pens "roses," people may not realize what they are good for. If you call our operating system "Linux," that conveys a mistaken idea of the system's origin, history, and purpose. If you call it "GNU/Linux," that conveys (though not in detail) an accurate idea.

But does this matter for our community? Is it important whether people know the system's origin, history, and purpose? Yes—because people who forget history are often condemned to repeat it. The Free World that has developed around GNU/Linux is not secure; the problems that led us to develop GNU are not completely eradicated, and they threaten to come back.

When I explain why it's appropriate to call the operating system "GNU/Linux" rather than "Linux," people sometimes respond this way:

> Granted that the GNU Project deserves credit for this work, is it really
> worth a fuss when people don't give credit? Isn't the important thing that
> the job was done, not who did it? You ought to relax, take pride in the
> job well done, and not worry about the credit.

This would be wise advice, if only the situation were like that—if the job were done and it were time to relax. If only that were true! But challenges abound, and this is no time to take the future for granted. Our community's strength rests on commitment to freedom and cooperation. Using the name GNU/Linux is a way for people to remind themselves and inform others of these goals.

It is possible to write good free software without thinking of GNU; much good work has been done in the name of Linux also. But "Linux" has been associated ever since it was first coined with a philosophy that does not make a commitment to the freedom to cooperate. As the name becomes used increasingly by business, we will have even more trouble making it connect with community spirit.

A great challenge to the future of free software comes from the tendency of the "Linux" distribution companies to add non-free software to GNU/Linux in the name of convenience and power. All the major commercial distribution developers do this; none produces a distribution that is entirely free. Most of them do not clearly identify the non-free packages in their distributions. Many even develop non-free software and add it to the system. Some outrageously advertise "Linux"

Originally written in 2000, this printed version is part of *Free Software, Free Society: Selected Essays of Richard M. Stallman*, 2002, GNU Press (http://www.gnupress.org); ISBN 1-882114-98-1.

systems that are "licensed per seat," which give the user as much freedom as Microsoft Windows.

People justify adding non-free software in the name of the "popularity of Linux"—in effect, valuing popularity above freedom. Sometimes this is openly admitted. For instance, *Wired* magazine says that Robert McMillan, editor of *Linux Magazine*, "feels that the move toward open source software should be fueled by technical, rather than political, decisions." And Caldera's CEO openly urged users to drop the goal of freedom and work instead for the "popularity of Linux."

Adding non-free software to the GNU/Linux system may increase the popularity, if by popularity we mean the number of people using some of GNU/Linux in combination with non-free software. But at the same time, it implicitly encourages the community to accept non-free software as a good thing, and forget the goal of freedom. It is no use driving faster if you can't stay on the road.

When the non-free "add-on" is a library or programming tool, it can become a trap for free software developers. When they write free software that depends on the non-free package, their software cannot be part of a completely free system.[1]

If our community keeps moving in this direction, it could redirect the future of GNU/Linux into a mosaic of free and non-free components. Five years from now, we will surely still have plenty of free software; but if we are not careful, it will hardly be usable without the non-free software that users expect to find with it. If this happens, our campaign for freedom will have failed.

If releasing free alternatives were simply a matter of programming, solving future problems might become easier as our community's development resources increase. But we face obstacles which threaten to make this harder: laws that prohibit free software. As software patents mount up and as laws like the DMCA[2] are used to prohibit the development of free software for important jobs such as viewing a DVD or listening to a RealAudio stream, we will find ourselves with no clear way to fight the patented and secret data formats except to reject the non-free programs that use them.

Meeting these challenges will require many different kinds of effort. But what we need above all, to confront any kind of challenge, is to remember the goal of freedom to cooperate. We can't expect a mere desire for powerful, reliable software to motivate people to make great efforts. We need the kind of determination that people have when they fight for their freedom and their community, determination to keep on for years and not give up.

In our community, this goal and this determination emanate mainly from the GNU Project. We're the ones who talk about freedom and community as some-

---

[1] The Motif and Qt GUI libraries trapped large amounts of free software in this way in the past, creating problems whose solutions took years. The Qt problem is solved because Qt is now free; the Motif problem is still not entirely solved, since its free replacement, LessTif, needs some polishing (please volunteer!). Sun's non-free Java implementation and standard Java libraries are now causing a similar problem, and replacing them with free software is a major GNU effort now.

[2] The Digital Millennium Copyright Act of 1998 seeks to update U.S. copyright law; topics included in the DMCA are provisions concerning the circumvention of copyright protection systems, fair use, and online service provider liability. See Chapter 12 [Misinterpreting Copyright—A Series of Errors], page 77, for more details about the DMCA.

thing to stand firm for; the organizations that speak of "Linux" normally don't say this. The magazines about "Linux" are typically full of ads for non-free software; the companies that package "Linux" add non-free software to the system; other companies "support Linux" with non-free applications; the user groups for "Linux" typically invite salesman to present those applications. The main place people in our community are likely to come across the idea of freedom and determination is in the GNU Project.

But when people come across it, will they feel it relates to them?

People who know they are using a system that came out of the GNU Project can see a direct relationship between themselves and GNU. They won't automatically agree with our philosophy, but at least they will see a reason to think seriously about it. In contrast, people who consider themselves "Linux users," and believe that the GNU Project "developed tools which proved to be useful in Linux," typically perceive only an indirect relationship between GNU and themselves. They may just ignore the GNU philosophy when they come across it.

The GNU Project is idealistic, and anyone encouraging idealism today faces a great obstacle: the prevailing ideology encourages people to dismiss idealism as "impractical." Our idealism has been extremely practical: it is the reason we have a free GNU/Linux operating system. People who love this system ought to know that it is our idealism made real.

If "the job" really were done, if there were nothing at stake except credit, perhaps it would be wiser to let the matter drop. But we are not in that position. To inspire people to do the work that needs to be done, we need to be recognized for what we have already done. Please help us, by calling the operating system GNU/Linux.

6 Why "Free Software" is Better than "Open Source"

While free software by any other name would give you the same freedom, it makes a big difference which name we use: different words *convey different* ideas.

In 1998, some of the people in the free software community began using the term "open source software"[1] instead of "free software" to describe what they do. The term "open source" quickly became associated with a different approach, a different philosophy, different values, and even a different criterion for which licenses are acceptable. The Free Software movement and the Open Source movement are today separate movements with different views and goals, although we can and do work together on some practical projects.

The fundamental difference between the two movements is in their values, their ways of looking at the world. For the Open Source movement, the issue of whether software should be open source is a practical question, not an ethical one. As one person put it, "Open source is a development methodology; free software is a social movement." For the Open Source movement, non-free software is a suboptimal solution. For the Free Software movement, non-free software is a social problem and free software is the solution.

Relationship Between the Free Software Movement and Open Source Movement

The Free Software movement and the Open Source movement are like two political camps within the free software community.

Radical groups in the 1960s developed a reputation for factionalism: organizations split because of disagreements on details of strategy, and then treated each other as enemies. Or at least, such is the image people have of them, whether or not it was true.

The relationship between the Free Software movement and the Open Source movement is just the opposite of that picture. We disagree on the basic principles, but agree more or less on the practical recommendations. So we can and do work together on many specific projects. We don't think of the Open Source movement as an enemy. The enemy is proprietary software.

We are not against the Open Source movement, but we don't want to be lumped in with them. We acknowledge that they have contributed to our community, but we created this community, and we want people to know this. We want people to

---

[1] http://www.opensource.org

Originally written in 1998, this version is part of *Free Software, Free Society: Selected Essays of Richard M. Stallman*, 2002, GNU Press (http://www.gnupress.org); ISBN 1-882114-98-1.

associate our achievements with our values and our philosophy, not with theirs. We want to be heard, not obscured behind a group with different views.

So please mention the Free Software movement when you talk about the work we have done, and the software we have developed—such as the GNU/Linux operating system.

Comparing the Two Terms

This rest of this article compares the two terms "free software" and "open source." It shows why the term "open source" does not solve any problems, and in fact creates some.

Ambiguity

The term "free software" has an ambiguity problem: an unintended meaning, "Software you can get for zero price," fits the term just as well as the intended meaning, "software which gives the user certain freedoms." We address this problem by publishing a more precise definition of free software (see the "Free Software Definition,") but this is not a perfect solution; it cannot completely eliminate the problem. An unambiguously correct term would be better, if it didn't have other problems.

Unfortunately, all the alternatives in English have problems of their own. We've looked at many alternatives that people have suggested, but none is so clearly "right" that switching to it would be a good idea. Every proposed replacement for "free software" has a similar kind of semantic problem, or worse—and this includes "open source software."

The official definition of "open source software," as published by the Open Source Initiative, is very close to our definition of free software; however, it is a little looser in some respects, and they have accepted a few licenses that we consider unacceptably restrictive of the users. However, the obvious meaning for the expression "open source software" is "You can look at the source code." This is a much weaker criterion than free software; it includes free software, but also includes semi-free programs such as Xv, and even some proprietary programs, including Qt under its original license (before the QPL).

That obvious meaning for "open source" is not the meaning that its advocates intend. The result is that most people misunderstand what those advocates are advocating. Here is how writer Neal Stephenson defined "open source":

Linux is "open source" software meaning, simply, that anyone can get copies of its source code files.

I don't think he deliberately sought to reject or dispute the "official" definition. I think he simply applied the conventions of the English language to come up with a meaning for the term. The state of Kansas published a similar definition:

Make use of open-source software (OSS). OSS is software for which the source code is freely and publicly available, though the specific licensing agreements vary as to what one is allowed to do with that code.

Of course, the open source people have tried to deal with this by publishing a precise definition for the term, just as we have done for "free software."

But the explanation for "free software" is simple—a person who has grasped the idea of "free speech, not free beer" will not get it wrong again. There is no succinct way to explain the proper meaning of "open source" and show clearly why the natural definition is the wrong one.

Fear of Freedom

The main argument for the term "open source software" is that "free software" makes some people uneasy. That's true: talking about freedom, about ethical issues, about responsibilities as well as convenience, is asking people to think about things they might rather ignore. This can trigger discomfort, and some people may reject the idea for that. It does not follow that society would be better off if we stop talking about these things.

Years ago, free software developers noticed this discomfort reaction, and some started exploring an approach for avoiding it. They figured that by keeping quiet about ethics and freedom, and talking only about the immediate practical benefits of certain free software, they might be able to "sell" the software more effectively to certain users, especially business. The term "open source" is offered as a way of doing more of this—a way to be "more acceptable to business." The views and values of the Open Source movement stem from this decision.

This approach has proved effective, in its own terms. Today many people are switching to free software for purely practical reasons. That is good, as far as it goes, but that isn't all we need to do! Attracting users to free software is not the whole job, just the first step.

Sooner or later these users will be invited to switch back to proprietary software for some practical advantage. Countless companies seek to offer such temptation, and why would users decline? Only if they have learned to *value the freedom* free software gives them, for its own sake. It is up to us to spread this idea—and in order to do that, we have to talk about freedom. A certain amount of the "keep quiet" approach to business can be useful for the community, but we must have plenty of freedom talk too.

At present, we have plenty of "keep quiet," but not enough freedom talk. Most people involved with free software say little about freedom—usually because they seek to be "more acceptable to business." Software distributors especially show this pattern. Some GNU/Linux operating system distributions add proprietary packages to the basic free system, and they invite users to consider this an advantage, rather than a step backwards from freedom.

We are failing to keep up with the influx of free software users, failing to teach people about freedom and our community as fast as they enter it. This is why non-free software (which Qt was when it first became popular), and partially non-free operating system distributions, find such fertile ground. To stop using the word "free" now would be a mistake; we need more, not less, talk about freedom.

If those using the term "open source" draw more users into our community, that is a contribution, but the rest of us will have to work even harder to bring the issue of freedom to those users' attention. We have to say, "It's free software and it gives you freedom!"—more and louder than ever before.

Would a Trademark Help?

The advocates of "open source software" tried to make it a trademark, saying this would enable them to prevent misuse. The attempt went awry when the application was allowed to lapse in 1999; thus, the legal status of "open source" is the same as that of "free software": there is no legal constraint on using it. I have heard reports of a number of companies' calling software packages "open source" even though they did not fit the official definition; I have observed some instances myself.

But would it have made a big difference to use a term that is a trademark? Not necessarily.

Companies also made announcements that give the impression that a program is "open source software" without explicitly saying so. For example, one IBM announcement, about a program that did not fit the official definition, said this: As is common in the open source community, users of the. . . technology will also be able to collaborate with IBM. . .

This did not actually say that the program was "open source," but many readers did not notice that detail. (I should note that IBM was sincerely trying to make this program free software, and later adopted a new license which does make it free software and "open source"; but when that announcement was made, the program did not qualify as either one.)

And here is how Cygnus Solutions, which was formed to be a free software company and subsequently branched out (so to speak) into proprietary software, advertised some proprietary software products: "Cygnus Solutions is a leader in the open source market and has just launched two products into the [GNU/]Linux marketplace."

Unlike IBM, Cygnus was not trying to make these packages free software, and the packages did not come close to qualifying. But Cygnus didn't actually say that these are "open source software," they just made use of the term to give careless readers that impression.

These observations suggest that a trademark would not have truly prevented the confusion that comes with the term "open source."

Misunderstandings(?) of "Open Source"

The Open Source Definition is clear enough, and it is quite clear that the typical non-free program does not qualify. So you would think that "Open Source company" would mean one whose products are free software (or close to it), right? Alas, many companies are trying to give it a different meaning.

At the "Open Source Developers Day" meeting in August 1998, several of the commercial developers invited said they intend to make only a part of their work free software (or "open source"). The focus of their business is on developing proprietary add-ons (software or manuals) to sell to the users of this free software.

They ask us to regard this as legitimate, as part of our community, because some of the money is donated to free software development.

In effect, these companies seek to gain the favorable cachet of "open source" for their proprietary software products—even though those are not "open source software"—because they have some relationship to free software or because the same company also maintains some free software. (One company founder said quite explicitly that they would put, into the free package they support, as little of their work as the community would stand for.)

Over the years, many companies have contributed to free software development. Some of these companies primarily developed non-free software, but the two activities were separate; thus, we could ignore their non-free products, and work with them on free software projects. Then we could honestly thank them afterward for their free software contributions, without talking about the rest of what they did.

We cannot do the same with these new companies, because they won't go let us. These companies actively try to lead the public to lump all their activities together; they want us to regard their non-free software as favorably as we would regard a real contribution, although it is not one. They present themselves as "open source companies," hoping that we will get a warm fuzzy feeling about them, and that we will be fuzzy-minded in applying it.

This manipulative practice would be no less harmful if it were done using the term "free software." But companies do not seem to use the term "free software" that way; perhaps its association with idealism makes it seem unsuitable. The term "open source" opened the door for this.

At a trade show in late 1998, dedicated to the operating system often referred to as "Linux," the featured speaker was an executive from a prominent software company. He was probably invited on account of his company's decision to "support" that system. Unfortunately, their form of "support" consists of releasing non-free software that works with the system—in other words, using our community as a market but not contributing to it.

He said, "There is no way we will make our product open source, but perhaps we will make it 'internal' open source. If we allow our customer support staff to have access to the source code, they could fix bugs for the customers, and we could provide a better product and better service." (This is not an exact quote, as I did not write his words down, but it gets the gist.)

People in the audience afterward told me, "He just doesn't get the point." But is that so? Which point did he not get?

He did not miss the point of the Open Source movement. That movement does not say users should have freedom, only that allowing more people to look at the source code and help improve it makes for faster and better development. The executive grasped that point completely; unwilling to carry out that approach in full, users included, he was considering implementing it partially, within the company.

The point that he missed is the point that "open source" was designed not to raise: the point that users deserve freedom.

Spreading the idea of freedom is a big job—it needs your help. That's why we stick to the term "free software" in the GNU Project, so we can help do that job.

If you feel that freedom and community are important for their own sake—not just for the convenience they bring—please join us in using the term "free software."[2]

---

[2] Joe Barr wrote an article called Live and let license that gives his perspective on this issue.

7 Releasing Free Software if You Work at a University

In the Free Software Movement, we believe computer users should have the freedom to change and redistribute the software that they use. The "free" in free software refers to freedom: it means users have the freedom to run, modify and redistribute the software. Free software contributes to human knowledge, while non-free software does not. Universities should therefore encourage free software for the sake of advancing human knowledge, just as they should encourage scientists and scholars to publish their work.

Alas, many university administrators have a grasping attitude towards software (and towards science); they see programs as opportunities for income, not as opportunities to contribute to human knowledge. Free software developers have been coping with this tendency for almost 20 years.

When I started developing the GNU operating system in 1984, my first step was to quit my job at MIT. I did this specifically so that the MIT licensing office would be unable to interfere with releasing GNU as free software. I had planned an approach for licensing the programs in GNU that ensures that all modified versions must be free software as well, an approach that developed into the GNU General Public License (GNU GPL), and I did not want to have to beg the MIT administration to let me use it.

Over the years, university affiliates have often come to the Free Software Foundation for advice on how to cope with administrators who see software only as something to sell. One good method, applicable even for specifically funded projects, is to base your work on an existing program that was released under the GNU GPL. Then you can tell the administrators, "We're not allowed to release the modified version except under the GNU GPL—any other way would be copyright infringement." After the dollar signs fade from their eyes, they will usually consent to releasing it as free software.

You can also ask your funding sponsor for help. When a group at NYU developed the GNU Ada Compiler, with funding from the U.S. Air Force, the contract explicitly called for donating the resulting code to the Free Software Foundation. Work out the arrangement with the sponsor first, then politely show the university administration that it is not open to renegotiation. They would rather have a contract to develop free software than no contract at all, so they will most likely go along.

Whatever you do, raise the issue early—certainly before the program is half finished. At this point, the university still needs you, so you can play hardball: tell the administration you will finish the program, make it usable, if they have agreed

Originally written in 2002, this version is part of *Free Software, Free Society: Selected Essays of Richard M. Stallman*, 2002, GNU Press (http://www.gnupress.org); ISBN 1-882114-98-1.

in writing to make it free software (and agreed to your choice of free software license). Otherwise you will work on it only enough to write a paper about it, and never make a version good enough to release. When the administrators know their choice is to have a free software package that brings credit to the university or nothing at all, they will usually choose the former.

Not all universities have grasping policies. The University of Texas has a policy that, by default, all software developed there is released as free software under the GNU General Public License. Univates in Brazil, and the Indian Institute of Information Technology in Hyderabad, India, both have policies in favor of releasing software under the GPL. By developing faculty support first, you may be able to institute such a policy at your university. Present the issue as one of principle: does the university have a mission to advance human knowledge, or is its sole purpose to perpetuate itself?

Whatever approach you use, it helps to have determination and adopt an ethical perspective, as we do in the Free Software Movement. To treat the public ethically, the software should be free—as in freedom—for the whole public.

Many developers of free software profess narrowly practical reasons for doing so: they advocate allowing others to share and change software as an expedient for making software powerful and reliable. If those values motivate you to develop free software, well and good, and thank you for your contribution. But those values will not give you a good footing to stand firm when university administrators try to tempt you to make the program non-free.

For instance, they may argue that "We could make it even more powerful and reliable with all the money we can get." This claim may or may not come true in the end, but it is hard to disprove in advance. They may suggest a license to offer copies "free of charge, for academic use only," which would tell the general public they don't deserve freedom, and argue that this will obtain the cooperation of academia, which is all (they say) you need.

If you start from "pragmatic" values, it is hard to give a good reason for rejecting these dead-end proposals, but you can do it easily if you base your stand on ethical and political values. What good is it to make a program powerful and reliable at the expense of users' freedom? Shouldn't freedom apply outside academia as well as within it? The answers are obvious if freedom and community are among your goals. Free software respects the users' freedom, while non-free software negates it.

Nothing strengthens your resolve like knowing that the community's freedom depends, in one instance, on you.

8 Selling Free Software

Many people believe that the spirit of the GNU project is that you should not charge money for distributing copies of software, or that you should charge as little as possible—just enough to cover the cost.

Actually, we encourage people who redistribute free software to charge as much as they wish or can. If this seems surprising to you, please read on.

The word "free" has two legitimate general meanings; it can refer either to freedom or to price. When we speak of "free software," we're talking about freedom, not price.[1] Specifically, it means that a user is free to run the program, change the program, and redistribute the program with or without changes.

Free programs are sometimes distributed gratis, and sometimes for a substantial price. Often the same program is available in both ways from different places. The program is free regardless of the price, because users have freedom in using it.

Non-free programs are usually sold for a high price, but sometimes a store will give you a copy at no charge. That doesn't make it free software, though. Price or no price, the program is non-free because users don't have freedom.

Since free software is not a matter of price, a low price isn't more free, or closer to free. So if you are redistributing copies of free software, you might as well charge a substantial fee and make some money. Redistributing free software is a good and legitimate activity; if you do it, you might as well make a profit from it.

Free software is a community project, and everyone who depends on it ought to look for ways to contribute to building the community. For a distributor, the way to do this is to give a part of the profit to the Free Software Foundation or some other free software development project. By funding development, you can advance the world of free software.

Distributing free software is an opportunity to raise funds for development. Don't waste it!

In order to contribute funds, you need to have some extra. If you charge too low a fee, you won't have anything to spare to support development.

Will a higher distribution price hurt some users?

People sometimes worry that a high distribution fee will put free software out of range for users who don't have a lot of money. With proprietary software, a high price does exactly that—but free software is different.

The difference is that free software naturally tends to spread around, and there are many ways to get it.

---

[1] Remember to think of "free" as in "free speech," not as in "free beer."

Originally written in 1996, this version is part of *Free Software, Free Society: Selected Essays of Richard M. Stallman*, 2002, GNU Press (http://www.gnupress.org); ISBN 1-882114-98-1.

Software hoarders try their damnedest to stop you from running a proprietary program without paying the standard price. If this price is high, that does make it hard for some users to use the program.

With free software, users don't have to pay the distribution fee in order to use the software. They can copy the program from a friend who has a copy, or with the help of a friend who has network access. Or several users can join together, split the price of one CD-ROM, then each in turn can install the software. A high CD-ROM price is not a major obstacle when the software is free.

Will a higher distribution price discourage use of free software?

Another common concern is for the popularity of free software. People think that a high price for distribution would reduce the number of users, or that a low price is likely to encourage users.

This is true for proprietary software—but free software is different. With so many ways to get copies, the price of distribution service has less effect on popularity.

In the long run, how many people use free software is determined mainly by how much free software can do, and how easy it is to use. Many users will continue to use proprietary software if free software can't do all the jobs they want to do. Thus, if we want to increase the number of users in the long run, we should above all develop more free software.

The most direct way to do this is by writing needed free software or manuals yourself. But if you do distribution rather than writing, the best way you can help is by raising funds for others to write them.

The term "selling software" can be confusing too

Strictly speaking, "selling" means trading goods for money. Selling a copy of a free program is legitimate, and we encourage it.

However, when people think of "selling software," they usually imagine doing it the way most companies do it: making the software proprietary rather than free.

So unless you're going to draw distinctions carefully, the way this article does, we suggest it is better to avoid using the term "selling software" and choose some other wording instead. For example, you could say "distributing free software for a fee"—that is unambiguous.

High or low fees, and the GNU GPL

Except for one special situation, the GNU General Public License (GNU GPL) has no requirements about how much you can charge for distributing a copy of free software. You can charge nothing, a penny, a dollar, or a billion dollars. It's up to you, and the marketplace, so don't complain to us if nobody wants to pay a billion dollars for a copy.

The one exception is in the case where binaries are distributed without the corresponding complete source code. Those who do this are required by the GNU GPL to provide source code on subsequent request. Without a limit on the fee for the source code, they would be able set a fee too large for anyone to pay—such as a billion dollars—and thus pretend to release source code while in truth concealing it. So in this case we have to limit the fee for source, to ensure the user's freedom. In ordinary situations, however, there is no such justification for limiting distribution fees, so we do not limit them.

Sometimes companies whose activities cross the line of what the GNU GPL permits plead for permission, saying that they "won't charge money for the GNU software" or such like. They don't get anywhere this way. Free software is about freedom, and enforcing the GPL is defending freedom. When we defend users' freedom, we are not distracted by side issues such as how much of a distribution fee is charged. Freedom is the issue, the whole issue, and the only issue.

9 Free Software Needs Free Documentation

The biggest deficiency in free operating systems is not in the software—it is the lack of good free manuals that we can include in these systems. Many of our most important programs do not come with full manuals. Documentation is an essential part of any software package; when an important free software package does not come with a free manual, that is a major gap. We have many such gaps today.

Once upon a time, many years ago, I thought I would learn Perl. I got a copy of a free manual, but I found it hard to read. When I asked Perl users about alternatives, they told me that there were better introductory manuals—but those were not free.

Why was this? The authors of the good manuals had written them for O'Reilly Associates, which published them with restrictive terms—no copying, no modification, source files not available—which exclude them from the free software community.

That wasn't the first time this sort of thing has happened, and (to our community's great loss) it was far from the last. Proprietary manual publishers have enticed a great many authors to restrict their manuals since then. Many times I have heard a GNU user eagerly tell me about a manual that he is writing, with which he expects to help the GNU project—and then had my hopes dashed, as he proceeded to explain that he had signed a contract with a publisher that would restrict it so that we cannot use it.

Given that writing good English is a rare skill among programmers, we can ill afford to lose manuals this way.

Free documentation, like free software, is a matter of freedom, not price. The problem with these manuals was not that O'Reilly Associates charged a price for printed copies—that in itself is fine. (The Free Software Foundation sells printed copies of free GNU manuals, too.) But GNU manuals are available in source code form, while these manuals are available only on paper. GNU manuals come with permission to copy and modify; the Perl manuals do not. These restrictions are the problems.

The criterion for a free manual is pretty much the same as for free software: it is a matter of giving all users certain freedoms. Redistribution (including commercial redistribution) must be permitted, so that the manual can accompany every copy of the program, on-line or on paper. Permission for modification is crucial too.

As a general rule, I don't believe that it is essential for people to have permission to modify all sorts of articles and books. The issues for writings are not necessarily the same as those for software. For example, I don't think you or I are obliged to give permission to modify articles like this one, which describe our actions and our views.

Originally written in 2000, this version is part of *Free Software, Free Society: Selected Essays of Richard M. Stallman*, 2002, GNU Press (http://www.gnupress.org); ISBN 1-882114-98-1.

But there is a particular reason why the freedom to modify is crucial for documentation for free software. When people exercise their right to modify the software, and add or change its features, if they are conscientious they will change the manual too—so they can provide accurate and usable documentation with the modified program. A manual that forbids programmers to be conscientious and finish the job, or more precisely requires them to write a new manual from scratch if they change the program, does not fill our community's needs.

While a blanket prohibition on modification is unacceptable, some kinds of limits on the method of modification pose no problem. For example, requirements to preserve the original author's copyright notice, the distribution terms, or the list of authors, are OK. It is also no problem to require modified versions to include notice that they were modified, even to have entire sections that may not be deleted or changed, as long as these sections deal with nontechnical topics. (Some GNU manuals have them.)

These kinds of restrictions are not a problem because, as a practical matter, they don't stop the conscientious programmer from adapting the manual to fit the modified program. In other words, they don't block the free software community from making full use of the manual.

However, it must be possible to modify all the technical content of the manual, and then distribute the result in all the usual media, through all the usual channels; otherwise, the restrictions do block the community, the manual is not free, and so we need another manual.

Unfortunately, it is often hard to find someone to write another manual when a proprietary manual exists. The obstacle is that many users think that a proprietary manual is good enough—so they don't see the need to write a free manual. They do not see that the free operating system has a gap that needs filling.

Why do users think that proprietary manuals are good enough? Some have not considered the issue. I hope this article will do something to change that.

Other users consider proprietary manuals acceptable for the same reason so many people consider proprietary software acceptable: they judge in purely practical terms, not using freedom as a criterion. These people are entitled to their opinions, but since those opinions spring from values which do not include freedom, they are no guide for those of us who do value freedom.

Please spread the word about this issue. We continue to lose manuals to proprietary publishing. If we spread the word that proprietary manuals are not sufficient, perhaps the next person who wants to help GNU by writing documentation will realize, before it is too late, that he must above all make it free.

We can also encourage commercial publishers to sell free, copylefted manuals instead of proprietary ones. One way you can help this is to check the distribution terms of a manual before you buy it, and prefer copylefted manuals to non-copylefted ones.

[Note: The Free Software Foundation maintains a Web page (http://www.gnu.org/doc/other-free-books.html) that lists free books available from other publishers]

10 Free Software Song

To the melody of the Bulgarian folk song "Sadi Moma."

whistle

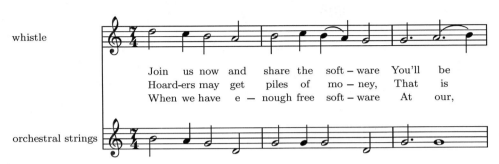

Join us now and share the soft — ware You'll be
Hoard-ers may get piles of mo — ney, That is
When we have e — nough free soft — ware At our,

orchestral strings

free hack — ers, you'll be free_____ Join us now and
true, hack — ers, that is true_____ But they can — not
call, hack — ers, at our call,_____ We'll kick out those

share the soft — ware You'll be — free hack — ers, you'll be free.
help their neigh-bors That's not___ good, hack — ers, that's not good.
dir — ty li-cens-es Ev — er more, hack — ers, Ev — er more.

Originally written in 1993, this version is part of *Free Software, Free Society: Selected Essays of Richard M. Stallman*, 2002, GNU Press (http://www.gnupress.org); ISBN 1-882114-98-1.

Section Two
Copyright, Copyleft, and Patents

11 The Right to Read

From "The Road To Tycho," a collection of articles about the antecedents of the Lunarian Revolution, published in Luna City in 2096

For Dan Halbert, the road to Tycho began in college—when Lissa Lenz asked to borrow his computer. Hers had broken down, and unless she could borrow another, she would fail her midterm project. There was no one she dared ask, except Dan.

This put Dan in a dilemma. He had to help her—but if he lent her his computer, she might read his books. Aside from the fact that you could go to prison for many years for letting someone else read your books, the very idea shocked him at first. Like everyone, he had been taught since elementary school that sharing books was nasty and wrong—something that only pirates would do.

And there wasn't much chance that the SPA—the Software Protection Authority—would fail to catch him. In his software class, Dan had learned that each book had a copyright monitor that reported when and where it was read, and by whom, to Central Licensing. (They used this information to catch reading pirates, but also to sell personal interest profiles to retailers.) The next time his computer was networked, Central Licensing would find out. He, as computer owner, would receive the harshest punishment—for not taking pains to prevent the crime.

Of course, Lissa did not necessarily intend to read his books. She might want the computer only to write her midterm. But Dan knew she came from a middle-class family and could hardly afford the tuition, let alone her reading fees. Reading his books might be the only way she could graduate. He understood this situation; he himself had had to borrow to pay for all the research papers he read. (10% of those fees went to the researchers who wrote the papers; since Dan aimed for an academic career, he could hope that his own research papers, if frequently referenced, would bring in enough to repay this loan.)

Later on, Dan would learn there was a time when anyone could go to the library and read journal articles, and even books, without having to pay. There were independent scholars who read thousands of pages without government library grants. But in the 1990s, both commercial and nonprofit journal publishers had begun charging fees for access. By 2047, libraries offering free public access to scholarly literature were a dim memory.

There were ways, of course, to get around the SPA and Central Licensing. They were themselves illegal. Dan had had a classmate in software, Frank Martucci, who had obtained an illicit debugging tool, and used it to skip over the copyright

This article appeared in the February 1997 issue of *Communications of the ACM* (Volume 40, Number 2). The "Author's Note" was updated in 2002. This version is part of *Free Software, Free Society: Selected Essays of Richard M. Stallman*, 2002, GNU Press (http://www.gnupress.org); ISBN 1-882114-98-1.

monitor code when reading books. But he had told too many friends about it, and one of them turned him in to the SPA for a reward (students deep in debt were easily tempted into betrayal). In 2047, Frank was in prison, not for pirate reading, but for possessing a debugger.

Dan would later learn that there was a time when anyone could have debugging tools. There were even free debugging tools available on CD or downloadable over the net. But ordinary users started using them to bypass copyright monitors, and eventually a judge ruled that this had become their principal use in actual practice. This meant they were illegal; the debuggers' developers were sent to prison.

Programmers still needed debugging tools, of course, but debugger vendors in 2047 distributed numbered copies only, and only to officially licensed and bonded programmers. The debugger Dan used in software class was kept behind a special firewall so that it could be used only for class exercises.

It was also possible to bypass the copyright monitors by installing a modified system kernel. Dan would eventually find out about the free kernels, even entire free operating systems, that had existed around the turn of the century. But not only were they illegal, like debuggers—you could not install one if you had one, without knowing your computer's root password. And neither the FBI nor Microsoft Support would tell you that.

Dan concluded that he couldn't simply lend Lissa his computer. But he couldn't refuse to help her, because he loved her. Every chance to speak with her filled him with delight. And that she chose him to ask for help, that could mean she loved him too.

Dan resolved the dilemma by doing something even more unthinkable—he lent her the computer, and told her his password. This way, if Lissa read his books, Central Licensing would think he was reading them. It was still a crime, but the SPA would not automatically find out about it. They would only find out if Lissa reported him.

Of course, if the school ever found out that he had given Lissa his own password, it would be curtains for both of them as students, regardless of what she had used it for. School policy was that any interference with their means of monitoring students' computer use was grounds for disciplinary action. It didn't matter whether you did anything harmful—the offense was making it hard for the administrators to check on you. They assumed this meant you were doing something else forbidden, and they did not need to know what it was.

Students were not usually expelled for this—not directly. Instead they were banned from the school computer systems, and would inevitably fail all their classes.

Later, Dan would learn that this kind of university policy started only in the 1980s, when university students in large numbers began using computers. Previously, universities maintained a different approach to student discipline; they punished activities that were harmful, not those that merely raised suspicion.

Lissa did not report Dan to the SPA. His decision to help her led to their marriage, and also led them to question what they had been taught about piracy as children. The couple began reading about the history of copyright, about the Soviet Union and its restrictions on copying, and even the original United States Constitution. They moved to Luna, where they found others who had likewise gravitated away from the long arm of the SPA. When the Tycho Uprising began in 2062, the universal right to read soon became one of its central aims.

Author's Note

The right to read is a battle being fought today. Although it may take 50 years for our present way of life to fade into obscurity, most of the specific laws and practices described above have already been proposed; many have been enacted into law in the U.S. and elsewhere. In the U.S., the 1998 Digital Millennium Copyright Act established the legal basis to restrict the reading and lending of computerized books (and other data too). The European Union imposed similar restrictions in a 2001 copyright directive.

There is one exception: the idea that the FBI and Microsoft will keep the root passwords for personal computers, and not let you have them, has not been proposed. This is an extrapolation from the Clipper chip and similar U.S. government key-escrow proposals, together with a long-term trend: computer systems are increasingly set up to give absentee operators control over the people actually using the computer system.

But we are coming steadily closer to that point. In 2001, Disney-funded Senator Hollings proposed a bill called the SSSCA (now renamed the CBDTPA) that would require every new computer to have mandatory copy-restriction facilities that the user cannot bypass.

In 2001 the U.S. began attempting to use the proposed Free Trade Area of the Americas treaty to impose the same rules on all the countries in the Western Hemisphere. The FTAA is one of the so-called "free trade" treaties, actually designed to give business increased power over democratic governments; imposing laws like the DMCA is typical of this spirit. The Electronic Frontier Foundation asks people to explain to the other governments why they should oppose this plan.

The SPA, which actually stands for Software Publisher's Association, has been replaced in this police-like role by the BSA or Busines Software Alliance. It is not, today, an official police force; unofficially, it acts like one. Using methods reminiscent of the erstwhile Soviet Union, it invites people to inform on their coworkers and friends. A BSA terror campaign in Argentina in 2001 made veiled threats that people sharing software would be raped in prison.

When this story was written, the SPA was threatening small Internet Service Providers (ISPs), demanding they permit the SPA to monitor all users. Most ISPs surrender when threatened, because they cannot afford to fight back in court, (*Atlanta Journal-Constitution*, 1 Oct 96, D3). At least one ISP, Community ConneXion in Oakland, California, refused the demand and was actually sued. The SPA later dropped the suit, but obtained the DMCA, which gave them the power they sought.

The university security policies described above are not imaginary. For example, a computer at one Chicago-area university prints this message when you log in:

> "This system is for the use of authorized users only. Individuals using
> this computer system without authority or in the excess of their author-

ity are subject to having all their activities on this system monitored and recorded by system personnel. In the course of monitoring individuals improperly using this system or in the course of system maintenance, the activities of authorized users may also be monitored. Anyone using this system expressly consents to such monitoring and is advised that if such monitoring reveals possible evidence of illegal activity or violation of University regulations system personnel may provide the evidence of such monitoring to University authorities and/or law enforcement officials."

This is an interesting approach to the Fourth Amendment: pressure most everyone to agree, in advance, to waive their rights under it.

References

- The administration's White Paper: "Information Infrastructure Task Force, Intellectual Property and the National Information Infrastructure: The Report of the Working Group on Intellectual Property Rights" (1995).
- An explanation of the White Paper: "The Copyright Grab," Pamela Samuelson, *Wired*, Jan. 1996 (http://www.wired.com/wired/archive/4.01/white.paper_pr.html)
- "Sold Out," James Boyle, *The New York Times*, 31 March 1996
- "Public Data or Private Data," *The Washington Post*, 4 Nov 1996. (We used to have a link to this on our Web site, but the *The Washington Post* has decided to start charging users who wishes to read articles on the Web site and therefore we have decided to remove the link.)
- Union for the Public Domain—an organization that aims to resist and reverse the overextension of copyright and patent powers, (http://www.public-domain.org/).

12 Misinterpreting Copyright—A Series of Errors

Something strange and dangerous is happening in copyright law. Under the U.S. Constitution, copyright exists to benefit users—those who read books, listen to music, watch movies, or run software—not for the sake of publishers or authors. Yet even as people tend increasingly to reject and disobey the copyright restrictions imposed on them "for their own benefit," the U.S. government is adding more restrictions, and trying to frighten the public into obedience with harsh new penalties.

How did copyright policies come to be diametrically opposed to their stated purpose? And how can we bring them back into alignment with that purpose? To understand, we should start by looking at the root of United States copyright law: the U.S. Constitution.

Copyright in the U.S. Constitution

When the U.S. Constitution was drafted, the idea that authors were entitled to a copyright monopoly was proposed—and rejected. The founders of our country adopted a different premise, that copyright is not a natural right of authors, but an artificial concession made to them for the sake of progress. The Constitution gives permission for a copyright system with this paragraph (Article I, Section 8):

[Congress shall have the power] to promote the progress of science and the useful arts, by securing for limited times to authors and inventors the exclusive right to their respective writings and discoveries.

The Supreme Court has repeatedly affirmed that promoting progress means benefit for the users of copyrighted works. For example, in Fox Film v. Doyal, the court said,

The sole interest of the United States and the primary object in conferring the [copyright] monopoly lie in the general benefits derived by the public from the labors of authors.

This fundamental decision explains why copyright is not *required* by the Constitution, only *permitted* as an option—and why it is supposed to last for "limited times." If copyright were a natural right, something that authors have because they deserve it, nothing could justify terminating this right after a certain period of time, any more than everyone's house should become public property after a certain lapse of time from its construction.

This is the first published version of this essay and is part of *Free Software, Free Society: Selected Essays of Richard M. Stallman*, 2002, GNU Press (http://www.gnupress.org); ISBN 1-882114-98-1.

The "copyright bargain"

The copyright system works by providing privileges and thus benefits to publishers and authors; but it does not do this for their sake. Rather, it does this to modify their behavior: to provide an incentive for authors to write more and publish more. In effect, the government spends the public's natural rights, on the public's behalf, as part of a deal to bring the public more published works. Legal scholars call this concept the "copyright bargain." It is like a government purchase of a highway or an airplane using taxpayer's money, except that the government spends our freedom instead of our money.

But is the bargain as it exists actually a good deal for the public? Many alternative bargains are possible; which one is best? Every issue of copyright policy is part of this question. If we misunderstand the nature of the question, we will tend to decide the issues badly.

The Constitution authorizes granting copyright powers to authors. In practice, authors typically cede them to publishers; it is usually the publishers, not the authors, who exercise these powers and get most of the benefits, though authors may get a small portion. Thus it is usually the publishers that lobby to increase copyright powers. To better reflect the reality of copyright rather than the myth, this article refers to publishers rather than authors as the holders of copyright powers. It also refers to the users of copyrighted works as "readers," even though using them does not always mean reading, because "the users" is remote and abstract.

The first error: "striking a balance"

The copyright bargain places the public first: benefit for the reading public is an end in itself; benefits (if any) for publishers are just a means toward that end. Readers' interests and publishers' interests are qualitatively unequal in priority. The first step in misinterpreting the purpose of copyright is the elevation of the publishers to the same level of importance as the readers.

It is often said that U.S. copyright law is meant to "strike a balance" between the interests of publishers and readers. Those who cite this interpretation present it as a restatement of the basic position stated in the Constitution; in other words, it is supposed to be equivalent to the copyright bargain.

But the two interpretations are far from equivalent; they are different conceptually, and different in their implications. The balance concept assumes that the readers' and publishers' interests differ in importance only quantitatively, in "how much weight" we should give them, and in what actions they apply to. The term "stakeholders" is often used to frame the issue in this way; it assumes that all kinds of interest in a policy decision are equally important. This view rejects the qualitative distinction between the readers' and publishers' interests which is at the root of the government's participation in the copyright bargain.

The consequences of this alteration are far-reaching, because the great protection for the public in the copyright bargain—the idea that copyright privileges can be justified only in the name of the readers, never in the name of the publishers—is discarded by the "balance" interpretation. Since the interest of the publishers is regarded as an end in itself, it can justify copyright privileges; in other words, the "balance" concept says that privileges can be justified in the name of someone other than the public.

As a practical matter, the consequence of the "balance" concept is to reverse the burden of justification for changes in copyright law. The copyright bargain places the burden on the publishers to convince the readers to cede certain freedoms. The concept of balance reverses this burden, practically speaking, because there is generally no doubt that publishers will benefit from additional privilege. So unless harm to the readers can be proved, sufficient to "outweigh" this benefit, we are led to conclude that the publishers are entitled to almost any privilege they request.

Since the idea of "striking a balance" between publishers and readers denies the readers the primacy they are entitled to, we must reject it.

Balancing against what?

When the government buys something for the public, it acts on behalf of the public; its responsibility is to obtain the best possible deal—best for the public, not for the other party in the agreement.

For example, when signing contracts with construction companies to build highways, the government aims to spend as little as possible of the public's money. Government agencies use competitive bidding to push the price down.

As a practical matter, the price cannot be zero, because contractors will not bid that low. Although not entitled to special consideration, they have the usual rights of citizens in a free society, including the right to refuse disadvantageous contracts; even the lowest bid will be high enough for some contractor to make money. So there is indeed a balance, of a kind. But it is not a deliberate balancing of two interests each with claim to special consideration. It is a balance between a public goal and market forces. The government tries to obtain for the taxpaying motorists the best deal they can get in the context of a free society and a free market.

In the copyright bargain, the government spends our freedom instead of our money. Freedom is more precious than money, so government's responsibility to spend our freedom wisely and frugally is even greater than its responsibility to spend our money thus. Governments must never put the publishers' interests on a par with the public's freedom.

Not "balance" but "trade-off"

The idea of balancing the readers' interests against the publishers' is the wrong way to judge copyright policy, but there are indeed two interests to be weighed: two interests *of the readers*. Readers have an interest in their own freedom in using published works; depending on circumstances, they may also have an interest in encouraging publication through some kind of incentive system.

The word "balance," in discussions of copyright, has come to stand as shorthand for the idea of "striking a balance" between the readers and the publishers. Therefore, to use the word "balance" in regard to the readers' two interests would be confusing—we need another term.

In general, when one party has two goals that partly conflict, and cannot completely achieve both of them, we call this a "trade-off." Therefore, rather than speaking of "striking the right balance" between parties, we should speak of "finding the right trade-off between spending our freedom and keeping it."

The second error: maximizing one output

The second mistake in copyright policy consists of adopting the goal of maximizing—not just increasing—the number of published works. The erroneous concept of "striking a balance" elevated the publishers to parity with the readers; this second error places them far above the readers.

When we purchase something, we do not generally buy the whole quantity in stock or the most expensive model. Instead we conserve funds for other purchases, by buying only what we need of any particular good, and choosing a model of sufficient rather than highest quality. The principle of diminishing returns suggests that spending all our money on one particular good is likely to be inefficient allocation of resources; we generally choose to keep some money for another use.

Diminishing returns applies to copyright just as to any other purchase. The first freedoms we should trade away are those we miss the least, while giving the largest encouragement to publication. As we trade additional freedoms that cut closer to home, we find that each trade is a bigger sacrifice than the last, while bringing a smaller increment in literary activity. Well before the increment becomes zero, we may well say it is not worth its incremental price; we would then settle on a bargain whose overall result is to increase the amount of publication, but not to the utmost possible extent.

Accepting the goal of maximizing publication rejects all these wiser, more advantageous bargains in advance—it dictates that the public must cede nearly all of its freedom to use published works, for just a little more publication.

The rhetoric of maximization

In practice, the goal of maximizing publication regardless of the cost to freedom is supported by widespread rhetoric which asserts that public copying is illegitimate, unfair, and intrinsically wrong. For instance, the publishers call people who copy "pirates," a smear term designed to equate sharing information with your neighbor with attacking a ship. (This smear term was formerly used by authors to describe publishers who found lawful ways to publish unauthorized editions; its modern use by the publishers is almost the reverse.) This rhetoric directly rejects the Constitutional basis for copyright, but presents itself as representing the unquestioned tradition of the American legal system.

The "pirate" rhetoric is typically accepted because it blankets the media so that few people realize that it is radical. It is effective because if copying by the public is fundamentally illegitimate, we can never object to the publishers' demand that we surrender our freedom to do so. In other words, when the public is challenged to show why publishers should not receive some additional power, the most important reason of all—"We want to copy"—is disqualified in advance.

This leaves no way to argue against increasing copyright power except using side issues. Hence opposition to stronger copyright powers today almost exclusively cites side issues, and never dares cite the freedom to distribute copies as a legitimate public value.

As a practical matter, the goal of maximization enables publishers to argue that "A certain practice is reducing our sales—or we think it might—so we presume it diminishes publication by some unknown amount, and therefore it should be prohibited." We are led to the outrageous conclusion that the public good is measured by publishers' sales: What's good for General Media is good for the U.S.A.

The third error: maximizing publishers' power

Once the publishers have obtained assent to the policy goal of maximizing publication output at any cost, their next step is to infer that this requires giving them the maximum possible powers—making copyright cover every imaginable use of a work, or applying some other legal tool such as "shrink wrap" licenses to equivalent effect. This goal, which entails the abolition of "fair use" and the "right of first sale," is being pressed at every available level of government, from states of the U.S. to international bodies.

This step is erroneous because strict copyright rules obstruct the creation of useful new works. For instance, Shakespeare borrowed the plots of some of his plays from other plays published a few decades before, so if today's copyright law had been in effect, his plays would have been illegal.

Even if we wanted the highest possible rate of publication, regardless of cost to the public, maximizing publishers' power is the wrong way to get it. As a means of promoting progress, it is self-defeating.

The results of the three errors

The current trend in copyright legislation is to hand publishers broader powers for longer periods of time. The conceptual basis of copyright, as it emerges distorted from the series of errors, rarely offers a basis for saying no. Legislators give lip service to the idea that copyright serves the public, while in fact giving publishers whatever they ask for.

For example, here is what Senator Hatch said when introducing S. 483, a 1995 bill to increase the term of copyright by 20 years:

> I believe we are now at such a point with respect to the question of whether the current term of copyright adequately protects the interests of authors and the related question of whether the term of protection continues to provide a sufficient incentive for the creation of new works of authorship.

This bill extended the copyright on already-published works written since the 1920s. This change was a giveaway to publishers with no possible benefit to the public, since there is no way to retroactively increase now the number of books published back then. Yet it cost the public a freedom that is meaningful today—the freedom to redistribute books from that era.

The bill also extended the copyrights of works yet to be written. For works made for hire, copyright would last 95 years instead of the present 75 years. Theoretically this would increase the incentive to write new works; but any publisher that claims to need this extra incentive should substantiate the claim with projected balance sheets for the year 2075.

Needless to say, Congress did not question the publishers' arguments: a law extending copyright was enacted in 1998. It was called the Sonny Bono Copyright Term Extension Act, named after one of its sponsors who died earlier that year. His widow, who served the rest of his term, made this statement:

> Actually, Sonny wanted copyright to last forever. I am informed by staff that such a change would violate the Constitution. I invite all of you to work with me to strengthen our copyright laws in all ways available to us. As you know, there is also Jack Valenti's proposal to last forever less one day. Perhaps the committee may look at that next Congress.

The Supreme Court has agreed to hear a case that seeks to overturn the law on the grounds that the retroactive extension fails to serve the Constitution's goal of promoting progress.

Another law, passed in 1996, made it a felony to make sufficiently many copies of any published work, even if you give them away to friends just to be nice. Previously this was not a crime in the U.S. at all.

An even worse law, the Digital Millennium Copyright Act (DMCA), was designed to bring back copy protection (which computer users detest) by making it a crime to break copy protection, or even publish information about how to break it. This law ought to be called the "Domination by Media Corporations Act" because it effectively offers publishers the chance to write their own copyright law. It says they can impose any restrictions whatsoever on the use of a work, and these restrictions take the force of law provided the work contains some sort of encryption or license manager to enforce them.

One of the arguments offered for this bill was that it would implement a recent treaty to increase copyright powers. The treaty was promulgated by the World Intellectual Property Organization, an organization dominated by copyright-holding and patent-holding interests, with the aid of pressure from the Clinton administration; since the treaty only increases copyright power, whether it serves the public interest in any country is doubtful. In any case, the bill went far beyond what the treaty required.

Libraries were a key source of opposition to this bill, especially to the aspects that block the forms of copying that are considered "fair use." How did the publishers respond? Former representative Pat Schroeder, now a lobbyist for the Association of American Publishers, said that the publishers "could not live with what [the libraries are] asking for." Since the libraries were asking only to preserve part of the status quo, one might respond by wondering how the publishers had survived until the present day.

Congressman Barney Frank, in a meeting with me and others who opposed this bill, showed how far the U.S. Constitution's view of copyright has been disregarded. He said that new powers, backed by criminal penalties, were needed urgently because the "movie industry is worried," as well as the "music industry" and other "industries." I asked him, "But is this in the public interest?" His response was telling: "Why are you talking about the public interest? These creative people don't have to give up their rights for the public interest!" The "industry" has been identified with the "creative people" it hires, copyright has been treated as its entitlement, and the Constitution has been turned upside down.

The DMCA was enacted in 1998. As enacted, it says that fair use remains nominally legitimate, but allows publishers to prohibit all software or hardware that you could practice it with. Effectively, fair use is prohibited.

Based on this law, the movie industry has imposed censorship on free software for reading and playing DVDs, and even on the information about how to read them. In April 2001, Professor Edward Felten of Princeton University was intimidated by lawsuit threats from the Recording Industry Association of America (RIAA) into withdrawing a scientific paper stating what he had learned about a proposed encryption system for restricting access to recorded music.

We are also beginning to see e-books that take away many of readers' traditional freedoms—for instance, the freedom to lend a book to your friend, to sell it to a used book store, to borrow it from a library, to buy it without giving your name to a corporate data bank, even the freedom to read it twice. Encrypted e-books generally restrict all these activities—you can read them only with special secret software designed to restrict you.

I will never to buy one of these encrypted, restricted e-books, and I hope you will reject them too. If an e-book doesn't give you the same freedoms as a traditional paper book, don't accept it!

Anyone independently releasing software that can read restricted e-books risks prosecution. A Russian programmer, Dmitry Sklyarov, was arrested in 2001 while visiting the U.S. to speak at a conference, because he had written such a program in Russia, where it was lawful to do so. Now Russia is preparing a law to prohibit it too, and the European Union recently adopted one.

Mass-market e-books have been a commercial failure so far, but not because readers chose to defend their freedom; they were unattractive for other reasons, such as that computer display screens are not easy surfaces to read from. We can't rely on this happy accident to protect us in the long term; the next attempt to promote e-books will use "electronic paper"—book-like objects into which an encrypted, restricted e-book can be downloaded. If this paper-like surface proves more appealing than today's display screens, we will have to defend our freedom in order to keep it. Meanwhile, e-books are making inroads in niches: NYU and other dental schools require students to buy their textbooks in the form of restricted e-books.

The media companies are not satisfied yet. In 2001, Disney-funded Senator Hollings proposed a bill called the "Security Systems Standards and Certification

Act" (SSSCA),[1] which would require all computers (and other digital recording and playback devices) to have government-mandated copy restriction systems. That is their ultimate goal, but the first item on their agenda is to prohibit any equipment that can tune digital HDTV unless it is designed to be impossible for the public to "tamper with" (i.e., modify for their own purposes). Since free software is software that users can modify, we face here for the first time a proposed law that explicitly prohibits free software for a certain job. Prohibition of other jobs will surely follow. If the FCC adopts this rule, existing free software such as GNU Radio would be censored.

To block these bills and rules requires political action.[2]

Finding the right bargain

What is the proper way to decide copyright policy? If copyright is a bargain made on behalf of the public, it should serve the public interest above all. The government's duty when selling the public's freedom is to sell only what it must, and sell it as dearly as possible. At the very least, we should pare back the extent of copyright as much as possible while maintaining a comparable level of publication.

Since we cannot find this minimum price in freedom through competitive bidding, as we do for construction projects, how can we find it?

One possible method is to reduce copyright privileges in stages, and observe the results. By seeing if and when measurable diminutions in publication occur, we will learn how much copyright power is really necessary to achieve the public's purposes. We must judge this by actual observation, not by what publishers say will happen, because they have every incentive to make exaggerated predictions of doom if their powers are reduced in any way.

Copyright policy includes several independent dimensions, which can be adjusted separately. After we find the necessary minimum for one policy dimension, it may still be possible to reduce other dimensions of copyright while maintaining the desired publication level.

One important dimension of copyright is its duration, which is now typically on the order of a century. Reducing the monopoly on copying to ten years, starting from the date when a work is published, would be a good first step. Another aspect of copyright, which covers the making of derivative works, could continue for a longer period.

Why count from the date of publication? Because copyright on unpublished works does not directly limit readers' freedom; whether we are free to copy a work is moot when we do not have copies. So giving authors a longer time to get a work published does no harm. Authors (who generally do own the copyright prior to

---

[1] Since renamed to the unpronounceable CBDTPA, for which a good mnemonic is, "Consume, But Don't Try Programming Anything," but it really stands for the "Consumer Broadband and Digital Television Promotion Act."

[2] If you would like to help, I recommend the Web sites `digitalspeech.org` and `www.eff.org`

publication) will rarely choose to delay publication just to push back the end of the copyright term.

Why ten years? Because that is a safe proposal; we can be confident on practical grounds that this reduction would have little impact on the overall viability of publishing today. In most media and genres, successful works are very profitable in just a few years, and even successful works are usually out of print well before ten. Even for reference works, whose useful life may be many decades, ten-year copyright should suffice: updated editions are issued regularly, and many readers will buy the copyrighted current edition rather than copy a ten-year-old public domain version.

Ten years may still be longer than necessary; once things settle down, we could try a further reduction to tune the system. At a panel on copyright at a literary convention, where I proposed the ten-year term, a noted fantasy author sitting beside me objected vehemently, saying that anything beyond five years was intolerable.

But we don't have to apply the same time span to all kinds of works. Maintaining the utmost uniformity of copyright policy is not crucial to the public interest, and copyright law already has many exceptions for specific uses and media. It would be foolish to pay for every highway project at the rates necessary for the most difficult projects in the most expensive regions of the country; it is equally foolish to "pay" for all kinds of art with the greatest price in freedom that we find necessary for any one kind.

So perhaps novels, dictionaries, computer programs, songs, symphonies, and movies should have different durations of copyright, so that we can reduce the duration for each kind of work to what is necessary for many such works to be published. Perhaps movies over one hour long could have a twenty-year copyright, because of the expense of producing them. In my own field, computer programming, three years should suffice, because product cycles are even shorter than that.

Another dimension of copyright policy is the extent of fair use: some ways of reproducing all or part of a published work that are legally permitted even though it is copyrighted. The natural first step in reducing this dimension of copyright power is to permit occasional private small-quantity noncommercial copying and distribution among individuals. This would eliminate the intrusion of the copyright police into people's private lives, but would probably have little effect on the sales of published works. (It may be necessary to take other legal steps to ensure that shrink-wrap licenses cannot be used to substitute for copyright in restricting such copying.) The experience of Napster shows that we should also permit noncommercial verbatim redistribution to the general public—when so many of the public want to copy and share, and find it so useful, only draconian measures will stop them, and the public deserves to get what it wants.

For novels, and in general for works that are used for entertainment, noncommercial verbatim redistribution may be sufficient freedom for the readers. Computer programs, being used for functional purposes (to get jobs done), call for additional freedoms beyond that, including the freedom to publish an improved version. See "Free Software Definition," in this book, for an explanation of the freedoms that software users should have. But it may be an acceptable compromise for these freedoms to be universally available only after a delay of two or three years from the program's publication.

Changes like these could bring copyright into line with the public's wish to use digital technology to copy. Publishers will no doubt find these proposals "unbalanced"; they may threaten to take their marbles and go home, but they won't really do it, because the game will remain profitable and it will be the only game in town.

As we consider reductions in copyright power, we must make sure media companies do not simply replace it with end-user license agreements. It would be necessary to prohibit the use of contracts to apply restrictions on copying that go beyond those of copyright. Such limitations on what mass-market nonnegotiated contracts can require are a standard part of the U.S. legal system.

A personal note

I am a software designer, not a legal scholar. I've become concerned with copyright issues because there's no avoiding them in the world of computer networks[3]. As a user of computers and networks for thirty years, I value the freedoms that we have lost, and the ones we may lose next. As an author, I can reject the romantic mystique of the author as semidivine creator, often cited by publishers to justify increased copyright powers for authors, which authors will then sign away to publishers.

Most of this article consists of facts and reasoning that you can check, and proposals on which you can form your own opinions. But I ask you to accept one thing on my word alone: that authors like me don't deserve special power over you. If you wish to reward me further for the software or books I have written, I would gratefully accept a check—but please don't surrender your freedom in my name.

---

[3] The Internet being the largest of the world's computer networks

13 Science Must 'Push' Copyright Aside

It should be a truism that scientific literature exists to disseminate scientific knowledge, and that scientific journals exist to facilitate the process. It therefore follows that rules for use of scientific literature should be designed to help achieve that goal.

The rules we have now, known as copyright, were established in the age of the printing press, an inherently centralized method of mass-production copying. In a print environment, copyright on journal articles restricted only journal publishers, requiring them to obtain permission to publish an article, and would-be plagiarists. It helped journals to operate and disseminate knowledge, without interfering with the useful work of scientists or students, either as writers or readers of articles. These rules fit that system well.

The modern technology for scientific publishing, however, is the World Wide Web. What rules would best ensure the maximum dissemination of scientific articles, and knowledge, on the Web? Articles should be distributed in non-proprietary formats, with open access for all. And everyone should have the right to "mirror" articles; that is, to republish them verbatim with proper attribution.

These rules should apply to past as well as future articles, when they are distributed in electronic form. But there is no crucial need to change the present copyright system as it applies to paper publication of journals, because the problem is not in that domain.

Unfortunately, it seems that not everyone agrees with the truisms that began this article. Many journal publishers appear to believe that the purpose of scientific literature is to enable them to publish journals so as to collect subscriptions from scientists and students. Such thinking is known as "confusion of the means with the ends."

Their approach has been to restrict access even to read the scientific literature to those who can and will pay for it. They use copyright law, which is still in force despite its inappropriateness for computer networks, as an excuse to stop scientists from choosing new rules.

For the sake of scientific cooperation and humanity's future, we must reject that approach at its root—not merely the obstructive systems that have been instituted, but the mistaken priorities that inspired them.

Journal publishers sometimes claim that on-line access requires expensive high-powered server machines, and that they must charge access fees to pay for these servers. This "problem" is a consequence of its own "solution." Give everyone the freedom to mirror, and libraries around the world will set up mirror sites to meet

---

This essay originally appeared on http://www.nature.com in 1991 in their *Web Debates* section; this version is part of *Free Software, Free Society: Selected Essays of Richard M. Stallman*, 2002, GNU Press (http://www.gnupress.org); ISBN 1-882114-98-1.

the demand. This decentralized solution will reduce network bandwidth needs and provide faster access, all the while protecting the scholarly record against accidental loss.

Publishers also argue that paying the editors requires charging for access. Let us accept the assumption that editors must be paid; this tail need not wag the dog. The cost of editing for a typical paper is between 1% and 3% of the cost of funding the research to produce it. Such a small percentage of the cost can hardly justify obstructing the use of the results.

Instead, the cost of editing could be recovered, for example, through page charges to the authors, who can pass these on to the research sponsors. The sponsors should not mind, given that they currently pay for publication in a more cumbersome way through overhead fees for the university library's subscription to the journal. By changing the economic model to charge editing costs to the research sponsors, we can eliminate the apparent need to restrict access. The occasional author who is not affiliated with an institution or company, and who has no research sponsor, could be exempted from page charges, with costs levied on institution-based authors.

Another justification for access fees to on-line publications is to fund conversion of the print archives of a journal into on-line form. That work needs to be done, but we should seek alternative ways of funding it that do not involve obstructing access to the result. The work itself will not be any more difficult, or cost any more. It is self-defeating to digitize the archives and waste the results by restricting access.

The U.S. Constitution says that copyright exists "to promote the progress of science." When copyright impedes the progress of science, science must push copyright out of the way.

14 What is Copyleft?

Copyleft is a general method for making a program free software and requiring all modified and extended versions of the program to be free software as well.

The simplest way to make a program free is to put it in the public domain, uncopyrighted. This allows people to share the program and their improvements, if they are so minded. But it also allows uncooperative people to convert the program into proprietary software. They can make changes, many or few, and distribute the result as a proprietary product. People who receive the program in that modified form do not have the freedom that the original author gave them; the middleman has stripped it away.

In the GNU project, our aim is to give all users the freedom to redistribute and change GNU software. If middlemen could strip off the freedom, we might have many users, but those users would not have freedom. So instead of putting GNU software in the public domain, we "copyleft" it. Copyleft says that anyone who redistributes the software, with or without changes, must pass along the freedom to further copy and change it. Copyleft guarantees that every user has freedom.

Copyleft also provides an incentive for other programmers to add to free software. Important free programs such as the GNU C++ compiler exist only because of this.

Copyleft also helps programmers who want to contribute improvements to free software get permission to do that. These programmers often work for companies or universities that would do almost anything to get more money. A programmer may want to contribute her changes to the community, but her employer may want to turn the changes into a proprietary software product.

When we explain to the employer that it is illegal to distribute the improved version except as free software, the employer usually decides to release it as free software rather than throw it away.

To copyleft a program, we first state that it is copyrighted; then we add distribution terms, which are a legal instrument that gives everyone the rights to use, modify, and redistribute the program's code or any program derived from it but only if the distribution terms are unchanged. Thus, the code and the freedoms become legally inseparable.

Proprietary software developers use copyright to take away the users' freedom; we use copyright to guarantee their freedom. That's why we reverse the name, changing "copyright" into "copyleft."

Copyleft is a general concept; there are many ways to fill in the details. In the GNU Project, the specific distribution terms that we use are contained in the GNU General Public License. The GNU General Public License is of-

---

Originally written in 1996, this version is part of *Free Software, Free Society: Selected Essays of Richard M. Stallman*, 2002, GNU Press (http://www.gnupress.org); ISBN 1-882114-98-1.

ten called the GNU GPL for short. There is also a Frequently Asked Questions page (http://www.gnu.org/licenses/gpl-faq.html) about the GNU GPL. You can also read about why the FSF gets copyright assignments from contributors (http://www.gnu.org/copyleft/why-assign.html).

An alternate form of copyleft, the GNU Lesser General Public License (LGPL), applies to a few (but not all) GNU libraries. This license was formerly called the Library GPL, but we changed the name, because the old name encouraged developers to use this license more often than it should be used. For an explanation of why this change was necessary, read the article Why you shouldn't use the Library GPL for your next library.

The GNU Library General Public License is still available in HTML and text format although it has been superseded by the Lesser GPL.

The GNU Free Documentation License (FDL) is a form of copyleft intended for use on a manual, textbook or other document to assure everyone the effective freedom to copy and redistribute it, with or without modifications, either commercially or noncommercially.

The appropriate license is included in many manuals and in each GNU source code distribution.

The GNU GPL is designed so that you can easily apply it to your own program if you are the copyright holder. You don't have to modify the GNU GPL to do this, just add notices to your program which refer properly to the GNU GPL.

If you would like to copyleft your program with the GNU GPL or the GNU LGPL, please see the GPL instructions page for advice (http://www.gnu.org/copyleft/gpl-howto.html). Please note that you must use the entire text of the GPL, if you use it. It is an integral whole, and partial copies are not permitted. (Likewise for the LGPL.)

Using the same distribution terms for many different programs makes it easy to copy code between various different programs. Since they all have the same distribution terms, there is no need to think about whether the terms are compatible. The Lesser GPL includes a provision that lets you alter the distribution terms to the ordinary GPL, so that you can copy code into another program covered by the GPL.

If you would like to copyleft your manual with the GNU FDL, please see the instructions at the end of the FDL text, and the GFDL instructions page (http://www.gnu.org/copyleft/fdl-howto.html). As with the GNU GPL, you must use the entire license; partial copies are not permitted.

15 Copyleft: Pragmatic Idealism

Every decision a person makes stems from the person's values and goals. People can have many different goals and values; fame, profit, love, survival, fun, and freedom, are just some of the goals that a good person might have. When the goal is to help others as well as oneself, we call that idealism.

My work on free software is motivated by an idealistic goal: spreading freedom and cooperation. I want to encourage free software to spread, replacing proprietary software that forbids cooperation, and thus make our society better.

That's the basic reason why the GNU General Public License is written the way it is—as a copyleft. All code added to a GPL-covered program must be free software, even if it is put in a separate file. I make my code available for use in free software, and not for use in proprietary software, in order to encourage other people who write software to make it free as well. I figure that since proprietary software developers use copyright to stop us from sharing, we cooperators can use copyright to give other cooperators an advantage of their own: they can use our code.

Not everyone who uses the GNU GPL has this goal. Many years ago, a friend of mine was asked to rerelease a copylefted program under non-copyleft terms, and he responded more or less like this:

Sometimes I work on free software, and sometimes I work on proprietary software—but when I work on proprietary software, I expect to get paid.

He was willing to share his work with a community that shares software, but saw no reason to give a handout to a business making products that would be off limits to our community. His goal was different from mine, but he decided that the GNU GPL was useful for his goal too.

If you want to accomplish something in the world, idealism is not enough—you need to choose a method that works to achieve the goal. In other words, you need to be "pragmatic." Is the GPL pragmatic? Let's look at its results.

Consider GNU C++. Why do we have a free C++ compiler? Only because the GNU GPL said it had to be free. GNU C++ was developed by an industry consortium, MCC, starting from the GNU C compiler. MCC normally makes its work as proprietary as can be. But they made the C++ front end free software, because the GNU GPL said that was the only way they could release it. The C++ front end included many new files, but since they were meant to be linked with GCC, the GPL did apply to them. The benefit to our community is evident.

Consider GNU Objective C. NeXT[1] initially wanted to make this front end proprietary; they proposed to release it as .o files, and let users link them with the rest of GCC, thinking this might be a way around the GPL's requirements. But our

---

[1] An operating system created by Steve Jobs, eventually bought out by Apple.

Originally written in 1998, this version is part of *Free Software, Free Society: Selected Essays of Richard M. Stallman*, 2002, GNU Press (http://www.gnupress.org); ISBN 1-882114-98-1.

lawyer said that this would not evade the requirements, that it was not allowed. And so they made the Objective C front end free software.

Those examples happened years ago, but the GNU GPL continues to bring us more free software.

Many GNU libraries are covered by the GNU Library General Public License, but not all. One GNU library that is covered by the ordinary GNU GPL is Readline, which implements command-line editing. I once found out about a non-free program that was designed to use Readline, and told the developer this was not allowed. He could have taken command-line editing out of the program, but what he actually did was re-release it under the GPL. Now it is free software.

The programmers who write improvements to GCC (or Emacs, or Bash, or Linux, or any GPL-covered program) are often employed by companies or universities. When the programmer wants to return his improvements to the community, and see his code in the next release, the boss may say,

> Hold on there—your code belongs to us! We don't want to share it; we have decided to turn your improved version into a proprietary software product.

Here the GNU GPL comes to the rescue. The programmer shows the boss that this proprietary software product would be copyright infringement, and the boss realizes that he has only two choices: release the new code as free software, or not at all. Almost always he lets the programmer do as he intended all along, and the code goes into the next release.

The GNU GPL is not Mr. Nice Guy. It says "no" to some of the things that people sometimes want to do. There are users who say that this is a bad thing—that the GPL "excludes" some proprietary software developers who "need to be brought into the free software community."

But we are not excluding them from our community; they are choosing not to enter. Their decision to make software proprietary is a decision to stay out of our community. Being in our community means joining in cooperation with us; we cannot "bring them into our community" if they don't want to join.

What we can do is offer them an inducement to join. The GNU GPL is designed to make an inducement from our existing software: "If you will make your software free, you can use this code." Of course, it won't win 'em all, but it wins some of the time.

Proprietary software development does not contribute to our community, but its developers often want handouts from us. Free software users can offer free software developers strokes for the ego—recognition and gratitude—but it can be very tempting when a business tells you:

> Just let us put your package in our proprietary program, and your program will be used by many thousands of people!

The temptation can be powerful, but in the long run we are all better off if we resist it. The temptation and pressure are harder to recognize when they come indirectly, through free software organizations that have adopted a policy of catering to proprietary software. The X Consortium (and its successor, the Open Group) offers an example: funded by companies that made proprietary software, they have strived for a decade to persuade programmers not to use copyleft. Now that the Open Group has made X11R6.4 non-free software, those of us who resisted that pressure are glad that we did.[2]

Pragmatically speaking, thinking about greater long-term goals will strengthen your will to resist this pressure. If you focus your mind on the freedom and community that you can build by staying firm, you will find the strength to do it. "Stand for something, or you will fall for nothing."

And if cynics ridicule freedom, ridicule community. . . if "hard-nosed realists" say that profit is the only ideal. . . just ignore them, and use copyleft all the same.

---

[2] In September 1998, several months after X11R6.4 was released with non-free distribtion terms, the Open Group reversed its decision and rereleased it under the same non-copyleft free software license that was used for X11R6.3. Thank you, Open Group—but this subsequent reversal does not invalidate the conclusions we draw from the fact that adding the restrictions was possible.

16 The Danger of Software Patents

You might have been familiar with my work on free software. This speech is not about that. This speech is about a way of misusing laws to make software development a dangerous activity. This is about what happens when patent law gets applied to the field of software.

It is not about patenting software. That is a very bad way, a misleading way, to describe it, because it is not a matter of patenting individual programs. If it were, it would make no difference, it would be basically harmless. Instead, it is about patenting ideas. Every patent covers some idea. Software patents are patents which cover software ideas, ideas you would use in developing software. That is what makes them a dangerous obstacle to all software development.

You may have heard people using a misleading term, "intellectual property." This term, as you can see, is biased: it makes an assumption that, whatever it is you are talking about, the way to treat it is as a kind of property, which is actually one among many alternatives. This term "intellectual property" prejudges the most basic question in whatever area you are dealing with. This is not conducive to clear and open-minded thinking.

There is an additional problem in the term, which has nothing to do with the promotion of any one opinion: it gets in the way of understanding even the facts. The term "intellectual property" is a catch-all: it lumps together completely disparate areas of law such as copyrights and patents, which are completely different. Every detail is different. It also lumps together trademarks, which are even more different, and various other things less commonly encountered. None of them has anything in common with any of the others. Their origins historically are completely separate; the laws were designed independently; they covered different areas of life and activities. The public policy issues they raise are completely unrelated, so if you try to think about them by lumping them together, you are guaranteed to come to foolish conclusions. There is literally no sensible, intelligent opinion you can have about "intellectual property." So if you want to think clearly, don't lump them together. Think about copyrights, and then think about patents. Learn about copyright law, and separately learn about patent law.

To give you some of the biggest differences between copyrights and patents:

- Copyrights cover the details of expression of a work; copyrights don't cover any ideas. Patents only cover ideas and the use of ideas.

- Copyrights happen automatically. Patents are issued by a patent office in response to an application.

This speech was given at University of Cambridge, London, on the 25th of March, 2002; this version is part of *Free Software, Free Society: Selected Essays of Richard M. Stallman*, 2002, GNU Press (http://www.gnupress.org); ISBN 1-882114-98-1.

- Patents cost a lot of money. They cost even more paying the lawyers to write the application than they cost to actually apply. It typically takes some years for the application to get considered, even though patent offices do an extremely sloppy job of considering them.

- Copyrights last tremendously long. In some cases they can last as long as 150 years. Patents last 20 years, which is long enough that you can outlive them but still quite long by the timescale of a field such as software. Think back about 20 years ago when the PC was a new thing. Imagine being constrained to develop software using only the ideas that were known in 1982.

- Copyrights cover copying only. If you write a novel that turns out to be word-for-word the same as *Gone With The Wind*, and you can prove you never saw *Gone With The Wind*, that would be a defense to any accusation of copyright infringement.

  A patent is an absolute monopoly on using an idea. Even if you could prove you had the idea on your own, that would be entirely irrelevant if the idea is patented by somebody else.

I hope you will forget about copyrights for the rest of this talk, because this talk is about patents, and you should never lump together copyrights and patents—for the sake of understanding these legal issues clearly.

Imagine what would happen in your understanding of practical chemistry [or cooking] if you confused water and ethanol.

When you hear people describe the patent system, they usually describe it from the point of view of somebody who is hoping to get a patent—what it would be like for you to get a patent, what it would be like for you to be walking down the street with a patent in your pocket, so that every so often you can pull it out and point it at somebody and say "Give me your money!"

There is a reason for this bias, which is that most of the people who will tell you about the patent system have a stake in it, so they want you to like it. There is another reason: the patent system is a lot like a lottery, because only a tiny fraction of patents actually bring any benefit to those who hold the patents. In fact, *The Economist* once compared it to a "time-consuming lottery." If you have seen ads for lotteries, they always invite you to think about winning. They don't invite you to think about losing, even though losing is far more likely. It is the same with ads for the patent system: they always invite you to think about being the one who wins.

To balance this bias, I am going to describe the patent system from the point of view of its victims—that is, from the point of view of somebody who wants to develop software but is forced to contend with a system of software patents that might result in getting sued.

So, what is the first thing you are going to do after you have had an idea of what kind of program you are going to write?

The first thing you might want to try to do, to deal with the patent system, is find out what patents may cover the program you want to write. This is impossible.

The reason is that some of the patent applications that are pending are secret. After a certain amount of time they may get published, like 18 months. But that is plenty of time for you to write a program, and even release it, not knowing that there is going to be a patent and you are going to get sued.

This is not just academic. In 1984, the compress program was written, a program for data compression. At the time, there was no patent on the LZW compression algorithm it used. Then, in 1985, the U.S. issued a patent on this algorithm, and over the next few years those who distributed the compress program started getting threats.

There was no way that the author of compress could have realized that he was likely to get sued. All he did was use an idea that he found in a journal, just as programmers had always done. He hadn't realized that you could no longer safely use ideas that you found in a journal.

Let's forget about that problem. The issued patents are published by the patent office, so you can find the whole long list of them and see exactly what they say.

Of course, you couldn't actually read the whole list, as there are too many of them. In the U.S., there are hundreds of thousands of software patents. There is no way you can keep track of what they are all about. You would have to try to search for relevant ones.

Some people say that should be easy in these modern days of computers. You could search for key words and so on, but that only works to a certain extent. You will find some patents in the area. However, you won't necessarily find them all.

For instance, there was a software patent (which may have expired by now) on natural-order recalculation in spreadsheets. This means basically that when you make certain cells depend on other cells, it always recalculates everything after things it depends on, so that after one recalculation, everything is up to date. The first spreadsheets did their recalculation top-down, so if you made a cell depend on a cell lower down, and you had a few such steps, you had to recalculate several times to get the new values to propagate upwards. (You were supposed to have things depend on cells above them.)

Then someone realized, why don't I do the recalculation so that each thing gets recalculated after the things it depends on? This algorithm is called topological sorting. The first reference I could find to it is in 1963. The patent covered several dozen different ways you could implement topological sorting.

But you wouldn't have found this patent by searching for "spreadsheet." You couldn't have found it by searching for "natural order" or "topological sort." It didn't have any of those terms in it. In fact, it was described as a method of "compiling formulas into object code." When I first saw it, I thought it was the wrong patent.

Let's suppose that you got a list of patents and you want to see what you are not allowed to do. When you try studying these patents, you will discover they are very hard to understand, as they are written in tortuous legal language whose meaning is very hard to understand. The things patent offices say often don't mean what they seem to mean.

There was an Australian government study of the patent system in the 1980's. It concluded that aside from international pressure, there was no reason to have a patent system—it did no good for the public—and recommended abolishing it if not for international pressure. One of the things they cited was that engineers don't try reading patents to learn anything, as it is too hard to understand them. They quoted one engineer saying "I can't recognize my own inventions in patentese."

This is not just theoretical. Around 1990, a programmer named Paul Heckel sued Apple, claiming that Hypercard infringed a couple of his patents. When he first saw Hypercard, he didn't think it had anything to do with his patents, with his "inventions." It didn't look similar. When his lawyer told him that you could read the patents as covering part of Hypercard, he decided to attack Apple. When I gave a speech about this at Stanford, he was in the audience. He said, "That's not true, I just didn't understand the extent of my protection!" I said, "Yes, that's what I said."

So, in fact, you will have to spend a lot of time talking with lawyers to figure out what these patents prohibit you from doing. Ultimately they are going to say something like this: "If you do something in here, you are sure to lose; if you do something here (RMS gestures, sweeping out a large area), there is a substantial chance of losing, and if you really want to be safe, stay out of this area (he gestures again, sweeping out an even larger area). And, by the way, there is a substantial element of chance in the outcome of any lawsuit."

Now that you have a predictable terrain for doing business(!), what are you going to do? Well, there are three approaches you might try, any of which is applicable in some cases. They are,

1. avoiding the patent,

2. licensing the patent, and

3. overturning a patent in court.

Let me describe these three approaches and what makes them workable or unworkable.

Avoiding the Patent

"Avoiding the patent"—that means don't use the idea that the patent covers. This can be easy or hard, depending on what that idea is.

In some cases, a feature is patented. Then you avoid the patent by not implementing that feature. Then it just matters how important that feature is.

In some cases, you can live without it. A while ago, the users of the word processor XyWrite got a downgrade in the mail. The downgrade removed a feature that allowed you to predefine abbreviations. That is, when you typed an abbreviation followed by a punctuation character, it would immediately replace itself with some expansion of the abbreviation. That way, you could define the abbreviation for some long phrase, type the abbreviation, and then the phrase would be in your document. They (the developers) wrote to me about this because they knew the Emacs editor has a similar feature. In fact, it had it since the 70's. This was interesting as it showed me that I had at least one patentable idea in my life. I know it was patentable because somebody else patented it afterward!

Actually they considered all three approaches. First they tried negotiating with the patent holder, who turned out not to negotiate in good faith. Then they looked at whether they could have a chance at overturning the patent. What they decided to do was to take out the feature.

You can live without this feature. If the word processor lacks only this feature, maybe people will still use it. But as various features start getting hit, eventually you end up with a program people think is not very good, and they are likely to reject it.

That is a rather narrow patent on a very specific feature. What do you do with the British Telecom patent on traversing hyperlinks together with dial-up access? Traversing hyperlinks is absolutely essential to a major use of computers these days. Dial-up access is also essential. How do you do without this feature? Which, by the way, isn't even one feature—it is really a combination of two features arbitrarily juxtaposed. It is rather like having a patent on a sofa and television in the same room.

Sometimes the idea that's patented will be so broad and basic that it basically rules out an entire field. For instance, the idea of public key encryption, which was patented in the U.S. The patent expired in 1997. Until then, it largely blocked the use of public key encryption in the U.S. A number of programs that people started to develop got crushed—they were never really available because the patent holders threatened them. Then, one program got away, the program PGP, which initially was released as free software. Apparently, the patent holders, by the time they got around to attacking, realized they might get too much bad publicity. So they imposed restrictions, making it for non-commercial use only, which meant it couldn't catch on too much. So they greatly limited the use of Public Key Encryption for a decade or more. There was no way around that patent. There was nothing else you could do like public key encryption.

Sometimes a specific algorithm gets patented. For instance, there is a patent on an optimized version of the Fast Fourier Transform (FFT). It runs about twice as fast. You can avoid that by using an ordinary FFT in your program. That part of the program will take twice as long. Maybe that doesn't matter, maybe that is a small part of the program's running time. Maybe if it is twice as slow, you won't really notice. Or maybe your program won't run at all as it will take twice real time to do its job. The effects vary.

In some cases, you can find a better algorithm. This may or may not do you any good. Because we couldn't use compress in the GNU Project, we started looking for an alternative algorithm for data compression. Somebody wrote to us saying he had one; he had written a program and decided to contribute it to us. We were going to release it. Just by chance, I happened to see a copy of the *New York Times*, it happened to have the weekly patent column in it. (I didn't see a copy of the *Times* more than once every few months.) So I looked at it and it said someone had got a patent for "inventing a new method of compressing data." I figured I'd better take a look at this patent. I got a copy and it turned out to cover the program that we were just a week away from releasing. That program died before it was born.

Later on we did find another algorithm, which was unpatented. That became the program gzip, which is now effectively the de facto standard for data compression. As an algorithm to use in a program for data compression, it was fine. Anyone who wanted to do data compression could use gzip instead of compress.

The same patented LZW compression algorithm was also used in image formats such as the GIF format. But there, because the job people wanted to do was not to simply compress data but to make an image that people could display with their software, it turned out extremely hard to switch over to a different algorithm. We have not been able to do it in 10 years! Yes, people used the gzip algorithm to define another image format, once people started getting threatened with lawsuits for using GIF files. When we started saying to people stop using GIF files, switch over to this, people said "We can't switch. The browsers don't support the new format yet." The browser developers said "We're not in a hurry about this. After all, nobody is using this new file format."

In effect, society had so much inertia in the use of the GIF format, we have not been able to get people to switch. Essentially, the community's use of the GIF format is still pushing sites into using GIF format, with the result that they are vulnerable to these threats.

In fact, the situation is even more bizarre. There are in fact two patents covering the LZW compression algorithm. The patent office couldn't even tell they were issuing two patents on the same thing; they couldn't keep track. There is a reason for this: it takes a while of studying these two patents to see that they really cover the same thing.

If they were patents on some chemical process, it would be much easier. You could see what substances were being used, what the inputs were, what the outputs were, which physical actions were being taken. No matter how they were described, you'd see what they were and then you would see they were similar. If something is purely mathematical, there are many ways of describing it, which are a lot more different. They are not superficially similar. You have to really understand them to see that they are really talking about the same thing. The patent office doesn't have time. The U.S. patent office, as of a few years ago, was spending on average 17 hours per patent. This is not long enough to think carefully about them, so of course they make mistakes like that. In fact, I told you about the program that died before it was born. That algorithm also had two patents issued for it in the U.S., apparently, it is not that unusual.

Avoiding the patents may be easy, or it may be impossible. It may be easy but make your program useless—it varies depending on the situation.

Here is another point I should mention: Sometimes a company or consortium can make a format or protocol the de facto standard. Then if that format or protocol is patented, that is a real disaster for you. There are even official standards that are restricted by patents. There was a big political uproar in September of 2001 when the World Wide Web Consortium was proposing to start adopting standards that were covered by patents. The community objected, so they reversed themselves. They went back to insisting that any patents had to be freely implementable by anyone and that the standards had to be free for anyone to implement. That is an interesting victory. I think that was the first time any standards body has made that decision. It is normal for standards bodies to be willing to put something in a standard that is restricted by patents and people are not allowed to go ahead and implement freely. We need to go to other standards bodies and call on them to change their rules.

Licensing the Patent

The second possibility instead of avoiding the patent is to get a license for the patent. This is not necessarily an option. The patent holder does not have to offer you a license; it is not required. Ten years ago, the League for Programming Freedom got a letter asking for help from somebody whose family business was making gambling machinery for casinos, and they [already] used computers back then. He received a threat from another company that said, "We have a patent. You are not allowed to make these things. Shut down!"

I looked at that patent. It covered having a number of computers on a network for playing games such that each computer supported more than one game and allowed you to play more than one game at a time.

You will find that the patent office really thinks there is something brilliant about doing more than one of anything. They don't realize that in computer science, that's the most obvious way to generalize anything. You did it once, so now you can do it any number of times, you can make a subroutine. They think that if you do anything more than once, that somehow means you are brilliant and that nobody can possibly argue with you and that you have the right to boss them around.

Anyway, he was not offered a license. He had to shut down. He couldn't even afford to go to court. I would say that particular patent was an obvious idea. It is possible that a judge might have agreed, but we will never know because he could not afford to go to court.

However, a lot of patent holders do offer licenses. They often charge a lot of money for that, though. The company licensing the natural-order recalculation patent was demanding 5% of the gross sales of every spreadsheet in the U.S. I am told that was the cheap pre-lawsuit price—if you actually made them sue you and they won, they'd demand more.

You might be able to afford that 5% for licensing this one patent, but what if you need to license 20 different patents to make the program? Then all the money you take in goes on patents. What if you need to license 21 patents? People in business told me that practically speaking, two or three such patent licenses would make any business unfeasible.

There is a situation where licensing patents is a very good solution. That is if you are a multinational mega-corporation. Because these companies own a lot of patents, and they cross-license with each other. That way, they escape most of the harm that the patent system does and they get only the good.

IBM published an article in *Think* magazine—I believe it was issue No. 5 of 1990—on IBM's patent portfolio, which said that IBM got two kinds of benefit from its 9000 U.S. patents. (I believe the number is larger today.) These were, first, collecting royalties and second, getting "access to the patents of others." They said that the latter benefit is an order of magnitude greater. So the benefit that IBM got from being allowed to use the ideas that were patented by others was ten times the direct benefit IBM could get from licensing patents.

What does this really mean? What is the benefit that IBM gets from this "access to the patents of others"? It is basically the benefit of being excused from the trouble that the patent system can cause you. The patent system is like a lottery:

what happens with any given patent could be nothing, could be a windfall for some patent holder, or a disaster for everyone else. But IBM being so big, it averages out for them. They get to measure the average harm and good of the patent system. For them, the trouble of the patent system would have been ten times the good.

I say "would have been" because IBM through cross-licensing avoids experiencing that trouble. That trouble is only potential, it doesn't really happen to them. But when they measure the benefits of avoiding that trouble, they estimate it as ten times the value of the money they collect from their patents.

This phenomenon of cross-licensing refutes a common myth, the myth of the "starving genius," the myth that patents "protect" the "small inventor." (Those terms are propaganda terms. You shouldn't use them.)

The scenario is like this: Suppose there is a "brilliant" designer of whatever. Suppose he has spent "years starving in the attic" designing a new wonderful kind of whatever, and now wants to manufacture it. Isn't it a shame the big companies are going to go into competition with him, take away all the business, and he'll "starve"?

I have to point out that people in high-tech fields are not generally working on their own, that ideas don't come in a vacuum—they are based on ideas of others—and these people have pretty good chances of getting a job if they need to these days. So this scenario—the idea that a brilliant idea came from this brilliant person working alone—is unrealistic, and the idea that he is in danger of starving is unrealistic.

But it is conceivable that somebody could have an idea and this idea along with 100 or 200 other ideas can be the basis of making some kind of product, and that big companies might want to compete with him. So let's see what happens if he tries to use a patent to stop them. He says "Oh no, IBM, You cannot compete with me. I've got this patent." IBM says, "Let's see. Let's look at your product. Hmmm. I've got this patent, and this one, and this one and this one and this one and this one, which parts of your product infringe. If you think you can fight against all of them in court, I will just go back and find some more. So, why don't you cross-license with me?" And then the brilliant small inventor says "Well, OK, I'll cross-license." So he can go back and make these wonderful whatever-it-is, but so can IBM. IBM gets "access" to his patent, and gets the right to compete with him, which means this patent didn't "protect" him at all. The patent system doesn't really do that.

The mega-corporations avoid, for the most part, the harm of the patent system; they see mainly the good side. That is why they want to have software patents: they are the ones who will benefit from it. But if you are a small inventor or work for a small company, the small company will not be able to do this. They try. The problem is that small companies cannot get enough patents to do this (make everyone cross-license with them).

Any given patent is pointing in a certain direction. So if a small company has patents pointing there, there, and there, and somebody over there (Stallman indicates to a different place) points a patent at them and says give me your money, the small company is helpless. IBM can do it, because with 9000 patents, they are pointing everywhere; no matter where you are, there is probably an IBM patent pointing at you. So IBM can almost always make you cross-license. Small companies can only occasionally make someone cross-license. They will say they want patents for defensive purposes, but they won't get enough to be able to defend themselves.

There are cases where even IBM cannot make someone cross-license. That is when there is a company whose sole business is taking a patent and squeezing money out of people. The company that had the natural-order recalculation patent was exactly such a company. Their sole business was to threaten to sue people and collect money from people who were really developing something.

There are no patents on legal procedures. I guess the lawyers understand what a pain it would be to have to deal with the patent system themselves. The result is that there is no way to get a patent to make that company cross-license with you. So they go around squeezing everyone. But I guess companies like IBM figure that is part of the price of doing business so they can live with it.

So that is the possibility of licensing a patent, which may or may not be possible, and you may or may not be able to afford it—which leads us to our third possibility.

Overturning a Patent in Court

Supposedly, in order to be patented, something has to be new, useful, and unobvious. (That is the language used in the U.S.; I think other countries have other language which is pretty much equivalent to it.) Of course, when the patent office gets into the game, they start interpreting "new" and "unobvious." "New" turns out to mean "we don't have it in our files," and "unobvious" tends to mean "unobvious to someone with an I.Q of 50."

Somebody who studies most of the software patents issued in the U.S.—or at least he used to, I don't know if he can still keep up with them—said 90% of them wouldn't have passed the "Crystal City test," which meant if the people in the patent office went outside to the newsstand and got some computer magazines, they would see that these ideas are already known.

The patent office does things that are so obviously foolish, you wouldn't even have to know the state of the art to see they are foolish. This is not limited to software. I once saw the famous Harvard mouse patent, that was obtained after Harvard genetically engineered a mouse with a cancer-causing gene. The cancer-causing gene was already known, and was inserted using known techniques into an already existing strain of mouse. The patent they got covered inserting any cancer-causing gene into any kind of mammal using any method whatsoever. You don't have to know anything about genetic engineering to realize that is ridiculous. I am told that this "overclaiming" is normal practice, and that the U.S. patent office sometimes invites patent applicants to make their claims broader. Basically, you make the claims broader until you think they are running into something else that's unambiguous prior art. See how much land grab in mental space you can get away with.

When programmers look at a lot of software patents, they say "this is ridiculously obvious!" Patent bureaucrats have all sorts of excuses to justify ignoring what programmers think. They say "Oh! but you have to consider it in terms of the way things were ten or twenty years ago." Then they discovered that if they talk something to death then you can eventually lose your bearings. Anything can look unobvious if you tear it apart enough, analyze it enough. You simply lose all standard of obviousness, or at least lose the ability to justify any standard of obvious or unobvious. Then, of course, they describe the patent holders as brilliant inventors, all of them; therefore we can't question their entitlement to power over what we do.

If you go to court, the judges are likely to be a little more stringent about what is obvious or not. But the problem is that it costs millions of dollars to do that.

I heard of one patent case, the defendant I remember was Qualcomm, and I believe the ruling was ultimately $13 million (USD) of which most went to pay the lawyers on both sides. There were a few million dollars left over for the plaintiff (because Qualcomm lost).

To a large extent, the question of the validity of a patent will depend on historical accidents. Lots of historical accidents, such as precisely what was published when, and which of those things somebody manages to find, which of them didn't get lost, precise dates, and so on. Many historical accidents determine whether a patent is valid.

In fact, it is a weird thing that the British Telecom "following hyperlinks together with telephone access" patent was applied for in 1975. I think it was in 1974 that I developed the Info package for the first time. The Info package allows you to traverse hyperlinks, and people did use telephones to dial up and access the system. So in fact, I did produce a piece of prior art for this patent. This is the second patentable idea I know I have produced in my life.

But I don't think I have any proof of that. I didn't think this was interesting enough to publish it. After all, the idea of following hyperlinks I got from the demo of Englebart's editor. He is the one who had an idea that was interesting to publish. What I had done I called "poor man's hypertext," as I had to implement it in the context of TECO. It was not as powerful as his hypertext, but it was at least useful for browsing documentation, which is all it was meant for. And as for there being dial-up access to the system, well, there was, but it didn't occur to me that the one had anything particular to do with the other. I wasn't going to publish a paper saying, "Oh! I implemented this poor man's hypertext, and guess what! There are dial-up lines on the computer too!"

I suspect there is no way to tell precisely on what date I implemented this. Was it published in any sense? Well, we invited guests to come in across the ARPANET, and log in on our machine—so they could have browsed documentation using Info and seen the thing. If they had asked us, they would have found we had dial-up access. As you can see, historical accident determines whether you have prior art.

Now of course, there is a publication made by Englebart about hypertext, which they, the defendants, are going to show. I don't think it says anything about having dial-ups on the computer, however, so whether it will suffice is not clear.

The possibility of going to court to overturn the patent is an option. Because of the expense, it is often out of the question even if you can find solid prior art which ought to be sufficient to overturn the patent. As a result, an invalid patent, a patent that nominally shouldn't have existed (but in fact lots and lots of them do), is a dangerous weapon. If someone attacks you with an invalid patent, that can really cause a lot of trouble for you. You might be able to bluff them away by showing them the prior art. It depends on whether they can get scared off that way. They might think, "Well, you are just bluffing, we figure you can't really go to court; you can't afford it, so we'll sue you anyway."

All of these three options are things that sometimes you can manage to use, but often you can't. So you have to face patent after patent after patent. Each time you may be able to find one of these three possibilities you can use, then there is another patent, then another and another. It gets like crossing a minefield. Each step you take, each design decision, probably won't step on a patent, so you can take a few steps and probably there won't be an explosion. But the chance you can get all the way through the minefield and develop the program you want to develop without ever stepping on a patent gets less and less as the program gets bigger.

Now, people used to say to me, "Well, there are patents in other fields, why should software be exempt?" Note the bizarre assumption in there, that somehow we are all supposed to suffer through the patent system. It is like saying "Some people get cancer. Why should you be exempt?" As I see it, each person who doesn't get cancer is a good thing.

But there is, behind that, a less biased question, a good question, which is: Is software different from other fields? Should patent policy be different in different fields? If so, why?

Let me address that question: patents relate to different fields differently because, in different fields, patents relate to products differently.

On one extreme we have pharmaceuticals, where a given chemical formula would be patented, so that patent covers one and only one product. A new drug wouldn't be covered by the existing patent. If there is to be a patent for this new product, the patent holder would be whoever developed the new product.

That fits in with the naive idea of the patent system that we have, that if you are designing a new product, you are going to get "the patent." The idea is that there is one patent per product and that it covers the idea of the product. In some fields it is closer to being true; in other fields it is further from being true.

The software field is at the latter extreme: one program intersects many patents. This is because software packages are usually very big. They use many different ideas in combination. If the program is new and not just copied, then it is probably using a different combination of ideas—embodied, of course, in newly written code, because you can't just magically say the names of these ideas and have them work. You have to implement them all. You have to implement them all in that combination.

The result is that even when you write a program, you are using lots of different ideas, any one of which might be patented by somebody. A pair of them may be patented as a combination by somebody. There might be several different ways of describing one idea, which might be patented by various different people. So there are possibly thousands of things, thousands of points of vulnerability in your program, that might be patented by somebody else already.

This is why software patents tend to obstruct the progress of software—the work of software development. If it were "one patent, one product," then these patents wouldn't obstruct the development of products because if you develop a new product, it wouldn't be patented by somebody else already. But when one product corresponds to many different ideas combined, it gets very likely your new product (either part or all of your product) is going to be patented by somebody else already.

In fact, there is economic research now showing just how imposing a patent system on a field where there is incremental innovation can retard progress. You see, the advocates of software patents say "Well, yes, there may be problems, but more important than any problems, the patents must promote innovation, and that is so important it doesn't matter what problems they cause." Of course, they don't say that out loud because it is ridiculous, but implicitly they want you to believe that as long as the patent system promotes progress, that outweighs any possible cost. But actually, there is no reason to believe it does promote progress. We now have a model showing precisely how patents can retard progress. The case where that model applies describes the software field pretty well; incremental innovation.

Why is software on that extreme of the spectrum? The reason is that in software we are developing idealized mathematical objects. You can build a complicated castle and have it rest on a thin line and it will stay up because it doesn't weigh anything. In other fields, people have to cope with the perversity of matter—of physical objects. Matter does what it is going to do. You can try to model it, but if the actual behaviour doesn't fit the model then tough on you, because the challenge is to make physical objects that really work.

If I want to put an if-statement in a while-statement, I don't have to worry about whether the if-statement will oscillate at a certain frequency and rub against the while-statement and eventually they will fracture. I don't have to worry whether it will oscillate at a certain high frequency and induce a signal in the value of some other variable. I don't have to worry about how much current that if-statement will draw, and whether it can dissipate the heat there inside that while-statement, or whether there will be a voltage drop across the while-statement that will make the if-statement not function. I don't have to worry that if I run this program in a salt water environment, the salt water may get in between the if-statement and the while-statement and cause corrosion. [The audience laughs all through this.]

I don't have to worry, when I refer to the value of a variable, whether I am exceeding the fan-out limit by referring to it 20 times. I don't have to worry how much capacitance it has, and whether there has been sufficient time to charge up the value.

I don't have to worry, when I write the program, about how I am going to physically assemble each copy and whether I can manage to get access to put that if-statement inside the while-statement. I don't have to worry about how I am going to gain access in case that if-statement breaks, to remove it and replace it with a new one. There are so many problems that we don't have to worry about in software; that makes it fundamentally easier to write a program than to design a physical object that's going to work.

This may seem strange, because you have probably heard people talking about how hard software is to design and how this is a big problem and considering how we are going to solve it. They are not really talking about the same question as I am. I am comparing physical and software systems of the same complexity, the same number of parts. I am saying the software system is much easier to design than the physical system. But the intelligence of people in these various fields is the same, so what do we do when we are confronted with an easy field? We push it further! We push our abilities to the limit. If systems of the same size are easy, let's make systems that are ten times as big—then it will be hard! That's what we do: we make software systems that are far bigger in terms of number of parts than physical systems.

A physical system whose design has a million different pieces in it is a megaproject. A computer program whose design has a million pieces in it is maybe 300,000 lines; a few people will write that in a couple of years. That is not a particularly giant program. GNU Emacs now has several million pieces in its design, I think. It has a million lines of code. This is a project done with essentially no funding whatsoever, mostly done by people in their spare time.

There is another big saving. If you have designed a physical product, the next thing you have to do is design the factory to make it. To build this factory may cost millions or tens of millions, whereas to make copies of the program you just have to type "copy." The same copy command will copy any program. You want copies on CD, then fine, you burn a master CD and send it off to a CD plant. They will use the same equipment that will copy any contents on a CD. You don't have to build a specialized factory to make each particular product. This is tremendous simplification and tremendous reduction in costs of designing things.

An automobile company, which will spend $50 million to build a factory to build a new model of auto, can hire some lawyers to cope with patent license negotiations. They can even cope with a lawsuit if they wanted to. To design a program of the same complexity may cost $50,000 or $100,000. By comparison, the cost of dealing with the patent system is crushing—actually designing a program with the same complexity as the mechanical design of an auto is probably a month's work. How many parts does an auto have. . . that is, if it is an auto which doesn't have computers in it.[1] That is not to say designing a good one is easy, but just that there are not that many different parts in it.

The result is that software really is different from other fields, because when we are working with mathematical stuff, designing something is far, far easier. The result is that we regularly make systems which are much, much larger and do so with just a few people. The result is that instead of being close to one product, one patent, we are in a system where one product involves many, many ideas that could be patented already.

The best way to explain this by analogy is with symphonies. A symphony is also long and has many notes in it, and probably uses many musical ideas. Imagine if the governments of Europe in the 1700's had decided they wanted to promote the progress of symphonic music by establishing a European Musical Patent Office that would give patents for any kind of musical ideas that you could state in words.

---

[1] There are approximatly 300–400 unique parts in an automatic transmission, and a transmission is generally the most complicated component of an auto. To design a transmission may take six months to a year, and even then it may take longer to actually get it built and functioning. However, a program with 500 to 800 functional parts would have 200 to 300 lines of actual code, and would probably take a good programmer a day to a week to write, test and debug.

Then imagine it is around 1800, and you are Beethoven and you want to write a symphony. You will find that getting your symphony so that it doesn't infringe any patents is going to be harder than writing a good symphony.

When you complain about this, the patent holders would say "Aw Beethoven, you are just bitching because you have no ideas of your own. All you want to do is rip off our inventions." Beethoven, as it happens, had a lot of new musical ideas—but he had to use a lot of existing musical ideas in order to make recognizable music, in order to make music that listeners could possibly like, that they could recognize as music. Nobody is so brilliant that he can re-invent music completely different and make something that people would want to listen to. Pierre Boulez said he would try to do that, but who listens to Pierre Boulez?

Nobody is so brilliant he can re-invent all of computer science, completely new. If he did, he would make something that the users would find so strange that they wouldn't want to use it. If you look at a word processor today, you would find, I think, hundreds of different features. If you develop a nice new innovative word processor, that means there are some new ideas in it, but there must be hundreds of old ideas in it. If you are not allowed to use them, you cannot make an innovative word processor. Because the work of software development is so big, the result is that we don't need any artificial scheme to incentivize new ideas. You just have people writing software and they will have some new ideas. If you want to write a program and you want to make it good, some ideas will come to you and you will see a way to use some of them.

What used to happen—because I was in the software field before there were software patents—was most of the developers would publish any new ideas that they thought were noteworthy, that they thought that they might get any credit or respect for. The ideas that were too small or not impressive enough, they would not publish because that would be silly. Now, the patent system is supposed to encourage disclosure of ideas. In fact, in the old days, nobody kept the ideas secret. They kept the code secret, it's true. The code, after all, represented the bulk of the work. They would keep the code secret and publish the ideas, so that way the employees would get some credit and feel good.

After software patents, they still kept the code secret and they patented the ideas, so in fact, disclosure has not been encouraged in any meaningful sense. The same things are kept secret now as were kept secret before, but the ideas that used to be published so that we could use them are now likely to be patented and off limits for 20 years.

What can a country do to change this? How should we change the policy to solve this problem?

There are two places you can attack it. One is the place where patents are being issued, in the patent office. The other is where patents are being applied. That is a question of what does a patent cover.

One way is to keep a good criterion for issuing patents. This can work in a country that has not authorized software patents before, for instance, for the most part, in Europe. Simply to clearly reinforce the European Patent Office's rules which say that software is not patentable is a good solution for Europe. Europe is now considering a directive on software patents. (The directive I suppose may be broader than that, but one of its important implications is for software patents.) Simply modifying this to say software ideas cannot be patented will keep the problem out of Europe for the most part, except for some countries that may have admitted the problem on their own, unfortunately one of them being the U.K. (unfortunately for you.)

That approach won't work in the U.S. The reason is that the U.S. already has large numbers of software patents, and any change in the criteria for issuing patents won't get rid of the existing ones.[2] So, in the U.S., the solution would have to be done through changing the applicability, the scope, of patents: saying that a pure software implementation, running on general-purpose computer hardware that does not in itself infringe the patent, is not covered by any patent, and you cannot get sued for it. That is the other kind of solution.

The first kind of solution, the solution that operates on what types of patents can be valid, is a good solution for Europe to use.

When the U.S. started having software patents, there was no political debate. In fact, nobody noticed. The software field, for the most part, didn't even notice. There was a Supreme Court decision in 1981 that considered a patent on a process for curing rubber. The ruling was that the fact that the apparatus included a computer and a program as part of the process to cure the rubber didn't make it unpatentable. The next year, the appeals court that considers all patent cases reversed the quantifiers: they said the fact that there is a computer and a program in this makes it patentable. The fact that there is a computer and program in anything makes it patentable. This is why the U.S. started having business procedure patents: because the business procedures were carried out on a computer and that made them patentable.

So this ruling was made, and I think the natural-order recalculating patent was one of the first or might have even been the first.

Throughout the 80's, we didn't know about this. It was around 1990 that programmers in the U.S. started to become aware that they were faced with a danger from software patents. I saw how the field worked before and how the field worked after. I saw no particular speed-up in progress after 1990.

There was no political debate in the U.S., but in Europe there has been a big political debate. Several years ago there was a push to amend the Munich treaty that established the European Patent Office. It has a clause saying that software is not patentable. The push was to amend that to start allowing software patents. But the community took notice of this. It was actually free software developers and free software users who took the lead. But we are not the only ones threatened by software patents. All software developers are threatened by software patents, and even software users are threatened by software patents.

For instance, Paul Heckel—when Apple wasn't very scared of his threats—threatened to start suing Apple's customers. Apple found that very scary. They

---

[2] I say "software patents" but what do I really mean? The U.S. patent office doesn't officially divide patents into software patents and other patents. So, in fact, any patent might conceivably get you sued for writing software if it could apply to some software. Software patents are patents that might potentially apply to software, patents that might potentially get you sued for writing software.

figured they couldn't afford to have their customers being sued like that, even if they would ultimately win. So the users can get sued too, either as a way of attacking a developer or just as a way to squeeze money out of them on their own or to cause mayhem. All software developers and users are vulnerable.

But it was the free software community in Europe that took the lead in organizing opposition. In fact, twice now the countries that govern the European Patent Office voted not to amend that treaty. Then the E.U. took a hand and the Directorates of the E.U were divided on the issue. The one whose job is to promote software is against software patents, it seems, but they were not in charge of this issue. It is the Open Market Directorate that is in charge, and it is run by somebody who is in favor of software patents. They basically disregarded public opinion that has been expressed to them. They have proposed a directive to allow software patents.

The French government has already said they are against it. People are working on various other governments in Europe to oppose software patents, and it is vital to start doing so here, in Britain. According to Hartmut Pilch, who is one of the leaders in the European struggle against software patents, the main impetus for them comes from the U.K. patent office. The U.K. patent office is simply biased in favor of software patents. It had a public consultation, and most of the responses were opposed to software patents. They then wrote a report saying people seem to be content with them, completely disregarding the answers. You see, the free software community said, "Please send the answers to them and to us too." So they published these answers, which were generally opposed. You'd have never guessed that from the report that the U.K. patent office published.

They use a term that they call "technical effect." This is a term that can stretch tremendously. You are supposed to think it means a program idea would be patentable only if it relates only to specific physical acts. If that is the interpretation, it would mostly solve the problem. If the only software ideas that can be patented were those that really did relate to a particular technical, physical result that you might have patented if you didn't use a program, that would be OK. The problem is that you can stretch that term. You can describe the result you get by running any program as a physical result. How does this physical result different from any other? Well it is as a result of this computation. The result is that the U.K. patent office is proposing something that looks as if it leads to mostly solving the problem but really gives carte blanche for patenting almost anything.

The people in the same ministry are also involved in the copyright issue, which really has nothing to do with software patents except that it is being handled by the same people. (Perhaps they have been led by the term "intellectual property" to lump the issues together.) It is a question of interpreting the recent E.U. copyright directive, a horrible law like the Digital Millennium Copyright Act (DMCA) in the U.S., but there is some latitude for countries to decide how to implement it. The U.K. is proposing the most draconian possible way of implementing this directive. You could greatly reduce the harm it does by implementing it properly. The U.K. wants to maximize the tyrannical effect of this directive. It seems there is a certain group—the Department of Trade and Industry?—who need to be reined in. It is necessary to put a check on their activities, stop their creating new forms of power.

Software patents tie up every software developer and every computer user in a new form of bureaucracy. If the businesses that use computers realized how much trouble this can cause for them, they would be up in arms, and I am sure they could stop it. Business doesn't like being tied up in bureaucracy. Sometimes, of course, it serves an important purpose. There are some areas where we wish the U.K. government did a more careful job in tying certain businesses up in bureaucracy, like when it involves moving animals around.[3] But in cases when it doesn't serve any purpose except to create artificial monopolies so that somebody can interfere with software development—squeeze money out of developers and users—then we should reject it. We need to make management aware of what software patents will do to them, and get their support in fighting against software patents in Europe.

The battle is not over. It still can be won.

---

[3] To make it harder for foot-and-mouth disease to spread.

Section Three
Freedom, Society, and Software

17 Can You Trust Your Computer?

Who should your computer take its orders from? Most people think their computers should obey them, not obey someone else. With a plan they call "trusted computing," large media corporations (including the movie companies and record companies), together with computer companies such as Microsoft and Intel, are planning to make your computer obey them instead of you. Proprietary programs have included malicious features before, but this plan would make it universal.

Proprietary software means, fundamentally, that you don't control what it does; you can't study the source code, or change it. It's not surprising that clever businessmen find ways to use their control to put you at a disadvantage. Microsoft has done this several times: one version of Windows was designed to report to Microsoft all the software on your hard disk; a recent "security" upgrade in Windows Media Player required users to agree to new restrictions. But Microsoft is not alone: the KaZaa music-sharing software is designed so that KaZaa's business partner can rent out the use of your computer to their clients. These malicious features are often secret, but even once you know about them it is hard to remove them, since you don't have the source code.

In the past, these were isolated incidents. "Trusted computing" would make it pervasive. "Treacherous computing" is a more appropriate name, because the plan is designed to make sure your computer will systematically disobey you. In fact, it is designed to stop your computer from functioning as a general-purpose computer. Every operation may require explicit permission.

The technical idea underlying treacherous computing is that the computer includes a digital encryption and signature device, and the keys are kept secret from you. (Microsoft's version of this is called "palladium.") Proprietary programs will use this device to control which other programs you can run, which documents or data you can access, and what programs you can pass them to. These programs will continually download new authorization rules through the Internet, and impose those rules automatically on your work. If you don't allow your computer to obtain the new rules periodically from the Internet, some capabilities will automatically cease to function.

Of course, Hollywood and the record companies plan to use treacherous computing for "DRM" (Digital Restrictions Management), so that downloaded videos and music can be played only on one specified computer. Sharing will be entirely impossible, at least using the authorized files that you would get from those companies. You, the public, ought to have both the freedom and the ability to share these things. (I expect that someone will find a way to produce unencrypted versions, and

---

This is the first published version and is part of *Free Software, Free Society: Selected Essays of Richard M. Stallman*, 2002, GNU Press (http://www.gnupress.org); ISBN 1-882114-98-1.

to upload and share them, so DRM will not entirely succeed, but that is no excuse for the system.)

Making sharing impossible is bad enough, but it gets worse. There are plans to use the same facility for email and documents—resulting in email that disappears in two weeks, or documents that can only be read on the computers in one company.

Imagine if you get an email from your boss telling you to do something that you think is risky; a month later, when it backfires, you can't use the email to show that the decision was not yours. "Getting it in writing" doesn't protect you when the order is written in disappearing ink.

Imagine if you get an email from your boss stating a policy that is illegal or morally outrageous, such as to shred your company's audit documents, or to allow a dangerous threat to your country to move forward unchecked. Today you can send this to a reporter and expose the activity. With treacherous computing, the reporter won't be able to read the document; her computer will refuse to obey her. Treacherous computing becomes a paradise for corruption.

Word processors such as Microsoft Word could use treacherous computing when they save your documents, to make sure no competing word processors can read them. Today we must figure out the secrets of Word format by laborious experiments in order to make free word processors read Word documents. If Word encrypts documents using treacherous computing when saving them, the free software community won't have a chance of developing software to read them—and if we could, such programs might even be forbidden by the Digital Millennium Copyright Act.

Programs that use treacherous computing will continually download new authorization rules through the Internet, and impose those rules automatically on your work. If Microsoft, or the U.S. government, does not like what you said in a document you wrote, they could post new instructions telling all computers to refuse to let anyone read that document. Each computer would obey when it downloads the new instructions. Your writing would be subject to 1984-style retroactive erasure. You might be unable to read it yourself.

You might think you can find out what nasty things a treacherous computing application does, study how painful they are, and decide whether to accept them. It would be short-sighted and foolish to accept, but the point is that the deal you think you are making won't stand still. Once you come depend on using the program, you are hooked and they know it; then they can change the deal. Some applications will automatically download upgrades that will do something different—and they won't give you a choice about whether to upgrade.

Today you can avoid being restricted by proprietary software by not using it. If you run GNU/Linux or another free operating system, and if you avoid installing proprietary applications on it, then you are in charge of what your computer does. If a free program has a malicious feature, other developers in the community will take it out, and you can use the corrected version. You can also run free application programs and tools on non-free operating systems; this falls short of fully giving you freedom, but many users do it.

Treacherous computing puts the existence of free operating systems and free applications at risk, because you may not be able to run them at all. Some versions of treacherous computing would require the operating system to be specifically authorized by a particular company. Free operating systems could not be installed. Some versions of treacherous computing would require every program to be specifically authorized by the operating system developer. You could not run free applications on such a system. If you did figure out how, and told someone, that could be a crime.

There are proposals already for U.S. laws that would require all computers to support treacherous computing, and to prohibit connecting old computers to the Internet. The CBDTPA (we call it the Consume But Don't Try Programming Act) is one of them. But even if they don't legally force you to switch to treacherous computing, the pressure to accept it may be enormous. Today people often use Word format for communication, although this causes several sorts of problems (see http://www.gnu.org/no-word-attachments.html). If only a treacherous computing machine can read the latest Word documents, many people will switch to it, if they view the situation only in terms of individual action (take it or leave it). To oppose treacherous computing, we must join together and confront the situation as a collective choice.

For further information about treacherous computing, see http://www.cl.cam.ac.uk/users/rja14/tcpa-faq.html.

To block treacherous computing will require large numbers of citizens to organize. We need your help! The Electronic Frontier Foundation (www.eff.org) and Public Knowledge (www.publicknowledge.org) are campaigning against treacherous computing, and so is the Digital Speech Project sponsored by the Free Software Foundation (www.digitalspeech.org). Please visit these Web sites so you can sign up to support their work. You can also help by writing to the public affairs offices of Intel, IBM, HP/Compaq, or anyone you have bought a computer from, explaining that you don't want to be pressured to buy "trusted" computing systems so you don't want them to produce any. This can bring consumer power to bear. If you do this on your own, please send copies of your letters to the organizations above.

Postscript:

The GNU Project distributes the GNU Privacy Guard, a program that implements public-key encryption and digital signatures, which you can use to send secure and private email. It is useful to explore how GPG differs from trusted computing, and see what makes one helpful and the other so dangerous.

When someone uses GPG to send you an encrypted document, and you use GPG to decode it, the result is an unencrypted document that you can read, forward, copy, and even re-encrypt to send it securely to someone else. A treacherous computing application would let you read the words on the screen, but would not let you produce an unencrypted document that you could use in other ways. GPG, a free software package, makes security features available to the users; *they* use *it*. Treacherous computing is designed to impose restrictions on the users; *it* uses *them*.

18 Why Software Should Be Free

The existence of software inevitably raises the question of how decisions about its use should be made. For example, suppose one individual who has a copy of a program meets another who would like a copy. It is possible for them to copy the program; who should decide whether this is done? The individuals involved? Or another party, called the "owner"?

Software developers typically consider these questions on the assumption that the criterion for the answer is to maximize developers' profits. The political power of business has led to the government adoption of both this criterion and the answer proposed by the developers: that the program has an owner, typically a corporation associated with its development.

I would like to consider the same question using a different criterion: the prosperity and freedom of the public in general.

This answer cannot be decided by current law—the law should conform to ethics, not the other way around. Nor does current practice decide this question, although it may suggest possible answers. The only way to judge is to see who is helped and who is hurt by recognizing owners of software, why, and how much. In other words, we should perform a cost-benefit analysis on behalf of society as a whole, taking account individual freedom as well as production of material goods.

In this essay, I will describe the effects of having owners, and show that the results are detrimental. My conclusion is that programmers have the duty to encourage others to share, redistribute, study, and improve the software we write: in other words, to write *free* software.[1]

How Owners Justify Their Power

Those who benefit from the current system where programs are property offer two arguments in support of their claims to own programs: the emotional argument and the economic argument.

The emotional argument goes like this: "I put my sweat, my heart, my soul into this program. It comes from *me*, it's *mine*!"

This argument does not require serious refutation. The feeling of attachment is one that programmers can cultivate when it suits them; it is not inevitable. Consider, for example, how willingly the same programmers usually sign over all rights to a large corporation for a salary; the emotional attachment mysteriously vanishes. By contrast, consider the great artists and artisans of medieval times, who didn't even

---

[1] The word "free" in "free software" refers to freedom, not to price; the price paid for a copy of a free program may be zero, or small, or (rarely) quite large.

Originally written in 1992, this version is part of *Free Software, Free Society: Selected Essays of Richard M. Stallman*, 2002, GNU Press (http://www.gnupress.org); ISBN 1-882114-98-1.

sign their names to their work. To them, the name of the artist was not important. What mattered was that the work was done—and the purpose it would serve. This view prevailed for hundreds of years.

The economic argument goes like this: "I want to get rich (usually described inaccurately as 'making a living'), and if you don't allow me to get rich by programming, then I won't program. Everyone else is like me, so nobody will ever program. And then you'll be stuck with no programs at all!" This threat is usually veiled as friendly advice from the wise.

I'll explain later why this threat is a bluff. First I want to address an implicit assumption that is more visible in another formulation of the argument.

This formulation starts by comparing the social utility of a proprietary program with that of no program, and then concludes that proprietary software development is, on the whole, beneficial, and should be encouraged. The fallacy here is in comparing only two outcomes—proprietary software vs. no software—and assuming there are no other possibilities.

Given a system of software copyright, software development is usually linked with the existence of an owner who controls the software's use. As long as this linkage exists, we are often faced with the choice of proprietary software or none. However, this linkage is not inherent or inevitable; it is a consequence of the specific social/legal policy decision that we are questioning: the decision to have owners. To formulate the choice as between proprietary software vs. no software is begging the question.

The Argument Against Having Owners

The question at hand is, "Should development of software be linked with having owners to restrict the use of it?"

In order to decide this, we have to judge the effect on society of each of those two activities *independently*: the effect of developing the software (regardless of its terms of distribution), and the effect of restricting its use (assuming the software has been developed). If one of these activities is helpful and the other is harmful, we would be better off dropping the linkage and doing only the helpful one.

To put it another way, if restricting the distribution of a program already developed is harmful to society overall, then an ethical software developer will reject the option of doing so.

To determine the effect of restricting sharing, we need to compare the value to society of a restricted (i.e., proprietary) program with that of the same program, available to everyone. This means comparing two possible worlds.

This analysis also addresses the simple counterargument sometimes made that "the benefit to the neighbor of giving him or her a copy of a program is canceled by the harm done to the owner." This counterargument assumes that the harm and the benefit are equal in magnitude. The analysis involves comparing these magnitudes, and shows that the benefit is much greater.

To elucidate this argument, let's apply it in another area: road construction.

It would be possible to fund the construction of all roads with tolls. This would entail having toll booths at all street corners. Such a system would provide a great incentive to improve roads. It would also have the virtue of causing the users of any given road to pay for that road. However, a toll booth is an artificial obstruction to smooth driving—artificial, because it is not a consequence of how roads or cars work.

Comparing free roads and toll roads by their usefulness, we find that (all else being equal) roads without toll booths are cheaper to construct, cheaper to run, safer, and more efficient to use.[2] In a poor country, tolls may make the roads unavailable to many citizens. The roads without toll booths thus offer more benefit to society at less cost; they are preferable for society. Therefore, society should choose to fund roads in another way, not by means of toll booths. Use of roads, once built, should be free.

When the advocates of toll booths propose them as *merely* a way of raising funds, they distort the choice that is available. Toll booths do raise funds, but they do something else as well: in effect, they degrade the road. The toll road is not as good as the free road; giving us more or technically superior roads may not be an improvement if this means substituting toll roads for free roads.

Of course, the construction of a free road does cost money, which the public must somehow pay. However, this does not imply the inevitability of toll booths. We who must in either case pay will get more value for our money by buying a free road.

I am not saying that a toll road is worse than no road at all. That would be true if the toll were so great that hardly anyone used the road—but this is an unlikely policy for a toll collector. However, as long as the toll booths cause significant waste and inconvenience, it is better to raise the funds in a less obstructive fashion.

To apply the same argument to software development, I will now show that having "toll booths" for useful software programs costs society dearly: it makes the programs more expensive to construct, more expensive to distribute, and less satisfying and efficient to use. It will follow that program construction should be encouraged in some other way. Then I will go on to explain other methods of encouraging and (to the extent actually necessary) funding software development.

The Harm Done by Obstructing Software

Consider for a moment that a program has been developed, and any necessary payments for its development have been made; now society must choose either to make it proprietary or allow free sharing and use. Assume that the existence of the program and its availability is a desirable thing.[3]

---

[2] The issues of pollution and traffic congestion do not alter this conclusion. If we wish to make driving more expensive to discourage driving in general, it is disadvantageous to do this using toll booths, which contribute to both pollution and congestion. A tax on gasoline is much better. Likewise, a desire to enhance safety by limiting maximum driving speed is not relevant; a free-access road enhances the average driving speed by avoiding stops and delays, for any given speed limit.

[3] One might regard a particular computer program as a harmful thing that should not be available at all, like the Lotus Marketplace database of personal information, which was withdrawn from sale due to public disapproval. Most of what I say does not apply to this case, but it makes little sense

Restrictions on the distribution and modification of the program cannot facilitate its use. They can only interfere. So the effect can only be negative. But how much? And what kind?

Three different levels of material harm come from such obstruction:

1. Fewer people use the program.
2. None of the users can adapt or fix the program.
3. Other developers cannot learn from the program, or base new work on it.

Each level of material harm has a concomitant form of psychosocial harm. This refers to the effect that people's decisions have on their subsequent feelings, attitudes, and predispositions. These changes in people's ways of thinking will then have a further effect on their relationships with their fellow citizens, and can have material consequences.

The three levels of material harm waste part of the value that the program could contribute, but they cannot reduce it to zero. If they waste nearly all the value of the program, then writing the program harms society by at most the effort that went into writing the program. Arguably a program that is profitable to sell must provide some net direct material benefit.

However, taking account of the concomitant psychosocial harm, there is no limit to the harm that proprietary software development can do.

Obstructing Use of Programs

The first level of harm impedes the simple use of a program. A copy of a program has nearly zero marginal cost (and you can pay this cost by doing the work yourself), so in a free market, it would have nearly zero price. A license fee is a significant disincentive to use the program. If a widely useful program is proprietary, far fewer people will use it.

It is easy to show that the total contribution of a program to society is reduced by assigning an owner to it. Each potential user of the program, faced with the need to pay to use it, may choose to pay, or may forgo use of the program. When a user chooses to pay, this is a zero-sum transfer of wealth between two parties. But each time someone chooses to forgo use of the program, this harms that person without benefitting anyone. The sum of negative numbers and zeros must be negative.

But this does not reduce the amount of work it takes to *develop* the program. As a result, the efficiency of the whole process, in delivered user satisfaction per hour of work, is reduced.

This reflects a crucial difference between copies of programs and cars, chairs, or sandwiches. There is no copying machine for material objects outside of science fiction. But programs are easy to copy; anyone can produce as many copies as are wanted, with very little effort. This isn't true for material objects because matter is conserved: each new copy has to be built from raw materials in the same way that the first copy was built.

---

to argue for having an owner on the grounds that the owner will make the program less available. The owner will not make it *completely* unavailable, as one would wish in the case of a program whose use is considered destructive.

With material objects, a disincentive to use them makes sense, because fewer objects bought means less raw material and work needed to make them. It's true that there is usually also a startup cost, a development cost, which is spread over the production run. But as long as the marginal cost of production is significant, adding a share of the development cost does not make a qualitative difference. And it does not require restrictions on the freedom of ordinary users.

However, imposing a price on something that would otherwise be free is a qualitative change. A centrally-imposed fee for software distribution becomes a powerful disincentive.

What's more, central production as now practiced is inefficient even as a means of delivering copies of software. This system involves enclosing physical disks or tapes in superfluous packaging, shipping large numbers of them around the world, and storing them for sale. This cost is presented as an expense of doing business; in truth, it is part of the waste caused by having owners.

Damaging Social Cohesion

Suppose that both you and your neighbor would find it useful to run a certain program. In ethical concern for your neighbor, you should feel that proper handling of the situation will enable both of you to use it. A proposal to permit only one of you to use the program, while restraining the other, is divisive; neither you nor your neighbor should find it acceptable.

Signing a typical software license agreement means betraying your neighbor: "I promise to deprive my neighbor of this program so that I can have a copy for myself." People who make such choices feel internal psychological pressure to justify them, by downgrading the importance of helping one's neighbors—thus public spirit suffers. This is psychosocial harm associated with the material harm of discouraging use of the program.

Many users unconsciously recognize the wrong of refusing to share, so they decide to ignore the licenses and laws, and share programs anyway. But they often feel guilty about doing so. They know that they must break the laws in order to be good neighbors, but they still consider the laws authoritative, and they conclude that being a good neighbor (which they are) is naughty or shameful. That is also a kind of psychosocial harm, but one can escape it by deciding that these licenses and laws have no moral force.

Programmers also suffer psychosocial harm knowing that many users will not be allowed to use their work. This leads to an attitude of cynicism or denial. A programmer may describe enthusiastically the work that he finds technically exciting; then when asked, "Will I be permitted to use it?," his face falls, and he admits the answer is no. To avoid feeling discouraged, he either ignores this fact most of the time or adopts a cynical stance designed to minimize the importance of it.

Since the age of Reagan,[4] the greatest scarcity in the United States is not technical innovation, but rather the willingness to work together for the public good. It makes no sense to encourage the former at the expense of the latter.

Obstructing Custom Adaptation of Programs

The second level of material harm is the inability to adapt programs. The ease of modification of software is one of its great advantages over older technology. But most commercially available software isn't available for modification, even after you buy it. It's available for you to take it or leave it, as a black box—that is all.

A program that you can run consists of a series of numbers whose meaning is obscure. No one, not even a good programmer, can easily change the numbers to make the program do something different.

Programmers normally work with the "source code" for a program, which is written in a programming language such as Fortran or C. It uses names to designate the data being used and the parts of the program, and it represents operations with symbols such as + for addition and - for subtraction. It is designed to help programmers read and change programs. Here is an example; a program to calculate the distance between two points in a plane:[5]

```
float
distance (p0, p1)
      struct point p0, p1;
{
   float xdist = p1.x - p0.x;
   float ydist = p1.y - p0.y;
   return sqrt (xdist * xdist + ydist * ydist);
}
```

Here is the same program in executable form,[6] on the computer I normally use:

1314258944	-232267772	-231844864	1634862
1411907592	-231844736	2159150	1420296208
-234880989	-234879837	-234879966	-232295424
1644167167	-3214848	1090581031	1962942495
572518958	-803143692	1314803317	

Source code is useful (at least potentially) to every user of a program. But most users are not allowed to have copies of the source code. Usually the source code for a proprietary program is kept secret by the owner, lest anybody else learn something from it. Users receive only the files of incomprehensible numbers that the computer will execute. This means that only the program's owner can change the program.

---

[4] Ronald Reagan, the 40th President of the United States, is famous for having made cuts to many social programs. He also created an economic policy, often called "trickle down economics," thought of by many as a failure.

[5] Understanding how this source code works is not important; what is important is to notice that the source code is written at a level of abstraction that is fairly comprehensible.

[6] Notice the incomprehensibleness of the executable code; it is clearly harder to make sense of than the source code above.

A friend once told me of working as a programmer in a bank for about six months, writing a program similar to something that was commercially available. She believed that if she could have gotten source code for that commercially available program, it could easily have been adapted to their needs. The bank was willing to pay for this, but was not permitted to—the source code was a secret. So she had to do six months of make-work, work that counts in the gross national product but was actually waste.

The MIT Artificial Intelligence Lab (AI Lab) received a graphics printer as a gift from Xerox around 1977. It was run by free software to which we added many convenient features. For example, the software would notify a user immediately on completion of a print job. Whenever the printer had trouble, such as a paper jam or running out of paper, the software would immediately notify all users who had print jobs queued. These features facilitated smooth operation.

Later Xerox gave the AI Lab a newer, faster printer, one of the first laser printers. It was driven by proprietary software that ran in a separate dedicated computer, so we couldn't add any of our favorite features. We could arrange to send a notification when a print job was sent to the dedicated computer, but not when the job was actually printed (and the delay was usually considerable). There was no way to find out when the job was actually printed; you could only guess. And no one was informed when there was a paper jam, so the printer often went for an hour without being fixed.

The system programmers at the AI Lab were capable of fixing such problems, probably as capable as the original authors of the program. Xerox was uninterested in fixing them, and chose to prevent us, so we were forced to accept the problems. They were never fixed.

Most good programmers have experienced this frustration. The bank could afford to solve the problem by writing a new program from scratch, but a typical user, no matter how skilled, can only give up.

Giving up causes psychosocial harm—to the spirit of self-reliance. It is demoralizing to live in a house that you cannot rearrange to suit your needs. It leads to resignation and discouragement, which can spread to affect other aspects of one's life. People who feel this way are unhappy and do not do good work.

Imagine what it would be like if recipes were hoarded in the same fashion as software. You might say, "How do I change this recipe to take out the salt?" and the great chef would respond, "How dare you insult my recipe, the child of my brain and my palate, by trying to tamper with it? You don't have the judgment to change my recipe and make it work right!"

"But my doctor says I'm not supposed to eat salt! What can I do? Will you take out the salt for me?"

"I would be glad to do that; my fee is only $50,000." (Since the owner has a monopoly on changes, the fee tends to be large.) "However, right now I don't have time. I am busy with a commission to design a new recipe for ship's biscuit for the Navy Department. I might get around to you in about two years."

Obstructing Software Development

The third level of material harm affects software development. Software development used to be an evolutionary process, where a person would take an existing program and rewrite parts of it for one new feature, and then another person would rewrite parts to add another feature; in some cases, this continued over a period of twenty years. Meanwhile, parts of the program would be "cannibalized" to form the beginnings of other programs.

The existence of owners prevents this kind of evolution, making it necessary to start from scratch when developing a program. It also prevents new practitioners from studying existing programs to learn useful techniques or even how large programs can be structured.

Owners also obstruct education. I have met bright students in computer science who have never seen the source code of a large program. They may be good at writing small programs, but they can't begin to learn the different skills of writing large ones if they can't see how others have done it.

In any intellectual field, one can reach greater heights by standing on the shoulders of others. But that is no longer generally allowed in the software field—you can only stand on the shoulders of the other people *in your own company*.

The associated psychosocial harm affects the spirit of scientific cooperation, which used to be so strong that scientists would cooperate even when their countries were at war. In this spirit, Japanese oceanographers abandoning their lab on an island in the Pacific carefully preserved their work for the invading U.S. Marines, and left a note asking them to take good care of it.

Conflict for profit has destroyed what international conflict spared. Nowadays scientists in many fields don't publish enough in their papers to enable others to replicate the experiment. They publish only enough to let readers marvel at how much they were able to do. This is certainly true in computer science, where the source code for the programs reported on is usually secret.

It Does Not Matter How Sharing Is Restricted

I have been discussing the effects of preventing people from copying, changing, and building on a program. I have not specified how this obstruction is carried out, because that doesn't affect the conclusion. Whether it is done by copy protection, or copyright, or licenses, or encryption, or ROM cards, or hardware serial numbers, if it *succeeds* in preventing use, it does harm.

Users do consider some of these methods more obnoxious than others. I suggest that the methods most hated are those that accomplish their objective.

Software Should Be Free

I have shown how ownership of a program—the power to restrict changing or copying it—is obstructive. Its negative effects are widespread and important. It follows that society shouldn't have owners for programs.

Another way to understand this is that what society needs is free software, and proprietary software is a poor substitute. Encouraging the substitute is not a rational way to get what we need.

Vaclav Havel has advised us to "Work for something because it is good, not just because it stands a chance to succeed." A business making proprietary software stands a chance of success in its own narrow terms, but it is not what is good for society.

Why People Will Develop Software

If we eliminate copyright as a means of encouraging people to develop software, at first less software will be developed, but that software will be more useful. It is not clear whether the overall delivered user satisfaction will be less; but if it is, or if we wish to increase it anyway, there are other ways to encourage development, just as there are ways besides toll booths to raise money for streets. Before I talk about how that can be done, first I want to question how much artificial encouragement is truly necessary.

Programming Is Fun

There are some lines of work that few will enter except for money; road construction, for example. There are other fields of study and art in which there is little chance to become rich, which people enter for their fascination or their perceived value to society. Examples include mathematical logic, classical music, and archaeology; and political organizing among working people. People compete, more sadly than bitterly, for the few funded positions available, none of which is funded very well. They may even pay for the chance to work in the field, if they can afford to.

Such a field can transform itself overnight if it begins to offer the possibility of getting rich. When one worker gets rich, others demand the same opportunity. Soon all may demand large sums of money for doing what they used to do for pleasure. When another couple of years go by, everyone connected with the field will deride the idea that work would be done in the field without large financial returns. They will advise social planners to ensure that these returns are possible, prescribing special privileges, powers, and monopolies as necessary to do so.

This change happened in the field of computer programming in the past decade. Fifteen years ago,[7] there were articles on "computer addiction": users were "on-lining" and had hundred-dollar-a-week habits. It was generally understood that people frequently loved programming enough to break up their marriages. Today, it is generally understood that no one would program except for a high rate of pay. People have forgotten what they knew fifteen years ago.

When it is true at a given time that most people will work in a certain field only for high pay, it need not remain true. The dynamic of change can run in reverse, if society provides an impetus. If we take away the possibility of great wealth, then

---

[7] Fifteen years before this article was written was in the year 1977.

after a while, when the people have readjusted their attitudes, they will once again be eager to work in the field for the joy of accomplishment.

The question "How can we pay programmers?" becomes an easier question when we realize that it's not a matter of paying them a fortune. A mere living is easier to raise.

Funding Free Software

Institutions that pay programmers do not have to be software houses. Many other institutions already exist that can do this.

Hardware manufacturers find it essential to support software development even if they cannot control the use of the software. In 1970, much of their software was free because they did not consider restricting it. Today, their increasing willingness to join consortiums shows their realization that owning the software is not what is really important for them.

Universities conduct many programming projects. Today they often sell the results, but in the 1970's they did not. Is there any doubt that universities would develop free software if they were not allowed to sell software? These projects could be supported by the same government contracts and grants that now support proprietary software development.

It is common today for university researchers to get grants to develop a system, develop it nearly to the point of completion and call that "finished," and then start companies where they really finish the project and make it usable. Sometimes they declare the unfinished version "free"; if they are thoroughly corrupt, they instead get an exclusive license from the university. This is not a secret; it is openly admitted by everyone concerned. Yet if the researchers were not exposed to the temptation to do these things, they would still do their research.

Programmers writing free software can make their living by selling services related to the software. I have been hired to port the GNU C compiler to new hardware, and to make user-interface extensions to GNU Emacs. (I offer these improvements to the public once they are done.) I also teach classes for which I am paid.

I am not alone in working this way; there is now a successful, growing corporation which does no other kind of work. Several other companies also provide commercial support for the free software of the GNU system. This is the beginning of the independent software support industry—an industry that could become quite large if free software becomes prevalent. It provides users with an option generally unavailable for proprietary software, except to the very wealthy.

New[8] institutions such as the Free Software Foundation can also fund programmers. Most of the Foundation's funds come from users buying disks and tapes through the mail. The software on the tapes is free, which means that every user has the freedom to copy it and change it, but many nonetheless pay to get copies. (Recall that "free software" refers to freedom, not to price.) Some users who already

---

[8] This article was written on April 24, 1992.

have a copy order tapes as a way of making a contribution they feel we deserve. The Foundation also receives sizable donations from computer manufacturers.

The Free Software Foundation is a charity, and its income is spent on hiring as many programmers as possible. If it had been set up as a business, distributing the same free software to the public for the same fee, it would now provide a very good living for its founder.

Because the Foundation is a charity, programmers often work for the Foundation for half of what they could make elsewhere. They do this because we are free of bureaucracy, and because they feel satisfaction in knowing that their work will not be obstructed from use. Most of all, they do it because programming is fun. In addition, volunteers have written many useful programs for us. (Even technical writers volunteer.)

This confirms that programming is among the most fascinating of all fields, along with music and art. We don't have to fear that no one will want to program.

What Do Users Owe to Developers?

There is a good reason for users of software to feel a moral obligation to contribute to its support. Developers of free software are contributing to the users' activities, and it is both fair and in the long-term interest of the users to give them funds to continue.

However, this does not apply to proprietary software developers, since obstructionism deserves a punishment rather than a reward.

We thus have a paradox: the developer of useful software is entitled to the support of the users, but any attempt to turn this moral obligation into a requirement destroys the basis for the obligation. A developer can either deserve a reward or demand it, but not both.

I believe that an ethical developer faced with this paradox must act so as to deserve the reward, but should also entreat the users for voluntary donations. Eventually the users will learn to support developers without coercion, just as they have learned to support public radio and television stations.

What Is Software Productivity?

If software were free, there would still be programmers, but perhaps fewer of them. Would this be bad for society?

Not necessarily. Today the advanced nations have fewer farmers than in 1900, but we do not think this is bad for society, because the few deliver more food to the consumers than the many used to do. We call this improved productivity. Free software would require far fewer programmers to satisfy the demand, because of increased software productivity at all levels:

- Wider use of each program that is developed.
- The ability to adapt existing programs for customization instead of starting from scratch.
- Better education of programmers.

- The elimination of duplicate development effort.

Those who object to cooperation claiming it would result in the employment of fewer programmers are actually objecting to increased productivity. Yet these people usually accept the widely-held belief that the software industry needs increased productivity. How is this?[9]

"Software productivity" can mean two different things: the overall productivity of all software development, or the productivity of individual projects. Overall productivity is what society would like to improve, and the most straightforward way to do this is to eliminate the artificial obstacles to cooperation that reduce it. But researchers who study the field of "software productivity" focus only on the second, limited, sense of the term, where improvement requires difficult technological advances.

Is Competition Inevitable?

Is it inevitable that people will try to compete, to surpass their rivals in society? Perhaps it is. But competition itself is not harmful; the harmful thing is *combat*.

There are many ways to compete. Competition can consist of trying to achieve ever more, to outdo what others have done. For example, in the old days, there was competition among programming wizards—competition for who could make the computer do the most amazing thing, or for who could make the shortest or fastest program for a given task. This kind of competition can benefit everyone, *as long as* the spirit of good sportsmanship is maintained.

Constructive competition is enough competition to motivate people to great efforts. A number of people are competing to be the first to have visited all the countries on Earth; some even spend fortunes trying to do this. But they do not bribe ship captains to strand their rivals on desert islands. They are content to let the best person win.

Competition becomes combat when the competitors begin trying to impede each other instead of advancing themselves—when "Let the best person win" gives way to "Let me win, best or not." Proprietary software is harmful, not because it is a form of competition, but because it is a form of combat among the citizens of our society.

Competition in business is not necessarily combat. For example, when two grocery stores compete, their entire effort is to improve their own operations, not to sabotage the rival. But this does not demonstrate a special commitment to business ethics; rather, there is little scope for combat in this line of business short of physical violence. Not all areas of business share this characteristic. Withholding information that could help everyone advance is a form of combat.

---

[9] According to Eric Raymond, 95% of the jobs in the software industry involve production of custom software, not intended for publication at all. It follows that even if we assume the theoretical worst, that there will be no jobs for free software development (and we already know there are some), the switch to free software can only have a small effect on the total number of software jobs. There is plenty of room for people to have jobs writing custom software and develop free software in their spare time. There is no way to know whether full conversion to free software would increase or decrease the number of jobs in the software field.

Business ideology does not prepare people to resist the temptation to combat the competition. Some forms of combat have been banned with anti-trust laws, truth–in–advertising laws, and so on, but rather than generalizing this to a principled rejection of combat in general, executives invent other forms of combat that are not specifically prohibited. Society's resources are squandered on the economic equivalent of factional civil war.

"Why Don't You Move to Russia?"

In the United States, any advocate of other than the most extreme form of laissez-faire selfishness has often heard this accusation. For example, it is leveled against the supporters of a national health care system, such as is found in all the other industrialized nations of the free world. It is leveled against the advocates of public support for the arts, also universal in advanced nations. The idea that citizens have any obligation to the public good is identified in America with Communism. But how similar are these ideas?

Communism as was practiced in the Soviet Union was a system of central control where all activity was regimented, supposedly for the common good, but actually for the sake of the members of the Communist party. And where copying equipment was closely guarded to prevent illegal copying.

The American system of software copyright exercises central control over distribution of a program, and guards copying equipment with automatic copying-protection schemes to prevent illegal copying.

By contrast, I am working to build a system where people are free to decide their own actions; in particular, free to help their neighbors, and free to alter and improve the tools that they use in their daily lives. A system based on voluntary cooperation and on decentralization.

Thus, if we are to judge views by their resemblance to Russian Communism, it is the software owners who are the Communists.

The Question of Premises

I make the assumption in this paper that a user of software is no less important than an author, or even an author's employer. In other words, their interests and needs have equal weight, when we decide which course of action is best.

This premise is not universally accepted. Many maintain that an author's employer is fundamentally more important than anyone else. They say, for example, that the purpose of having owners of software is to give the author's employer the advantage he deserves—regardless of how this may affect the public.

It is no use trying to prove or disprove these premises. Proof requires shared premises. So most of what I have to say is addressed only to those who share the premises I use, or at least are interested in what their consequences are. For those who believe that the owners are more important than everyone else, this paper is simply irrelevant.

But why would a large number of Americans accept a premise that elevates certain people in importance above everyone else? Partly because of the belief that this premise is part of the legal traditions of American society. Some people feel that doubting the premise means challenging the basis of society.

It is important for these people to know that this premise is not part of our legal tradition. It never has been.

Thus, the Constitution says that the purpose of copyright is to "promote the progress of science and the useful arts." The Supreme Court has elaborated on this, stating in *Fox Film vs. Doyal* that "The sole interest of the United States and the primary object in conferring the [copyright] monopoly lie in the general benefits derived by the public from the labors of authors."

We are not required to agree with the Constitution or the Supreme Court. (At one time, they both condoned slavery.) So their positions do not disprove the owner supremacy premise. I hope that the awareness that this is a radical right-wing assumption rather than a traditionally recognized one will weaken its appeal.

Conclusion

We like to think that our society encourages helping your neighbor; but each time we reward someone for obstructionism, or admire them for the wealth they have gained in this way, we are sending the opposite message.

Software hoarding is one form of our general willingness to disregard the welfare of society for personal gain. We can trace this disregard from Ronald Reagan to Jim Bakker,[10] from Ivan Boesky[11] to Exxon,[12] from failing banks to failing schools. We can measure it with the size of the homeless population and the prison population. The antisocial spirit feeds on itself, because the more we see that other people will not help us, the more it seems futile to help them. Thus society decays into a jungle.

If we don't want to live in a jungle, we must change our attitudes. We must start sending the message that a good citizen is one who cooperates when appropriate, not one who is successful at taking from others. I hope that the free software movement will contribute to this: at least in one area, we will replace the jungle with a more efficient system that encourages and runs on voluntary cooperation.

---

[10] Jim Bakker raised millions of dollars over television for his religious groups Heritage USA, PTL, and the Inspirational Network in the 1980's. He was convicted of mail and wire fraud for fundraising efforts at PTL and sentenced to forty-five years in federal prison.

[11] Ivan Boesky was sent to prison for insider trading in the 1980's and fined $100 million. He is famous for having once said, "Greed is all right. I want you to know I think greed is healthy. You can be greedy and still feel good about yourself."

[12] In the 1980's Exxon Valdez caused the largest oil spill in the world off the Alaskan coast, causing immeasurable damage. Cleanups and fines have cost them over $1 billion to date.

19 Copyright and Globalization in the Age of Computer Networks

Introduction

David Thorburn, moderator: Our speaker today, Richard Stallman, is a legendary figure in the computing world, and my experience in trying to find a respondent to share the podium with him was instructive. One distinguished MIT professor told me that Stallman needs to be understood as a charismatic figure in a biblical parable—a kind of Old Testament anecdote-lesson. "Imagine," he said, "a Moses or a Jeremiah—better a Jeremiah." I said, "Well, that's very admirable. That sounds wonderful. It confirms my sense of the kind of contribution he has made to the world. Then why are you reluctant to share the podium with him?" His answer: "Like Jeremiah or Moses, he would simply overwhelm me. I won't appear on the same panel with him, but if you asked me to name five people alive in the world who have truly helped us all, Richard Stallman would be one of them."

The Speech

I should begin by explaining why I have refused to allow this forum to be Webcast, in case it wasn't clear fully what the issue is: the software they use for Web broadcasting requires the user to download certain software in order to receive the broadcast. That software is not free software. It's available at zero price but only as an executable, which is a mysterious bunch of numbers.

What it does is secret. You can't study it, you can't change it, and you certainly can not publish it in your own modified version. And, those are among the freedoms that are essential in the definition of "free software."

So if I am to be an honest advocate for free software, I can hardly go around giving speeches, then put pressure on people to use non-free software. I'd be undermining my own cause. If I don't show that I take my principles seriously, I can't expect anybody else to take them seriously.

However, this speech is not about free software. After I'd been working on the free software movement for several years and people started using some of the pieces of the GNU operating system, I began getting invited to give speeches at which people started asking me: "Well, how do the ideas about freedom for software users generalize to other kinds of things?"

The following is an edited transcript of a speech given at MIT in the Communications Forum on April 19, 2001, and is part of *Free Software, Free Society: Selected Essays of Richard M. Stallman*, 2002, GNU Press (http://www.gnupress.org); ISBN 1-882114-98-1.

And, of course, people asked silly questions like, "Well, should hardware be free?" "Should this microphone be free?"

Well, what does that mean? Should you be free to copy it and change it? Well, as for changing it, if you buy the microphone, nobody is going to stop you from changing it. As for copying it, nobody has a microphone copier. Outside of Star Trek, those things don't exist. Maybe some day there'll be nanotechnological analyzers and assemblers, and it really will be possible to copy a physical object, and then these issues of whether you're free to do that will start being really important. We'll see agribusiness companies trying to stop people from copying food, and that will become a major political issue, if that technological capability will ever exist. I don't know if it will; it's just speculation at this point.

But for other kinds of information, you can raise the issue because any kind of information that can be stored on a computer, conceivably, can be copied and modified. So, the ethical issues of free software, the issues of a user's right to copy and modify software, are the same as such questions for other kinds of published information. I'm not talking about private information, say, personal information, which is never meant to be available to the public at all. I'm talking about the rights you should have if you get copies of published things where there's no attempt to keep them secret.

The History of Copyright

In order to explain my ideas on the subject, I'd like to review the history of the distribution of information and of copyright. In the ancient world, books were written by hand with a pen, and anybody who knew how to read and write could copy a book about as efficiently as anybody else. Now somebody who did it all day would probably learn to be somewhat better at it, but there was not a tremendous difference. Because the copies were made one at a time, there was no great economy of scale. Making ten copies took ten times as long as making one copy. There was also nothing forcing centralization—a book could be copied anywhere.

Because of this technology, because it didn't force copies to be identical, there wasn't, in the ancient world, the same total divide between copying a book and writing a book. There are things in between that made sense. They did understand the idea of an author—they knew, say, that this play was written by Sophocles— but, in between writing a book and copying a book, there were other useful things you could do. For instance, you could copy a part of a book, then write some new words, copy some more, and write some new words, and on and on. This was called "writing a commentary." This was a common thing to do, and these commentaries were appreciated.

You could also copy a passage out of one book, then write some other words, and copy a passage from another book and write some more, and so on, and this was making a compendium. Compendia were also very useful. There are works that are lost, but parts of them survived when they were quoted into other books that got to be more popular than the original. Maybe they copied the most interesting parts. People made a lot of copies of these, but they didn't bother copying the original because it wasn't interesting enough.

Now as far as I can tell, there was no such thing as copyright in the ancient world. Anyone who wanted to copy a book could copy the book. Later on, the printing press was developed and books started to be copied on the printing press. Now the printing press was not just a quantitative improvement in the ease of copying. It affected different kinds of copying unevenly because it introduced an inherent economy of scale. It was a lot of work to set the type, and much less work to make many identical copies of the page. The result was that copying books tended to become a centralized, mass-production activity. Copies of any given book would probably be made in only a few places.

It also meant that ordinary readers couldn't copy books efficiently—only if you had a printing press could you do that. So it was an industrial activity.

Now for the first few centuries of printing, printed books did not totally replace hand-copying. Hand-copied books were still made, sometimes by rich people and sometimes by poor people. The rich people did this to get an especially beautiful copy that would show how rich they were, and poor people did it because maybe they didn't have enough money to buy a printed copy but they had the time to copy a book by hand. As the song says, "Time ain't money when all you got is time."

So hand-copying was still done to some extent. I think it was in the 1800's that printing actually got to be cheap enough that even poor people could afford printed books if they were literate.

Now copyright was developed along with the use of the printing press; and given the technology of the printing press, it had the effect of an industrial regulation. It didn't restrict what readers could do; it restricted what publishers and authors could do. Copyright in England was initially a form of censorship. You had to get government permission to publish the book. But the idea has changed. By the time of the U.S. Constitution, people came to a different idea of the purpose of copyright, and I think that that idea was accepted in England as well.

For the U.S. Constitution it was proposed that authors should be entitled to a copyright, a monopoly on copying their books. This proposal was rejected. Instead, a crucially different proposal was adopted, which is, that for the sake of promoting progress, Congress could optionally establish a copyright system that would create these monopolies. So the monopolies, according to the U.S. Constitution, do not exist for the sake of those who own them; they exist for the sake of promoting the progress of science. The monopolies are handed out to authors as a way of modifying their behavior to get them to do something that serves the public.

So the goal is to have more written and published books which other people can then read. And this [copyright] is believed to contribute to increased literary activity, and increased writing about science and other fields, and society then learns through this. That's the purpose to be served. The creation of private monopolies was a means to an end only, and the end is a public end.

Now copyright in the age of the printing press was fairly painless because it was an industrial regulation. It restricted only the activities of publishers and authors. In some strict sense, the poor people who copied books by hand may have been infringing copyright, too. But nobody ever tried to enforce copyright against them because it was understood as an industrial regulation.[1]

Copyright in the age of the printing press was also easy to enforce, because it had to be enforced only where there was a publisher, and publishers, by their nature, make themselves known. If you're trying to sell books, you've got to tell people where to come to buy them. You don't have to go into everybody's house to enforce copyright.

Finally, copyright may have been a beneficial system in that context. Copyright in the U.S. is considered by legal scholars as a trade, a bargain between the public and authors. The public trades away some of its natural rights to make copies, and in exchange gets the benefit of more books' being written and published.

Now, is this an advantageous trade? Well, when the general public can't make copies because they can only be efficiently made on printing presses, and most people don't own printing presses, the result is that the general public is trading away a freedom it is unable to exercise, a freedom that is of no practical value. If you have something that is a byproduct of your life and it's useless and you have the opportunity to exchange it for something else of any value, you're gaining. That's why copyright may have been an advantageous trade for the public in that time.

But the context is changing, and that has to change our ethical evaluation of copyright. Now, the basic principles of ethics are not changed by advances in technology; they're too fundamental to be touched by such contingencies. But our decision about any specific question is a matter of the consequences of the alternatives available, and the consequences of a given choice may change when the context changes. That is what is happening in the area of copyright law, because the age of the printing press is coming to an end, giving way gradually to the age of the computer networks.

Computer networks and digital information technology are bringing us back to a world more like the ancient world, where anyone who can read and use the information can also copy it and can make copies about as easily as anyone else could make them. They are perfect copies and they're just as good as the copies anyone else could make. So the centralization and economy of scale introduced by the printing press and similar technologies is going away.

This changing context changes the way copyright law works. You see, copyright law no longer acts as an industrial regulation; it is now a draconian restriction on a general public. It used to be a restriction on publishers for the sake of authors. Now, for practical purposes, it's a restriction on a public for the sake of publishers. Copyright used to be fairly painless and uncontroversial. It didn't restrict the general public. Now [today], that's not true. If you have a computer, the publishers consider restricting you to be their highest priority. Copyright was easy to enforce because it was a restriction only on publishers, who were easy to find—and what they published was easy to see. Now the copyright is a restriction on each and every one of you. To enforce it requires surveillance, an intrusion, and harsh

---

[1] The original statutes spoke of publishing and printing only. Copying by hand was completely unregulated—-most likely because the regulation was aimed at industry.

punishments, and we are seeing these being enacted into law in the U.S. and other countries.

Copyright used to be, arguably, an advantageous trade for the public to make, because the public was trading away freedoms it couldn't exercise. Well, now it can exercise these freedoms. What do you do if you have been producing a byproduct which was of no use to you and you were in the habit of trading it away, and then, all of a sudden, you discover a use for it? You can actually consume it, use it. What do you do? You don't trade it all; you keep some. And that's what the public would naturally want to do. That's what the public does whenever it's given a chance to voice its preference; it keeps some of this freedom and exercises it. Napster is a big example of that, the public deciding to exercise the freedom to copy instead of giving it up. The natural thing for us to do to make copyright law fit today's circumstances is to reduce the amount of copyright power that copyright owners get: to reduce the amount of restriction that they place on the public, and to increase the freedom that the public retains.

But this is not what the publishers want to do. What they want to do is exactly the opposite. They wish to increase copyright powers to the point where they can remain firmly in control of all use of information. This has led to laws that have given an unprecedented increase in the powers of copyright. Freedoms that the public used to have in the age of the printing press are being taken away.

For instance, let's look at e-books. There's a tremendous amount of hype about e-books; you can hardly avoid it. I took a flight in Brazil and in the in-flight magazine, there was an article saying that maybe it would take 10 or 20 years before we all switched to e-books. Clearly, this kind of campaign comes from somebody paying for it. Why are they doing that? I think I know. The reason is that e-books are the opportunity to take away some of the residual freedoms that readers of printed books have always had and still have—the freedom, for instance, to lend a book to your friend, or borrow it from the public library, or sell a copy to a used bookstore, or buy a copy anonymously without putting a record in the database of who bought that particular book. And maybe even the right to read it twice.

These are freedoms that the publishers would like to take away, but they can't do this for printed books because that would be too obvious a power grab and would raise an outcry. So they have found an indirect strategy. First, they obtain the legislation to take away these freedoms for e-books when there are no e-books; so there's no controversy. There are no pre-existing users of e-books who are accustomed to their freedoms and will defend them. That they obtained with the Digital Millennium Copyright Act in 1998. Then they introduce e-books and gradually get everybody to switch from printed books to e-books, and eventually the result is, readers have lost these freedoms without ever having an instant when those freedoms were being taken away and when they might have fought back to retain them.

We see at the same time efforts to take away people's freedom in using other kinds of published works. For instance, movies that are on DVDs are published in an encrypted format that used to be secret—it was meant to be secret—and the only way the movie companies would tell you the format, so that you could make a DVD player, was if you signed a contract to build certain restrictions into the player, with the result that the public would be stopped even from fully exercising their legal rights. Then a few clever programmers in Europe figured out the format of DVDs and they wrote a free software package that would read a DVD.[2] This made it possible to use free software on top of the GNU/Linux operating system to watch the DVD that you had bought, which is a perfectly legitimate thing to do. You ought to be able to do that with free software.

But the movie companies objected and they went to court. You see, the movie companies used to make a lot of films where there was a mad scientist and somebody was saying, "But, Doctor, there are some things Man was not meant to know." They must have watched their own films too much, because they came to believe that the format of DVDs is something that Man was not meant to know. And they obtained a ruling for total censorship of the software for playing DVDs. Even making a link to a site where this information is legally available outside the U.S. has been prohibited. An appeal has been made against this ruling. I signed a friend-of-the-court brief in that appeal, I'm proud to say, although I'm playing a fairly small role in that particular battle.

The U.S. government intervened directly on the other side. This is not surprising when you consider why the Digital Millennium Copyright Act was passed in the first place. The reason is the campaign finance system that we have in the U.S., which is essentially legalized bribery where the candidates are bought by business before they even get elected. And, of course, they know who their master is— they know whom they're working for, and they pass the laws to give business more power.

What will happen with that particular battle, we don't know. Meanwhile, Australia has passed a similar law and Europe is almost finished adopting one; so the plan is to leave no place on earth where this information can be made available to people. But the U.S. remains the world leader in trying to stop the public from distributing information that's been published.

However, the U.S. is not the first country to make a priority of this. The Soviet Union treated it as very important. There, unauthorized copying and redistribution was known as Samizdat, and to stamp it out, they developed a series of methods: First, guards watching every piece of copying equipment to check what people were copying to prevent forbidden copying. Second, harsh punishments for anyone caught doing forbidden copying—you could be sent to Siberia. Third, soliciting informers, asking everyone to rat on their neighbors and coworkers to the information police. Fourth, collective responsibility: "You! You're going to watch that group! If I catch any of them doing forbidden copying, you are going to prison. So watch them hard." And, fifth, propaganda, starting in childhood, to convince everyone that only a horrible enemy of the people would ever do this forbidden copying.

The U.S. is using all of these measures now. First, guards watching copying equipment. Well, in copy stores, they have human guards to check what you copy. But human guards to watch what you copy in your computer would be too expensive; human labor is too expensive. So they have robot guards. That's the purpose of the Digital Millennium Copyright Act. This software goes in your computer; it's the only way you can access certain data and it stops you from copying.

---

[2] There are many such packages now; the first was called "DeCSS."

There's a plan now to introduce this software into every hard disk, so that there could be files on your hard disk that you can't even access except by getting permission from some network server to access the file. And to bypass this software or even tell other people how to bypass it is a crime.

Second, harsh punishments. A few years ago, if you made copies of something and handed them out to your friends just to be helpful, this was not a crime; it had never been a crime in the U.S. Then they made it a felony, so you could be put in prisons for years for sharing with your neighbor.

Third, informers. Well, you may have seen the ads on TV, the ads in the Boston subways asking people to rat on their coworkers to the information police, which officially is called the Software Publishers Association.

And fourth, collective responsibility. In the U.S., this has been done by conscripting Internet service providers, making them legally responsible for everything their customers post. The only way they can avoid always being held responsible is if they have an invariable procedure to disconnect or remove the information within two weeks after a complaint. Just a few days ago, I heard that a clever protest site criticizing Citibank for some of its nasty policies was disconnected in this way. Nowadays, you don't even get your day in court; your site just gets unplugged.

And finally, propaganda starting in childhood. That's what the word "pirate" is used for. If you'll think back a few years, the term "pirate" was formerly applied to publishers that didn't pay the author. But now it's been turned completely around. It's now applied to members of the public who escape from the control of the publisher. It's being used to convince people that only a nasty enemy of the people would ever do this forbidden copying. It says that "sharing with your neighbor is the moral equivalent of attacking a ship." I hope that you don't agree with that and if you don't, I hope you will refuse to use the word in that way.

The publishers are purchasing laws to give themselves more power. In addition, they're also extending the length of time the copyright lasts. The U.S. Constitution says that copyright must last for a limited time, but the publishers want copyright to last forever. However, getting a constitutional amendment would be rather difficult, so they found an easier way that achieves the same result. Every 20 years they retroactively extend copyright by 20 years. So the result is, at any given time, copyright nominally lasts for a certain period and any given copyright will nominally expire some day. But that expiration will never be reached because every copyright will be extended by 20 years every 20 years; thus no work will ever go into the public domain again. This has been called "perpetual copyright on the installment plan."

The law in 1998 that extended copyright by 20 years is known as the "Mickey Mouse Copyright Extension Act"[3] because one of the main sponsors of this law was Disney. Disney realized that the copyright on Mickey Mouse was going to expire, and they don't want that to ever happen because they make a lot of money from that copyright.

---

[3] The official title is "The Sonny Bono Copyright Term Extension Act."

Globalization

Now the original title of this talk was supposed to be "Copyright and Globalization." If you look at globalization, what you see is that it's carried out by a number of policies which are done in the name of economic efficiency or so-called free-trade treaties, which really are designed to give business power over laws and policies. They're not really about free trade. They're about a transfer of power: removing the power to decide laws from the citizens of any country who might conceivably consider their own interests and giving that power to businesses who will not consider the interests of those citizens.

Democracy is the problem in their view, and these treaties are designed to put an end to the problem. For instance, NAFTA[4] actually contains provisions, I believe, allowing companies to sue another government to get rid of a law that they believe is interfering with their profits in the other country. So foreign companies have more power than citizens of the country.

There are attempts being made to extend this beyond NAFTA. For instance, this is one of the goals of the so-called free trade area of the Americas, to extend this principle to all the countries in South America and the Caribbean as well, and the multilateral agreement on investment was intended to spread it to the whole world.

One thing we've seen in the 1990's is that these treaties begin to impose copyright throughout the world, and in more powerful and restrictive ways. These treaties are not free-trade treaties. They're actually corporate-controlled trade treaties being used to give corporations control over world trade, in order to eliminate free trade.

When the U.S. was a developing country in the 1800's, the U.S. did not recognize foreign copyrights. This was a decision made carefully, and it was an intelligent decision. It was acknowledged that for the U.S. to recognize foreign copyrights would just be disadvantageous, that it would suck money out and wouldn't do much good.

The same logic would apply today to developing countries, but the U.S. has sufficient power to force them to go against their interests. Actually, it's a mistake to speak of the interests of countries in this context. In fact, I'm sure that most of you have heard about the fallacy of trying to judge the public interest by adding up everybody's wealth. If working Americans lost $1 billion and Bill Gates gained $2 billion, would Americans generally be better off? Would this be good for America? If you look only at the total, it looks like it's good. However, this example really shows that the total is the wrong way to judge because Bill Gates really doesn't need another $2 billion, but the loss of the $1 billion by other people who don't have as much to start with might be painful. Well, in a discussion about any of these trade treaties, when you hear people talk about the interests of this country or that country, what they're doing, within each country, is adding up everybody's income. The rich people and the poor people are being added up. So it's actually an excuse to apply that same fallacy to get you to ignore the effect on the distribution of wealth within the country and whether the treaty is going to make that more uneven, as it has done in the U.S.

---

[4] North American Free Trade Agreement.

So it's really not the U.S. interest that is being served by enforcing copyright around the world. It's the interests of certain business owners, many of whom are in the U.S. and some of whom are in other countries. It doesn't, in any sense, serve the public interest.

Rethinking Copyright

But what would make sense to do? If we believe in the goal of copyright stated, for instance, in the U.S. Constitution—the goal of promoting progress—what would be intelligent policies to use in the age of the computer network? Clearly, instead of increasing copyright powers, we have to pull them back so as to give the general public a certain domain of freedom where they can make use of the benefits of digital technology, make use of their computer networks. But how far should that go? That's an interesting question because I don't think we should necessarily abolish copyright totally. The idea of trading some freedoms for more progress might still be an advantageous trade at a certain level, even if traditional copyright gives up too much freedom. But, in order to think about this intelligently, the first thing we have to recognize is, there's no reason to make it totally uniform. There's no reason to insist on making the same deal for all kinds of work.

In fact, that already isn't the case because there are a lot of exceptions for music. Music is treated very differently under copyright law. But the arbitrary insistence on uniformity is used by the publishers in a certain clever way. They pick some peculiar special case and they make an argument that, in that special case, it would be advantageous to have this much copyright. Then they say that for uniformity's sake, there has to be this much copyright for everything. So, of course, they pick the special case where they can make the strongest argument, even if it's a rather rare special case and not really very important overall.

But maybe we should have that much copyright for that particular special case. We don't have to pay the same price for everything we buy. A thousand dollars for a new car might be a very good deal. A thousand dollars for a container of milk is a horrible deal. You wouldn't pay the special price for everything you buy in other areas of life. Why do it here?

We need to look at different kinds of works, and I'd like to propose a way of doing this.

The first class of work is that of functional works—that is, works whose use is to get a job done.

This includes recipes, computer programs, manuals and textbooks, and reference works like dictionaries and encyclopedias. For all these functional works, I believe that the issues are basically the same as they are for software and the same conclusions apply. People should have the freedom even to publish a modified version because it's very useful to modify functional works. People's needs are not all the same. If I wrote this work to do the job I think needs doing, your idea of a job you want to do may be somewhat different. So you want to modify this work to do what's good for you. At that point, there may be other people who have similar needs to yours, and your modified version might be good for them. Everybody who cooks knows this and has known this for hundreds of years. It's normal to make copies of recipes and hand them out to other people, and it's also normal to change a recipe. If you change the recipe and cook it for your friends and they like eating it, they might ask you, "Could I have the recipe?" Then maybe you'll write down your version and give them copies. That is exactly the same thing that we much later started doing in the free-software community.

So that's one class of work.

The second class of work is works whose purpose is to say what certain people think. Talking about those people is their purpose. This includes, for instance, memoirs, essays of opinion, scientific papers, offers to buy and sell, catalogues of goods for sale. The whole point of those works is that they tell you what somebody thinks or what somebody saw or what somebody believes. To modify them is to misrepresent the authors; so modifying these works is not a socially useful activity. So verbatim copying is the only thing that people really need to be allowed to do.

The next question is: Should people have the right to do commercial verbatim copying? Or is noncommercial enough? You see, these are two different activities we can distinguish, so that we can consider the questions separately—the right to do noncommercial verbatim copying and the right to do commercial verbatim copying. Well, it might be a good compromise policy to have copyright cover commercial verbatim copying but allow everyone the right to do noncommercial verbatim copying. This way, the copyright on the commercial verbatim copying, as well as on all modified versions—only the author could approve a modified version—would still provide the same revenue stream that it provides now to fund the writing of these works, to whatever extent it does.

By allowing the noncommercial verbatim copying, it means the copyright no longer has to intrude into everybody's home. It becomes an industrial regulation again, easy to enforce and painless, no longer requiring draconian punishments and informers for the sake of its enforcement. So we get most of the benefit, and avoid most of the horror, of the current system.

The third category of works is aesthetic or entertaining works, where the most important thing is just the sensation of looking at the work. Now for these works, the issue of modification is a very difficult one because on the one hand, there is the idea that these works reflect the vision of an artist and to change them is to mess up that vision. On the other hand, you have the fact that there is the folk process, where a sequence of people modifying a work can sometimes produce a result that is extremely rich. Even when you have artists producing the works, borrowing from previous works is often very useful. Some of Shakespeare's plays used a story that was taken from some other play. If today's copyright laws had been in effect back then, those plays would have been illegal. It's a hard question what we should do about publishing modified versions of an aesthetic or an artistic work, and we might have to look for further subdivisions of the category in order to solve this problem. For example, maybe computer game scenarios should be treated one way; maybe everybody should be free to publish modified versions of them. But perhaps a novel should be treated differently; perhaps for that, commercial publication should require an arrangement with the original author.

Now if commercial publication of these aesthetic works is covered by copyright, that will give most of the revenue stream that exists today to support the authors and musicians, to the limited extent that the present system supports them, because [the present system] does a very bad job. So that might be a reasonable compromise, just as in the case of the works which represent certain people.

If we look ahead to the time when the age of the computer networks will have fully begun, when we're past this transitional stage, we can envision another way for the authors to get money for their work. Imagine that we have a digital cash system that enables you to get money for your work. Imagine that we have a digital cash system that enables you to send somebody else money through the Internet; this can be done in various ways using encryption, for instance. And, imagine that verbatim copying of all these aesthetic works is permitted. But they're written in such a way that when you are playing one or reading one or watching one, a box appears on the side of your screen that says, "Click here to send a dollar to the author," or the musician or whatever. And it just sits there; it doesn't get in your way; it's on the side. It doesn't interfere with you, but it's there, reminding you that it's a good thing to support the writers and the musicians.

So if you love the work that you're reading or listening to, eventually you're going to say, "Why shouldn't I give these people a dollar? It's only a dollar. What's that? I won't even miss it." And people will start sending a dollar. The good thing about this is that it makes copying the ally of the authors and musicians. When somebody e-mails a friend a copy, that friend might send a dollar too. If you really love it, you might send a dollar more than once and that dollar is more than they're going to get today if you buy the book or buy the CD because they get a tiny fraction of the sale. The same publishers that are demanding total power over the public in the name of the authors and musicians are giving those authors and musicians the shaft all the time.

I recommend you read Courtney Love's article in Salon magazine, an article about pirates that plan to use musicians' work without paying them. These pirates are the record companies that pay musicians 4% of the sales figures, on the average. Of course, the very successful musicians have more clout. They get more than 4% of their large sales figures, which means that the great run of musicians who have a record contract get less than 4% of their small sales figures.

Here's the way it works: The record company spends money on publicity and they consider this expenditure as an advance to the musicians, although the musicians never see it. So nominally when you buy a CD, a certain fraction of that money is going to the musicians, but really it isn't. Really, it's going to pay back the publicity expenses, and only if the musicians are very successful do they ever see any of that money.

The musicians, of course, sign their record contracts because they hope they're going to be one of those few who strike it rich. So essentially a rolling lottery is being offered to the musicians to tempt them. Although they're good at music, they may not be good at careful, logical reasoning to see through this trap. So they sign and then probably all they get is publicity. Well, why don't we give them publicity in a different way, not through a system that's based on restricting the public and a system of the industrial complex that saddles us with lousy music that's easy to sell. Instead, why not make the listeners' natural impulse to share the music they love the ally of the musicians? If we have this box that appears in the player as a way to send a dollar to the musicians, then the computer networks could be the mechanism for giving the musicians this publicity, the same publicity which is all they get from record contracts now.

We have to recognize that the existing copyright system does a lousy job of supporting musicians, just as lousy as world trade does of raising living standards in the Philippines and China. You have these "enterprise zones" where everyone works in a sweatshop and all of the products are made in sweatshops. Globalization is a very inefficient way of raising living standards of people overseas. Say an American is getting paid twenty dollars an hour to make something, and you give that job to a Mexican who is getting paid maybe six dollars a day, what has happened here is that you've taken a large amount of money away from an American worker, given a tiny fraction, like a few percent, to a Mexican worker and given back the rest to the company. So if your goal is to raise the living standards of Mexican workers, this is a lousy way to do it.

It's interesting to see how the same phenomenon is going on in the copyright industry, the same general idea. In the name of these workers who certainly deserve something, you propose measures that give them a tiny bit and really mainly prop up the power of corporations to control our lives.

If you're trying to replace a very good system, you have to work very hard to come up with a better alternative. If you know that the present system is lousy, it's not so hard to find a better alternative; the standard of comparison today is very low. We must always remember that when we consider issues of copyright policy.

So I think I've said most of what I want to say. I'd like to mention that tomorrow[5] is Phone-In Sick Day in Canada. Tomorrow is the beginning of a summit to finish negotiating the Free Trade Area of the Americas, to try to extend corporate power throughout additional countries, and a big protest is being planned for Quebec. We've seen extreme methods being used to smash this protest. A lot of Americans are being blocked from entering Canada through the border that they're supposed to be allowed to enter through at any time. On the flimsiest of excuses, a wall has been built around the center of Quebec to be used as a fortress to keep protesters out. We've seen a large number of different dirty tricks used against public protest against these treaties. So whatever democracy remains to us after government powers have been taken away from democratically elected governors and given to businesses and to unelected international bodies, whatever is left after that may not survive the suppression of public protest against it.

I've dedicated seventeen years of my life to working on free software and allied issues. I didn't do this because I think it's the most important political issue in the world. I did it because it was the area where I saw I had to use my skills to do a lot of good. But what's happened is that the general issues of politics have evolved, and the biggest political issue in the world today is resisting the tendency to give business power over the public and governments. I see free software and the allied questions for other kinds of information that I've been discussing today as one part of that major issue. So I've indirectly found myself working on that issue. I hope I contribute something to the effort.

---

5 April 20, 2001.

Question and Answer Session

David Thorburn: We'll turn to the audience for questions and comments in a moment. But let me offer a brief general response. It seems to me that the strongest and most important practical guidance that Stallman offers us has two key elements. One is the recognition that old assumptions about copyright—old usages of copyright—are inappropriate; they are challenged or undermined by the advent of the computer and computer networks. That may be obvious, but it is essential.

Second is the recognition that the digital era requires us to reconsider how we distinguish and weigh forms of intellectual and creative labor. Stallman is surely right that certain kinds of intellectual enterprises justify more copyright protection than others. Trying to identify systematically these different kinds or levels of copyright protection seems to me a valuable way to engage with the problems for intellectual work posed by the advent of the computer.

But I think I detect another theme that lies beneath what Stallman has been saying and that isn't really directly about computers at all, but more broadly about questions of democratic authority and the power that government and corporations increasingly exercise over our lives. This populist and anti-corporate side to Stallman's discourse is nourishing but also reductive, potentially simplifying. And it is also perhaps overly idealistic. For example, how would a novelist or a poet or a songwriter or a musician or the author of an academic textbook survive in this brave new world where people are encouraged but not required to pay authors? In other words, it seems to me, the gap between existing practice and the visionary possibilities Stallman speculates about is still immensely wide.

So I'll conclude by asking if Stallman would like to expand a bit on certain aspects of his talk and, specifically, whether he has further thoughts about the way in which what we'll call "traditional creators" would be protected under his copyright system.

Richard M. Stallman: First of all, I have to point out that we shouldn't use the term "protection" to describe what copyright does. Copyright restricts people. The term "protection" is a propaganda term of the copyright-owning businesses. The term "protection" means stopping something from being somehow destroyed. Well, I don't think a song is destroyed if there are more copies of it being played more. I don't think that a novel is destroyed if more people are reading copies of it, either. So I won't use that word. I think it leads people to identify with the wrong party.

Also, it's a very bad idea to think about "intellectual property," for two reasons: First, it prejudges the most fundamental question in the area, which is: How should these things be treated and should they be treated as a kind of property? To use the term "intellectual property" to describe the area is to presuppose the answer is "yes," that that's the way to treat things, not some other way.

Second, it encourages over-generalization. Intellectual property is a catch-all for several different legal systems with independent origins, such as copyrights, patents, trademarks, trade secrets, and some other things as well. They are almost completely different; they have nothing in common. But people who hear the term "intellectual property" are led to a false picture where they imagine that there's a general principle of intellectual property that was applied to specific areas, so they assume that these various areas of the law are similar. This leads not only to confused thinking about what is right to do, it leads people to fail to understand what the law actually says, because they suppose that the copyright law and patent law and trademark law are similar, when, in fact, they are totally different.

So if you want to encourage careful thinking and clear understanding of what the law says, avoid the term "intellectual property." Talk about copyrights, or talk about patents, or talk about trademarks, or whichever subject you want to talk about. But don't talk about intellectual property. Opinion about intellectual property almost has to be a foolish one. I don't have an opinion about intellectual property. I have opinions about copyrights, patents, and trademarks, and they're different. I came to them through different thought processes because those systems of law are totally different.

Anyway, I made that digression, but it's terribly important.

So, let me now get to the point. Of course, we can't see now how well it would work, whether it would work to ask people to pay money voluntarily to the authors and musicians they love. One thing that's obvious is that how well such a system would work is proportional to the number of people who are participating in the network, and that number, we know, is going to increase by an order of magnitude over a number of years. If we tried it today, it might fail, and that wouldn't prove anything because with ten times as many people participating, it might work.

The other thing is, we do not have this digital cash payment system; so we can't really try it today. You could try to do something a little bit like it. There are services you can sign up for where you can pay money to someone—things like Pay Pal. But before you can pay anyone through Pay Pal, you have to go through a lot of rigmarole and give them personal information about you, and they collect records of whom you pay. Can you trust them not to misuse that?

The dollar might not discourage you, but the trouble it takes to pay might discourage you. The whole idea of this is that it should be as easy as falling off a log to pay when you get the urge, so that there's nothing to discourage you except the actual amount of money. And if that's small enough, why should it discourage you? We know, though, that fans can really love musicians, and we know that encouraging fans to copy and redistribute the music has been done by some bands that were, and are, quite successful, like *The Grateful Dead*. They didn't have any trouble making a living from their music because they encouraged fans to tape it and copy the tapes. They didn't even lose their record sales.

We are gradually moving from the age of the printing press to the age of the computer network, but it's not happening in a day. People are still buying lots of records, and that will probably continue for many years—maybe forever. As long as that continues, simply having copyrights that still apply to commercial sales of records ought to do about as good a job of supporting musicians as it does today. Of course, that's not very good, but at least it won't get any worse.

Question: [A comment and question about free downloading and about Stephen King's attempt[6] to market one of his novels serially over the Web.]

RMS: Yes, it's interesting to know what he did and what happened. When I first heard about that, I was elated. I thought, maybe he was taking a step towards a world that is not based on trying to maintain an iron grip on the public. Then I saw that he had actually written to ask people to pay. To explain what he did, he was publishing a novel as a serial, by installments, and he said, "If I get enough money, I'll release more." But the request he wrote was hardly a request. It browbeat the reader. It said, "If you don't pay, then you're evil. And if there are too many of you who are evil, then I'm just going to stop writing this."

Well, clearly that's not the way to make the public feel like sending you money. You've got to make them love you, not fear you.

Same Questioner: The details were that he required a certain percentage—I don't know the exact percentage, around 90% sounds correct—of people to send a certain amount of money, which, I believe, was a dollar or two dollars, or somewhere in that order of magnitude. You had to type in your name and your email address and some other information to get to download it and if that percentage of people was not reached after the first chapter, he said that he would not release another chapter. It was very antagonistic to the public downloading it.

Q: Isn't the scheme where there's no copyright but people are asked to make voluntary donations open to abuse by people plagiarizing?

RMS: No. That's not what I proposed. Remember, I'm proposing that there should be copyright covering commercial distribution and permitting only verbatim redistribution noncommercially. So anyone who modified it to put in a pointer to his Web site, instead of a pointer to the real author's Web site, would still be infringing the copyright and could be sued exactly as he could be sued today.

Q: I see. So you're still imagining a world in which there is copyright?

RMS: Yes. As I've said, for those kinds of works. I'm not saying that everything should be permitted. I'm proposing to reduce copyright powers, not abolish them.

Thorburn: I guess one question that occurred to me while you were speaking, Richard, and again now when you're responding here to this question is why you don't consider the ways in which the computer itself eliminates the middlemen completely—in the way that Stephen King refused to do—and might establish a personal relationship?

RMS: Well, they can and, in fact, this voluntary donation is one way.

Thorburn: You think of that as not involving going through a publisher at all?

RMS: Absolutely not. I hope it won't, you see, because the publishers exploit the authors terribly. When you ask the publishers' representatives about this, they say, "Well, yes, if an author or if a band doesn't want to go through us, they shouldn't be legally required to go through us." But, in fact, they're doing their utmost to set it up so that will not be feasible. For instance, they're proposing restricted-copying media formats, and in order to publish in these formats you'll have to go through the

---

6 Stephen King is a *New York Times* bestselling author who has written many books, most of which are in the category of horror. He attempted to sell a book online in a series of installments (you could buy a chapter at a time), but he ended the service before finishing the book.

big publishers, because they won't tell anyone else how to do it. So they're hoping for a world where the players will play these formats, and in order to get anything that you can play on those players, it'll have to come through the publishers. So, in fact, while there's no law against an author or a musician publishing directly, it won't be feasible. There's also the lure of maybe hitting it rich. They say, "We'll publicize you and maybe you'll hit it as rich as the Beatles" (take your pick of some very successful group), and of course only a tiny fraction of musicians are going to have that happen. But they may be drawn by that into signing contracts that will lock them down forever.

Publishers tend to be very bad at respecting their contracts with authors. For instance, book contracts typically have said that if a book goes out of print, the rights revert to the author, and publishers have generally not been very good about living up to that clause. They often have to be forced. Well, what they're starting to do now is use electronic publication as an excuse to say that it's never going out of print; so they never have to give the rights back. Their idea is, when the author has no clout, get him to sign up, and from then on he has no power; it's only the publisher that has the power.

Q: Would it be good to have free licenses for various kinds of works that protect for every user the freedom to copy them in whatever is the appropriate way for that kind of work?

RMS: Well, people are working on this. But for non-functional works, one thing doesn't substitute for another. Let's look at a functional kind of work—say, a word processor. Well, if somebody makes a free word processor, you can use that; you don't need the non-free word processors. But I wouldn't say that one free song substitutes for all the non-free songs or that one free novel substitutes for all the non-free novels. For those kinds of works, it's different. So what I think we simply have to do is to recognize that these laws do not deserve to be respected. It's not wrong to share with your neighbor, and if anyone tries to tell you that you cannot share with your neighbor, you should not listen to him.

Q: With regard to the functional works, how do you, in your own thinking, balance out the need for abolishing the copyright with the need for economic incentives in order to have these functional works developed?

RMS: Well, what we see is, first of all, that this economic incentive is a lot less necessary than people have been supposing. Look at the free-software movement, where we have over 100,000 part-time volunteers developing free software. We also see that there are other ways to raise money for this that are not based on stopping the public from copying and modifying these works. That's the interesting lesson of the free software movement. Aside from the fact that it gives you a way you can use a computer and keep your freedom to share and cooperate with other people, it also shows us that this negative assumption that people would never do these things unless they are given special powers to force people to pay them is simply wrong. A lot of people will do these things. Then if you look at, say, the writing of monographs, which serve as textbooks in many fields of science except for the ones that are very basic, the authors are not making money out of that. We now have a free encyclopedia project which is, in fact, a commercial free encyclopedia project, and it's making progress. We had a project for a GNU encyclopedia but we merged it into the commercial project when they adopted our license. In January, they switched to the GNU Free Documentation License for all the articles in their encyclopedia. So we said, "Well, let's join forces with them and urge people to contribute to them." It's called NUPEDIA, and you can find a link to it, if you look at http://www.gnu.org/encyclopedia. So here we've extended the community development of a free base of useful knowledge from software to encyclopedia. I'm pretty confident now that in all these areas of functional work, we don't need that economic incentive to the point where we have to mess up the use of these works.

Thorburn: Well, what about the other two categories [persons' thoughts, and entertainment]?

RMS: For the other two classes of work, I don't know. I don't know whether people will someday write novels without worrying about whether they make money from it. In a post-scarcity society, I guess they would. Maybe what we need to do in order to reach the post-scarcity society is to get rid of the corporate control over the economy and the laws. So, in effect, it's a chicken-or-the-egg problem, you know. Which do we do first? How do we get the world where people don't have to desperately get money except by removing the control by business? And how can we remove the control? I don't know, but that's why I'm trying to propose first a compromise copyright system and, second, the voluntary payment supported by a compromise copyright system as a way to provide a revenue stream to the people who write those works.

Q: How would you really expect to implement this compromise copyright system under the chokehold of corporate interests on American politicians due to their campaign-finance system?

RMS: It beats me. I wish I knew. It's a terribly hard problem. If I knew how to solve that problem, I would solve it and nothing in the world could make me prouder.

Q: How do you fight the corporate control? Because when you look at these sums of money going into corporate lobbying in the court case, it is tremendous. I think the DeCSS (Decryption of Contents Scrambling System) case that you're talking about is costing something like a million-and-a-half dollars on the defense side. Lord knows what it's costing on the corporate side. Do you have any idea how to deal with these huge sums of money?

RMS: I have a suggestion. If I were to suggest totally boycotting movies, I think people would ignore that suggestion. They might consider it too radical. So I would like to make a slightly different suggestion which comes to almost the same thing in the end, and that is, don't go to a movie unless you have some substantial reason to think it's good. Now this will lead in practice to almost the same result as a total boycott of Hollywood movies. In extension it's almost the same, but in intension it's very different. Now I've noticed that many people go to movies for reasons that have nothing to do with whether they think the movies are good. So if you change that, if you only go to a movie when you have some substantial reason to think it's good, you'll take away a lot of their money.

Thorburn: One way to understand all of this discourse today, I think, is to recognize that whenever radical, potentially transforming technologies appear in society, there's a struggle over who controls them. We today are repeating what has happened in the past. So from this angle, there may not be a reason for despair, or even pessimism, about what may occur in the longer run. But, in the shorter term, struggles over the control of text and images, over all forms of information are likely to be painful and extensive. For example, as a teacher of media, my access to images has been restricted in recent years in a way that had never been in place before. If I write an essay in which I want to use still images, even from films, they are much harder to get permission to use, and the prices charged to use those still images are much higher—even when I make arguments about intellectual inquiry and the the legal category of "fair use." So I think, in this moment of extended transformation, the longer-term prospects may, in fact, not be as disturbing as what's happening in the shorter term. But in any case, we need to understand the whole of our contemporary experience as a renewed version of a struggle over the control of technological resources that is a recurring principle of Western society.

It's also essential to understand that the history of older technologies is itself a complicated matter. The impact of the printing press in Spain, for example, is radically different from its impact in England or in France.

Q: One of the things that bothers me when I hear discussions of copyright is that often they start off with, "We want a 180-degree change. We want to do away with any sorts of control." It seems to me that part of what lay under the three categories that were suggested is an acknowledgement that there is some wisdom to copyright. Some of the critics of the way copyright is going now believe that, in fact, it ought to be backed up and function much more like patent and trademarks in terms of its duration. I wonder if our speaker would comment on that as a strategy.

RMS: I agree that shortening the time span of copyright is a good idea. There is absolutely no need in terms of encouraging publication for a possibility of copyrights' lasting as much as 150 years, which, in some cases, it can under present law. Now the companies were saying that a 75-year copyright on a work made for hire was not long enough to make possible the production of their works. I'd like to challenge those companies to present projected balance sheets for 75 years from now to back up that contention. What they really wanted was just to be able to extend the copyrights on the old works, so that they can continue restricting the use of them. But how you can encourage greater production of works in the 1920's by extending copyright today escapes me, unless they have a time machine somewhere. Of course, in one of their movies, they had a time machine. So maybe that's what affected their thinking.

Q: Have you given thought to extending the concept of "fair use," and are there any nuances there that you might care to lay out for us?

RMS: Well, the idea of giving everyone permission for noncommercial verbatim copying of two kinds of works, certainly, may be thought of as extending what fair use is. It's bigger than what's fair use currently. If your idea is that the public trades away certain freedoms to get more progress, then you can draw the line at various different places. Which freedoms does the public trade away and which freedoms does the public keep?

Q: To extend the conversation for just a moment, in certain entertainment fields, we have the concept of a public presentation. So, for example, copyright does not prevent us from singing Christmas carols seasonally but it prevents the public performance. And I'm wondering if it might be useful to think about instead of expanding fair use to unlimited noncommercial verbatim copying, to something less than that but more than the present concept of fair use.

RMS: I used to think that that might be enough, and then Napster convinced me otherwise because Napster is used by its users for noncommercial, verbatim redistribution. The Napster server, itself, is a commercial activity but the people who are actually putting things up are doing so noncommercially, and they could have done so on their Web sites just as easily. The tremendous excitement about, interest in, and use of Napster shows that that's very useful. So I'm convinced now that people should have the right to publicly, noncommercially, redistribute verbatim copies of everything.

Q: One analogy that was recently suggested to me for the whole Napster question was the analogy of the public library. I suppose some of you who have heard the Napster arguments have heard this analogy. I'm wondering if you would comment on it. The defenders of people who say Napster should continue and there shouldn't be restrictions on it sometimes say something like this: "When folks go into the public library and borrow a book, they're not paying for it, and it can be borrowed dozens of times, hundreds of time, without any additional payment. Why is Napster any different?"

RMS: Well, it's not exactly the same. But it should be pointed out that the publishers want to transform public libraries into pay-per-use, retail outlets. So they're against public libraries.

Q: Can these ideas about copyright suggest any ideas for certain issues about patent law such as making cheap, generic drugs for use in Africa?

RMS: No, there's absolutely no similarity. The issues of patents are totally different from the issues of copyrights. The idea that they have something to do with each other is one of the unfortunate consequences of using the term "intellectual property" and encouraging people to try to lump these issues together because, as you've heard, I've been talking about issues in which the price of a copy is not the crucial thing. But what's the crucial issue about making AIDS drugs for Africa? It's the price, nothing but the price.

Now the issue I've been talking about arises because digital information technology gives every user the ability to make copies. Well, there's nothing giving us all the ability to make copies of medicines. I don't have the ability to copy some medicine that I've got. In fact, nobody does; that's not how they're made. Those medicines can be made only in expensive centralized factories, whether they're generic drugs or imported from the U.S. Either way, they're going to be made in a small number of factories, and the issues are simply how much do they cost and are they available at a price that people in Africa can afford.

So that's a tremendously important issue, but it's a totally different issue. There's just one area where an issue arises with patents that is actually similar to these issues of freedom to copy, and that is in the area of agriculture. Because there are certain patented things that can be copies, more or less—namely, living things. They copy themselves when they reproduce. It's not necessarily exact copying; they re-shuffle the genes. But the fact is, farmers for millennia have been making use of this capacity of the living things they grow to copy themselves. Farming is, basically, copying the things that you grew, and you keep copying them every year. When plant and animal varieties get patented, when genes are patented and used in them, the result is that farmers are being prohibited from doing this.

There is a farmer in Canada who had a patented variety growing on his field and he said, "I didn't do that deliberately. The pollen blew, and the wind in those genes got into my stock of plants." And he was told that that doesn't matter; he has to destroy them anyway. It was an extreme example of how much government can side with a monopolist.

So I believe that, following the same principles that I apply to copying things on your computer, farmers should have an unquestioned right to save their seeds and breed their livestock. Maybe you could have patents covering seed companies, but they shouldn't cover farmers.

Q: There's more to making a model successful than just the licensing. Can you speak to that?

RMS: Absolutely. Well, you know, I don't know the answers. But part of what I believe is crucial for developing free, functional information is idealism. People have to recognize that it's important for this information to be free, that when the information is free, you can make full use of it. When it's restricted, you can't. They have to recognize that the non-free information is an attempt to divide them and keep them helpless and keep them down. Then they can get the idea, "Let's work together to produce the information we want to use, so that it's not under the control of some powerful person who can dictate to us what we can do."

This tremendously boosts [the development of the free software community]. I don't know how much it will work in various different areas, but I think that in the area of education, when you're looking for textbooks, I think I see a way it can be done. There are a lot of teachers in the world, teachers who are not at prestigious universities—maybe they're in high school; maybe they're in college where they don't write and publish a lot of things and there's not a tremendous demand for them. But, a lot of them are smart. A lot of them know their subjects well and they could write textbooks about lots of subjects and share them with the world and receive a tremendous amount of appreciation from the people who will have learned from them.

Q: That's what I proposed. But the funny thing is, I do know the history of education. That's what I do—educational, electronic media projects. I couldn't find an example. Do you know of one?

RMS: No, I don't. I started proposing this free encyclopedia and learning resource a couple of years ago, and I thought it would probably take a decade to get things rolling. Now we already have an encyclopedia that is rolling. So things are going faster than I hoped. I think what's needed is for a few people to start writing some free textbooks. Write one about whatever is your favorite subject or write a fraction of one. Write a few chapters of one and challenge other people to write the rest.

Q: Actually what I was looking for is something even more than that. What's important in your kind of structure is somebody that creates an infrastructure to which everybody else can contribute. There isn't a K-through-12 infrastructure out there in any place for a contribution for materials.

I can get information from lots of places but it's not released under free licenses, so I can't use it to make a free textbook.

RMS: Actually, copyright doesn't cover the facts. It only covers the way it's written. So you can learn a field from anywhere and then write a textbook, and you can make that textbook free, if you want.

Q: But I can't write by myself all the textbooks that a student needs going through school.

RMS: Well, it's true. And I didn't write a whole free operating system, either. I wrote some pieces and invited other people to join me by writing other pieces. So I set an example. I said, "I'm going in this direction. Join me and we'll get there." And enough people joined in that we got there. So if you think in terms of, how am I going to get this whole gigantic job done, it can be daunting. So the point is, don't look at it that way. Think in terms of taking a step and realizing that after you've taken a step, other people will take more steps and, together, it will get the job done eventually.

Assuming that humanity doesn't wipe itself out, the work we do today to produce the free educational infrastructure, the free learning resource for the world, will be useful for as long as humanity exists. If it takes 20 years to get it done, so what? So don't think in terms of the size of the whole job; think in terms of the piece that you're going to do. That will show people it can be done, so others will do other pieces.

20 Free Software: Freedom and Cooperation

Introduction

Mike Uretsky: I'm Mike Uretsky. I'm over at the Stern School of Business. I'm also one of the Co-Directors of the Center for Advanced Technology. And on behalf of all of us in the Computer Science Department, I want to welcome you here. I want to say a few comments, before I turn it over to Ed, who is going to introduce the speaker.

The role of a university is a place to foster debate and to have interesting discussions. And the role of a major university is to have particularly interesting discussions. And this particular presentation, this seminar falls right into that mold. I find the discussion of open source particularly interesting. In a sense. . . . [audience laughs]

Richard M. Stallman: I do free software. Open source is a different movement. [audience laughs] [applause]

Uretsky: When I first started in the field in the 1960's, basically software was free. And we went in cycles. It became free, and then software manufacturers, in the need to expand their markets, pushed it in other directions. A lot of the developments that took place with the entry of the PC moved in exactly the same kind of a cycle.

There's a very interesting French philosopher, Pierre Levy, who talks about movement to this direction and who talks about the move into cyberspace as not only relating to technology but also relating to social restructuring, to political restructuring, through a change in the kinds of relationships that will improve the well-being of mankind. And we're hoping that this debate is a movement in that direction, that this debate is something that cuts across a lot of the disciplines that normally act as solace within the University. We're looking forward to some very interesting discussions. Ed?

Ed Schonberg: I'm Ed Schonberg from the Computer Science Department at the Courant Institute. Let me welcome you all to this event. Introducers are usually, and particularly, a useless aspect of public presentations, but in this case, actually, they serve a useful purpose, as Mike easily demonstrated, because an introducer for instance, by making inaccurate comments, can allow [the speaker] to straighten out and correct and [audience laughs] sharpen considerably the parameters of the debate.

This is a transcript of a speech given at New York University on 29 May, 2001. This version is part of *Free Software, Free Society: Selected Essays of Richard M. Stallman*, 2002, GNU Press (http://www.gnupress.org); ISBN 1-882114-98-1.

So, let me make the briefest possible introduction to somebody who doesn't need one. Richard is the perfect example of somebody who, by acting locally, started thinking globally–from problems concerning the unavailability of source code for printer drivers at the M.I.T. AI Lab many years ago. He has developed a coherent philosophy that has forced all of us to reexamine our ideas of how software is produced, of what intellectual property means, and what the software community actually represents. Let me welcome Richard Stallman. [applause]

Free Software: Freedom and Cooperation

Richard M. Stallman: Can someone lend me a watch? [audience laughs] Thank you. So, I'd like to thank Microsoft for providing me the opportunity to [audience laughs] be on this platform. For the past few weeks, I have felt like an author whose book was fortuitously banned somewhere.[1] [audience laughs] Except that all the articles about it are giving the wrong author's name, because Microsoft describes the GNU GPL as an open source license, and most of the press coverage followed suit. Most people, of course just innocently don't realize that our work has nothing to do with open source, that in fact we did most of it before people even coined the term "open source."

We are in the free software movement, and I'm going to speak about what the free software movement is about, what it means, what we have done, and, because this is partly sponsored by a school of business, I'll say some things more than I usually do about how free software relates to business, and some other areas of social life.

Now, some of you may not ever write computer programs, but perhaps you cook. And if you cook, unless you're really great, you probably use recipes. And if you use recipes, you've probably had the experience of getting a copy of a recipe from a friend who's sharing it. And you've probably also had the experience–unless you're a total neophyte–of changing a recipe. It says certain things, but you don't have to do exactly that. You can leave out some ingredients. Add some mushrooms, 'cause you like mushrooms. Put in less salt because your doctor said you should cut down on salt – whatever. You can even make bigger changes, according to your skill. And if you've made changes in a recipe, and you cook it for your friends, and they like it, one of your friends might say, "Hey, could I have the recipe?" And then, what do you do? You could write down your modified version of the recipe and make a copy for your friend. These are the natural things to do with functionally useful recipes of any kind.

Now a recipe is a lot like a computer program. A computer program is a lot like a recipe: a series of steps to be carried out to get some result that you want. So it's just as natural to do those same things with computer programs–hand a copy to your friend. Make changes in it because the job it was written to do isn't exactly what you want. It did a great job for somebody else, but your job is a different job. And, after you've changed it, that is likely to be useful for other people. Maybe

---

[1] Less than a month before, Microsoft vice president Craig Mundie gave a speech attacking free software (calling it "open source").

they have a job to do that's like the job you do. So they ask, "Hey, can I have a copy?" Of course, if you're a nice person, you're going to give a copy. That's the way to be a decent person.

So imagine what it would be like if recipes were packaged inside black boxes. You couldn't see what ingredients they're using, let alone change them, and imagine if you made a copy for a friend, they would call you a pirate and try to put you in prison for years. That world would create tremendous outrage from all the people who are used to sharing recipes. But that is exactly what the world of proprietary software is like. A world in which common decency towards other people is prohibited or prevented.

Now, why did I notice this? I noticed this because I had the good fortune in the 1970's to be part of a community of programmers who shared software. Now, this community could trace its ancestry essentially back to the beginning of computing. In the 1970's, though, it was a bit rare for there to be a community where people shared software. And, in fact, this was sort of an extreme case, because in the lab where I worked, the entire operating system was software developed by the people in our community, and we'd share any of it with anybody. Anybody was welcome to come and take a look, and take away a copy, and do whatever he wanted to do. There were no copyright notices on these programs. Cooperation was our way of life. And we were secure in that way of life. We didn't fight for it. We didn't have to fight for it. We just lived that way. And, as far as we knew, we would just keep on living that way. So there was free software, but there was no free software movement.

But then our community was destroyed by a series of calamities that happened to it. Ultimately it was wiped out. Ultimately, the PDP-10 computer,[2] which we used for all our work, was discontinued. Our system—the *Incompatible Timesharing System*—was written starting in the '60's, so it was written in assembler language. That's what you used to write an operating system in the '60's. So, of course, assembler language is for one particular computer architecture; if that gets discontinued, all your work turns into dust—it's useless. And that's what happened to us. The 20 years or so of work of our community turned into dust.

But before this happened, I had an experience that prepared me, helped me see what to do, helped prepare me to see what to do when this happened, because at a certain point, Xerox gave the Artificial Intelligence Lab, where I worked, a laser printer, and this was a really handsome gift, because it was the first time anybody outside Xerox had a laser printer. It was very fast, printed a page a second, very fine in many respects, but it was unreliable, because it was really a high-speed office copier that had been modified into a printer. And, you know, copiers jam, but there's somebody there to fix them. The printer jammed and nobody saw. So it stayed jammed for a long time.

Well, we had an idea for how to deal with this problem. Change it so that whenever the printer gets a jam, the machine that runs the printer can tell our timesharing machine, and tell the users who are waiting for printouts, go fix the printer–because

---

[2] Programmed Data Processor model 10, a mainframe computer used by many top research and government organizations in the 1970's.

if they only knew it was jammed. . . of course, if you're waiting for a printout and you know that the printer is jammed, you don't want to sit and wait forever, you're going to go fix it.

But at that point, we were completely stymied, because the software that ran that printer was not free software. It had come with the printer, and it was just a binary. We couldn't have the source code; Xerox wouldn't let us have the source code. So, despite our skill as programmers–after all, we had written our own timesharing system–we were completely helpless to add this feature to the printer software.

And we just had to suffer with waiting. It would take an hour or two to get your printout because the machine would be jammed most of the time. You'd wait an hour figuring "I know it's going to be jammed. I'll wait an hour and go collect my printout," and then you'd see that it had been jammed the whole time, and in fact, nobody else had fixed it. So you'd fix it and you'd go wait another half hour. Then, you'd come back, and you'd see it jammed again–before it got to your output. It would print three minutes and be jammed thirty minutes. Frustration up the whazzoo. But the thing that made it worse was knowing that we could have fixed it, but somebody else, for his own selfishness, was blocking us, obstructing us from improving the software. So, of course, we felt some resentment.

And then I heard that somebody at Carnegie Mellon University had a copy of that software. I was visiting there later, so I went to his office and I said, "Hi, I'm from MIT. Could I have a copy of the printer source code?" And he said "No, I promised not to give you a copy." [audience laughs] I was stunned. I was so–I was angry, and I had no idea how I could do justice to it. All I could think of was to turn around on my heel and walk out of his room. Maybe I slammed the door. [audience laughs] And I thought about it later on, because I realized that I was seeing not just an isolated jerk, but a social phenomenon that was important and affected a lot of people.

I was lucky, I only got a taste of it. Other people had to live with this all the time. So I thought about it at length. See, he had promised to refuse to cooperate with us–his colleagues at MIT. He had betrayed us. But he didn't just do it to us. Chances are he did it to you too [Pointing at member of audience]. And I think, mostly likely, he did it to you too. [Pointing at another member of audience]. [audience laughs] And he probably did it to you as well [Pointing to third member of audience]. He probably did it to most of the people here in this room–except a few, maybe, who weren't born yet in 1980. Because he had promised to refuse to cooperate with just about the entire population of the planet Earth. He had signed a non-disclosure agreement.

Now, this was my first direct encounter with a non-disclosure agreement, and it taught me an important lesson–a lesson that's important because most program-mers never learn it. This was my first encounter with a non-disclosure agreement, and I was the victim. I, and my whole lab, were the victims. And the lesson it taught me was that non-disclosure agreements have victims. They're not innocent. They're not harmless. Most programmers first encounter a non-disclosure agree-ment when they're invited to sign one. And there's always some temptation–some goody they're going to get if they sign. So, they make up excuses. They say, "Well, he's never going to get a copy no matter what, so why shouldn't I join the conspiracy to deprive him?" They say, "This is the way it's always done. Who am I to go against it?" They say, "If I don't sign this, someone else will." Various excuses to gag their consciences.

But when somebody invited me to sign a non-disclosure agreement, my conscience was already sensitized. I remembered how angry I had been when somebody promised not to help me and my whole lab solve our problem. And I couldn't turn around and do the exact same thing to somebody else who had never done me any harm. If somebody asked me to promise not to share some useful information with a hated enemy, I would have said yes. If somebody's done something bad, he deserves it. But strangers–they haven't done me any harm. How could they deserve that kind of mistreatment? You can't let yourself start treating just anybody and everybody badly. Then you become a predator on society. So I said, "Thank you very much for offering me this nice software package. But I can't accept it in good conscience, on the conditions you are demanding, so I will do without it. Thank you so much." And so, I have never knowingly signed a non-disclosure agreement for generally useful technical information such as software.

Now there are other kinds of information, which raise different ethical issues. For instance, there's personal information. If you wanted to talk with me about what was happening between you and your boyfriend, and you asked me not to tell anybody–I could agree to keep that a secret for you, because that's not generally useful technical information.

At least, it's probably not generally useful [audience laughs]. There is a small chance–and it's a possibility though–that you might reveal to me some marvelous new sex technique, [audience laughs] and I would then feel a moral duty [audience laughs] to pass it on to the rest of humanity, so that everyone could get the benefit of it. So, I'd have to put a proviso in that promise.

If it's just details about who wants this, and who's angry at whom, and things like that soap opera. . .*that* I can keep private for you; but something that humanity could tremendously benefit from knowing, I mustn't withhold. You see, the purpose of science and technology is to develop useful information for humanity to help people live their lives better. If we promise to withhold that information–if we keep it secret–then we are betraying the mission of our field. And this, I decided, I shouldn't do.

But meanwhile my community had collapsed, and that left me in a bad situation. You see, the whole Incompatible Timesharing System was obsolete, because the PDP-10 was obsolete, and so there was no way that I could continue working as an operating system developer the way that I had been doing it. That depended on being part of the community, using the community's software and improving it. That no longer was a possibility, and that gave me a moral dilemma. What was I going to do? Because the most obvious possibility meant to go against that decision I had made. The most obvious possibility was to adapt myself to the change in the world. To accept that things were different, and that I'd just have to give up those principles and start signing non-disclosure agreements for proprietary operating systems, and most likely writing proprietary software as well. But I realized that that way I could have fun coding, and I could make money–especially if I did it other than at MIT–but at the end, I'd have to look back at my career and say, "I've spent my life building walls to divide people," and I would have been ashamed of my life.

So I looked for another alternative, and there was an obvious one. I could leave the software field and do something else. Now I had no other special noteworthy skills, but I'm sure I could have become a waiter. [audience laughs] Not at a fancy restaurant; they wouldn't hire me, [audience laughs] but I could be a waiter somewhere. And many programmers, they say to me, "The people who hire programmers demand this, this, and this. If I don't do those things, I'll starve." It's literally the word they use. Well, as a waiter, you're not going to starve. [audience laughs] So, really, they're in no danger. But–and this is important, you see–sometimes you can justify doing something that hurts other people by saying otherwise something worse is going to happen to me. If you were *really* going to starve, you'd be justified in writing proprietary software. [audience laughs] If somebody's pointing a gun at you, then I would say, it's forgivable. [audience laughs] But I had found a way that I could survive without doing something unethical, so that excuse was not available. I realized, though, that being a waiter would be no fun for me, and it would be wasting my skills as an operating system developer. It would avoid misusing my skills. Developing proprietary software would be misusing my skills. Encouraging other people to live in the world of proprietary software would be misusing my skills. So it's better to waste them than misuse them, but it's still not really good.

So for those reasons, I decided to look for some other alternative. What can an operating system developer do that would actually improve the situation, make the world a better place? And I realized that an operating system developer was exactly what was needed. The problem, the dilemma, existed for me and for everyone else because all of the available operating systems for modern computers were proprietary. The free operating systems were for old, obsolete computers, right? So for the modern computers–if you wanted to get a modern computer and use it, you were forced into a proprietary operating system. So if an operating system developer wrote another operating system, and then said, "Everybody come and share this; you're welcome to this"—that would give everybody a way out of the dilemma, another alternative. So I realized that there was something I could do that would solve the problem. I had just the right skills to be able to do it. And it was the most useful thing I could possibly imagine that I'd be able to do with my life. And it was a problem that no one else was trying to solve. It was just sort of sitting there, getting worse, and nobody was there but me. So I felt, "I'm elected. I have to work on this. If not me, who?" So I decided I would develop a free operating system, or die trying...of old age, of course. [audience laughs]

Of course I had to decide what kind of operating system it should be. There are some technical design decisions to be made. I decided to make the system compatible with Unix for a number of reasons. First of all, I had just seen one operating system that I really loved become obsolete because it was written for one particular kind of computer. I didn't want that to happen again. We needed to have a portable system. Well, Unix was a portable system. So if I followed the design of Unix, I had a pretty good chance that I could make a system that would also be portable and workable. And furthermore, why not be compatible with it in the details. The reason is, users hate incompatible changes. If I had just designed the system in my favorite way–which I would have loved doing, I'm sure–I would have produced something that was incompatible. The details would be different. So, if I wrote the system, then the users would have said to me, "Well, this is very nice, but it's incompatible. It will be too much work to switch. We can't afford that much trouble just to use your system instead of Unix, so we'll stay with Unix," they would have said.

Now, if I wanted to actually create a community where there would be people in it, people using this free system and enjoying the benefits of liberty and cooperation, I had to make a system people would use, a system that they would find easy to switch to, that would not have an obstacle making it fail at the very beginning. Now, making the system upward compatible with Unix actually made all the immediate design decisions, because Unix consists of many pieces, and they communicate through interfaces that are more or less documented. So if you want to be compatible with Unix, you have to replace each piece, one by one, with a compatible piece. So the remaining design decisions are inside one piece, and they could be made later by whoever decides to write that piece. They didn't have to be made at the outset.

All we had to do to start work was find a name for the system. Now, we hackers always look for a funny or naughty name for a program, because thinking of people being amused by the name is half the fun of writing the program. [audience laughs] And we had a tradition of recursive acronyms, to say that the program that you're writing is similar to some existing program. You can give it a recursive acronym name that says: this one's not the other. So, for instance, there were many Tico text editors in the '60's and '70's, and they were generally called something-or-other TECO. Then one clever hacker called his Tint, for Tint Is Not TECO–the first recursive acronym. In 1975, I developed the first Emacs text editor, and there were many imitations of Emacs, and a lot of them were called something-or-other Emacs, but one was called Fine, for Fine Is Not Emacs, and there was Sine, for Sine Is Not Emacs, and Eine for Eine Is Not Emacs, and MINCE for Mince Is Not Complete Emacs. [audience laughs] (That was a stripped-down imitation.) And then Eine was almost completely rewritten, and the new version was called Zwei, for Zwei Was Eine Initially.[3] [audience laughs]

So, I looked for a recursive acronym for Something is not Unix. And I tried all 26 letters, and discovered that none of them was a word. [audience laughs] Hmm, try another way. I made a contraction. That way I could have a three-letter acronym, for Something's not Unix. And I tried letters, and I came across the word "GNU"—the word "GNU" is the funniest word in the English language. [audience laughs] That was it. Of course, the reason it's funny is that according to the dictionary, it's pronounced "new." That's why people use it for a lot of wordplay. Let me tell you, this is the name of an animal that lives in Africa. And the African pronunciation had a click sound in it. [audience laughs] Maybe still does. And so, the European colonists, when they got there, they didn't bother learning to say this click sound. So they just left it out, and they wrote a 'g' which meant

---

[3] *Eine* and *Zwei* mean *one* and *two* in German respectively.

"there's another sound that's supposed to be here which we are not pronouncing." [audience laughs] So, tonight I'm leaving for South Africa, and I have begged them, I hope they're going to find somebody who can teach me to pronounce click sounds, [audience laughs] so that I'll know how to pronounce GNU the correct way, when it's the animal.

But, when it's the name of our system, the correct pronunciation is "guh-NEW"—pronounce the hard 'g'. If you talk about the "new" operating system, you'll get people very confused, because we've been working on it for 17 years now, so it is not new any more. [audience laughs] But it still is, and always will be, GNU–no matter how many people call it Linux by mistake. [audience laughs]

So, in January 1984, I quit my job at MIT to start writing pieces of GNU.[4] They were nice enough to let me keep using their facilities though. At the time, I thought we would write all these pieces, and make an entire GNU system, and then we'd say, "Come and get it," and people would start to use it. That's not what happened. The first pieces I wrote were just equally good replacements, with fewer bugs, for some pieces of Unix, but they weren't tremendously exciting. Nobody particularly wanted to get them and install them. But then, in September 1984, I started writing GNU Emacs, which was my second implementation of Emacs, and by early 1985, it was working. I could use it for all my editing, which was a big relief, because I had no intention of learning to use vi, the Unix editor. [audience laughs] So, until that time, I did my editing on some other machine, and saved the files through the network, so that I could test them. But when GNU Emacs was running well enough for me to use it, it was also–other people wanted to use it too.

So, I had to work out the details of distribution. Of course, I put a copy in the anonymous FTP directory, and that was fine for people who were on the net–they could just pull over a tar[5] file, but even a lot of programmers were not on the net in 1985. They were sending me email saying "How can I get a copy?" I had to decide what I would answer them. Well, I could have said: "I want to spend my time writing more GNU software, not writing tapes, so please find a friend who's on the Internet and who is willing to download it and put it on a tape for you," and I'm sure people would have found some friends, sooner or later. They would have got copies.

But I had no job. In fact, I've never had a job since quitting MIT in January 1984. So I was looking for some way I could make money through my work on free software, and therefore I started a free software business. I announced, "Send me 150 dollars, and I'll mail you a tape of Emacs." And the orders began dribbling in. By the middle of the year they were trickling in.

I was getting 8 to 10 orders a month. And, if necessary, I could have lived on just that, because I've always lived cheaply. I live like a student, basically. And I like that, because it means that money is not telling me what to do. I can do what I think is important for me to do. It freed me to do what seemed worth doing. So make a real effort to avoid getting sucked into all the expensive lifestyle habits of

---

[4] You can read the original announcement of the GNU project in "The GNU Manifesto"

[5] A Unix archiving program. Combined with gzip, it makes the GNU alternative to the non-free ZIP compression format.

typical Americans. Because if you do that, then people with the money will dictate what you do with your life. You won't be able to do what's really important to you.

So, that was fine, but people used to ask me, "What do you mean it's free software if it costs 150 dollars?" [audience laughs] Well, the reason they asked this was that they were confused by the multiple meanings of the English word "free." One meaning refers to price, and another meaning refers to freedom. When I speak of free software, I'm referring to freedom, not price. So think of free speech, not free beer. [audience laughs] Now, I wouldn't have dedicated so many years of my life to making sure programmers got less money. That's not my goal. I'm a programmer and I don't mind getting money myself. I won't dedicate my whole life to getting it, but I don't mind getting it. Therefore–since ethics is the same for everyone–I'm not against some other programmer getting money either. I don't want prices to be low. That's not the issue at all. The issue is freedom. Freedom for everyone who's using software, whether that person be a programmer or not.

At this point I should give you the definition of free software. I'd better get to some real details, because just saying "I believe in freedom" is vacuous. There are so many different freedoms you could believe in, and they conflict with each other, so the real political question is: Which are the important freedoms, the freedoms that we must make sure everybody has?

Now, I will give my answer to that question for the particular area of using software. A program is "free software" for you, a particular user, if you have the following freedoms:

- First, Freedom Zero is the freedom to run the program for any purpose, any way you like.
- Freedom One is the freedom to help yourself by changing the program to suit your needs.
- Freedom Two is the freedom to help your neighbor by distributing copies of the program.
- And Freedom Three is the freedom to help build your community by publishing an improved version so others can get the benefit of your work.

If you have all of these freedoms, the program is free software, for you–and that's crucial. That's why I phrase it that way. I'll explain why later, when I talk about the GNU General Public License, but right now I'm explaining what free software means, which is a more basic question.

So, **Freedom Zero** is pretty obvious. If you're not even allowed to run the program any way you like, it is a pretty damn restrictive program. But as it happens, most programs will at least give you Freedom Zero. And Freedom Zero follows, legally, as a consequence of Freedoms One, Two, and Three–that's the way that copyright law works. So the freedoms that distinguish free software from typical software are Freedoms One, Two, and Three, so I'll say more about them and why they are important.

Freedom One is the freedom to help yourself by changing the software to suit your needs. This could mean fixing bugs. It could mean adding new features. It could mean porting it to a different computer system. It could mean translating all the error messages into Navajo. Any change you want to make, you should be free to make.

Now, it's obvious that professional programmers can make use of this freedom very effectively, but not just them. Anybody of reasonable intelligence can learn a little programming. There are hard jobs, and there are easy jobs, and most people are not going to learn enough to do hard jobs. But lots of people can learn enough to do easy jobs, just the way 50 years ago, lots and lots of American men learned to repair cars, which is what enabled the U.S. to have a motorized army in World War II and win. It is very important to have lots of people tinkering.

And if you are a people person, and you really don't want to learn technology at all, that probably means that you have a lot of friends, and you're good at getting them to owe you favors. [audience laughs] Some of them are probably programmers. So you can ask one of your programmer friends. "Would you please change this for me? Add this feature?" So, lots of people can benefit from it.

Now, if you don't have this freedom, it causes practical, material harm to society. It makes you a prisoner of your software. I explained what that was like with regard to the laser printer. It worked badly for us, and we couldn't fix it, because we were prisoners of our software.

But it also affects people's morale. If the computer is constantly frustrating to use, and people are using it, their lives are going to be frustrating, and if they're using it in their jobs, their jobs are going to be frustrating; they're going to hate their jobs. And you know, people protect themselves from frustration by deciding not to care. So you end up with people whose attitude is, "Well, I showed up for work today. That's all I have to do. If I can't make progress, that's not my problem; that's the boss's problem." And when this happens, it's bad for those people, and it's bad for society as a whole. That's Freedom One, the freedom to help yourself.

Freedom Two is the freedom to help your neighbor by distributing copies of the program. Now, for beings that can think and learn, sharing useful knowledge is a fundamental act of friendship. When these beings use computers, this act of friendship takes the form of sharing software. Friends share with each other. Friends help each other. This is the nature of friendship. And, in fact, this spirit of goodwill–the spirit of helping your neighbor, voluntarily–is society's most important resource. It makes the difference between a livable society and a dog-eat-dog jungle. Its importance has been recognized by the world's major religions for thousands of years, and they explicitly try to encourage this attitude.

When I was going to kindergarten, the teachers were trying to teach us this attitude–the spirit of sharing–by having us do it. They figured if we did it, we'd learn. So they said, "If you bring candy to school, you can't keep it all for yourself; you have to share some with the other kids." The society was set up to teach this spirit of cooperation. And why do you have to do that? Because people are not totally cooperative. That's one part of human nature, and there are other parts of human nature. There are lots of parts of human nature. So, if you want a better society, you've got to work to encourage the spirit of sharing. It'll never get to be 100%. That's understandable. People have to take care of themselves too. But if we make it somewhat bigger, we're all better off.

Nowadays, according to the U.S. Government, teachers are supposed to do the exact opposite. "Oh, Johnny, you brought software to school. Well, don't share it. Oh no. Sharing is wrong. Sharing means you're a pirate." What do they mean when they say "pirate"? They're saying that helping your neighbor is the moral equivalent of attacking a ship. [audience laughs]

What would Buddha or Jesus say about that? Now, take your favorite religious leader. I don't know, maybe Manson would have said something different. [audience laughs] Who knows what L. Ron Hubbard would say? But ...

Question: [Inaudible]

Richard M. Stallman: Of course, he's dead. But they don't admit that. What?

Question: So are the others, also dead. [audience laughs] [Inaudible] Charles Manson's also dead. [audience laughs] They're dead, Jesus's dead, Buddha's dead...

RMS: Yes, that's true. [audience laughs] So I guess, in that regard, L. Ron Hubbard is no worse than the others. [audience laughs] Anyway – [Inaudible]

Question: L. Ron always used free software – it freed him from Zanu. [audience laughs]

RMS: Anyway, I think this is the most important reason why software should be free: we can't afford to pollute society's most important resource. It's true that it's not a physical resource like clean air and clean water. It's a psycho-social resource, but it's just as real for all that, and it makes a tremendous difference to our lives. The actions we take influence the thoughts of other people. When we go around telling people, "Don't share with each other," if they listen to us, we've had an effect on society, and it's not a good one. That's Freedom Two, the freedom to help your neighbor.

Oh, and by the way, if you don't have that freedom, it doesn't just cause this harm to society's psycho-social resource, it also causes waste–practical, material harm. If the program has an owner, and the owner arranges a state of affairs where each user has to pay in order to be able to use it, some people are going to say, "Never mind, I'll do without it." And that's waste, deliberately inflicted waste. And the interesting thing about software, of course, is that fewer users doesn't mean you have to make less stuff. If fewer people buy cars, you can make fewer cars. There's a saving there. There are resources to be allocated, or not allocated, into making cars. So that you can say that having a price on a car is a good thing. It prevents people from diverting lots of wasted resources into making cars that aren't really needed. But if each additional car used no resources, it wouldn't be doing any good saving the making of these cars. Well, for physical objects, of course, like cars, it is always going to take resources to make an additional one of them, each additional exemplar.

But for software that's not true. Anybody can make another copy. And it's almost trivial to do it. It takes no resources, except a tiny bit of electricity. So there's nothing we can save, no resource we're going to allocate better by putting this financial disincentive on the use of the software. You often find people taking the consequences of economic reasoning, based on premises that don't apply to software, and trying to transplant them from other areas of life where the premises may apply, and the conclusions may be valid. They just take the conclusions and assume that they're valid for software too, when the argument is based on nothing, in the case of software. The premises don't work in that case. It is very important to examine how you reach the conclusion, and what premises it depends on, to see where it might be valid. So, that is Freedom Two, the freedom to help your neighbor.

Freedom Three is the freedom to help build your community by publishing an improved version of the software. People used to say to me, "If the software's free, then nobody will get paid to work on it, so why should anybody work on it?" Well, of course, they were confusing the two meanings of *free*, so their reasoning was based on a misunderstanding. But, in any case, that was their theory. Today, we can compare that theory with empirical fact, and we find that hundreds of people are being paid to write free software, and over 100,000 are doing it as volunteers. We get lots of people working on free software, for various different motives.

When I first released GNU Emacs–the first piece of the GNU system that people actually wanted to use–and when it started having users, after a while, I got a message saying, "I think I saw a bug in the source code, and here's a fix." And I got another message, "Here's code to add a new feature." And another bug fix. And another new feature. And another, and another, and another, until they were pouring in on me so fast that just making use of all this help I was getting was a big job. Microsoft doesn't have this problem. [audience laughs]

Eventually, people noted this phenomenon. In the 1980's a lot of us thought that maybe free software wouldn't be as good as the non-free software, because we wouldn't have as much money to pay people. And of course people like me, who value freedom and community, said, "Well, we'll use the free software anyway." It's worth making a little sacrifice in some mere technical convenience to have freedom. But what people began to note, around 1990, was that our software was actually better. It was more powerful, and more reliable, than the proprietary alternatives.

In the early '90's, somebody found a way to do a scientific measurement of reliability of software. Here's what he did. He took several sets of comparable programs that did the same jobs–the exact same jobs–in different systems. Because there were certain basic Unix-like utilities. And the jobs that they did were more or less the same thing–or they were following the POSIX spec–so they were all the same in terms of what jobs they did; but they were maintained by different people, and written separately. The code was different. So they said, OK, we'll take these programs and run them with random data, and measure how often they crash or hang. So they measured it, and the most reliable set of programs was the GNU programs. All the commercial alternatives, which were proprietary software, were less reliable. So he published this and he told all the developers. A few years later he did the same experiment with the newest versions, and he got the same result. The GNU versions were the most reliable. You know, there are cancer clinics and 911 operations[6] that use the GNU system, because it's so reliable, and reliability is very important to them.

Anyway, there's even a group of people who focus on this particular benefit as the main reason why users should be permitted to do these various things, and to

---

[6]   In many areas of the United States 911 is the phone number for emergency help.

have these freedoms. If you've been listening to me, you've noticed that, speaking for the free software movement, I talk about issues of ethics, and what kind of a society we want to live in, what makes for a good society, as well as practical, material benefits. They're both important. That's the free software movement.

That other group of people–which is called the *open source movement*—they only cite the practical benefits. They deny that this is an issue of principle. They deny that people are entitled to the freedom to share with their neighbor and to see what the program's doing and change it if they don't like it. They say, however, that it's a useful thing to let people do that. So they go to companies and say to them, "You might make more money if you let people do this." So, what you can see is that to some extent, they lead people in a similar direction, but for totally different–for fundamentally different philosophical reasons.

On the deepest issue of all, on the ethical question, the two movements disagree. In the free software movement we say, "You're entitled to these freedoms. People shouldn't stop you from doing these things." In the open source movement, they say, "Yes, they can stop you if they want, but we'll try to convince them to deign to let you to do these things." Well, they have contributed–they have convinced a certain number of businesses to release substantial pieces of software as free software in our community. The open source movement has contributed substantially to our community, and we work together [with them] on practical projects. But philosophically, there's a tremendous disagreement.

Unfortunately, the open source movement is the one that gets the support of business the most, and so most articles about our work describe it as open source, and a lot of people just innocently think that we're all part of the open source movement. So that's why I'm mentioning this distinction. I want you to be aware that the free software movement, which brought our community into existence and developed the free operating system, is still here–and that we still stand for this ethical philosophy. I want you to know about this, so that you won't mislead someone else unknowingly.

But also, so that you can think about where you stand.

Which movement you support is up to you. You might agree with the free software movements and my views. You might agree with the open source movement. You might disagree with them both. You decide where you stand on these political issues.

But if you agree with the free software movement–if you see that there's an issue here that the people whose lives are controlled and directed by this decision deserve a say in it–then I hope you'll say that you agree with the free software movement, and one way you can do that is by using the term "free software" and just helping people know we exist.

So, Freedom Three is very important both practically and psycho-socially. If you don't have this freedom, it causes practical material harm, because this community development doesn't happen, and we don't make powerful, reliable software. But it also causes psycho-social harm, which affects the spirit of scientific cooperation–the idea that we're working together to advance human knowledge. You see, progress in science crucially depends on people being able to work together. Nowadays, though, you often find each little group of scientists acting as if it is a war with each other gang of scientists and engineers. But if they don't share with each other, they're all held back.

So, those are the three freedoms that distinguish free software from typical software. Freedom One is the freedom to help yourself, by making changes to suit your own needs. Freedom Two is the freedom to help your neighbor by distributing copies. And Freedom Three is the freedom to help build your community by making changes and publishing them for other people to use. If you have all of these freedoms, the program is free software for you. Now, why do I define it that way in terms of a particular user? Is it free software for you? [Pointing at member of audience.] Is it free software for you? [Pointing at another member of audience.] Is it free software for you? [Pointing at another member of audience.] Yes?

Question: Can you explain a bit about the difference between Freedom Two and Three? [inaudible]

RMS: Well, they certainly relate, because if you don't have freedom to redistribute at all, you certainly don't have freedom to distribute a modified version, but they're different activities.

Freedom Two is: you make an exact copy, and hand it to your friends, so now your friend can use it. Or maybe you make exact copies and you sell them to a bunch of people, and then they can use it.

Freedom Three is where you make improvements–or at least you think they're improvements, and some other people may agree with you. So that's the difference. Oh, and by the way, one crucial point. Freedoms One and Three depend on your having access to the source code. Because changing a binary-only program is extremely hard [audience laughs]—even trivial changes like using four digits for the date[7] [audience laughs]—if you don't have source. So, for compelling, practical reasons, access to the source code is a precondition, a requirement, for free software.

So, why do I define it in terms of whether it's free software "for you"? The reason is that sometimes the same program can be free software for some people, and non-free for others. Now, that might seem like a paradoxical situation, so let me give you an example to show you how it happens. A very big example–maybe the biggest ever–of this problem was the X Window System, which was developed at MIT and released under a license that made it free software. If you got the MIT version with the MIT license, you had Freedoms One, Two, and Three. It was free software for you. But among those who got copies were various computer manufacturers that distributed Unix systems, and they made the necessary changes in X to run on their systems. You know, probably just a few thousand lines out of the hundreds of thousands of lines of X. And then they compiled it, and they put the binaries into their Unix system and distributed it under the same non-disclosure agreement as the rest of the Unix system. And then millions of people got these

---

7　This refers to the "Y2K" problem in which many older programs stored the year in two digits; therefore it was unclear if the date "00" was 2000 or 1900, or any other year ending in 00. Millions of dollars were spent repairing this problem in thousands of computer systems before the year 2000.

copies. They had the X Window System, but they had none of these freedoms. It was not free software for *them*.

So, the paradox was that whether X was free software depended on where you made the measurement. If you made the measurement coming out of the developers' group, you'd say, "I observe all these freedoms. It's free software." If you made the measurements among the users you'd say, "Hmm, most users don't have these freedoms. It's not free software." Well, the people who developed X didn't consider this a problem, because their goal was just popularity–ego, essentially. They wanted a big professional success. They wanted to feel, "Ah, lots of people are using our software." And that was true. Lots of people were using their software but didn't have freedom.

Well, in the GNU Project, if that same thing had happened to GNU software, it would have been a failure, because our goal wasn't just to be popular; our goal was to give people liberty, and to encourage cooperation, to permit people to cooperate. Remember, never force anyone to cooperate with any other person, but make sure that everybody's allowed to cooperate, everyone has the freedom to do so, if he or she wishes. If millions of people were running non-free versions of GNU, that wouldn't be success at all. The whole thing would have been perverted into nothing like the goal.

So, I looked for a way to stop that from happening. The method I came up with is called "copyleft." It's called copyleft because it's sort of like taking copyright and flipping it over. [audience laughs] Legally, copyleft works based on copyright. We use the existing copyright law, but we use it to achieve a very different goal. Here's what we do. We say, "This program is copyrighted." And, of course, by default, that means it's prohibited to copy it, or distribute it, or modify it. But then we say, "You're authorized to distribute copies of this. You're authorized to modify it. You're authorized to distribute modified versions and extended versions. Change it any way you like."

But there is a condition. And the condition, of course, is the reason why we go to all this trouble, so that we could put the condition in. The condition says: Whenever you distribute anything that contains any piece of this program, that whole program must be distributed under these same terms, no more and no less. So you can change the program and distribute a modified version, but when you do, the people who get that from you must get the same freedom that you got from us. And not just for the parts of it that you copied from our program, but also for the other parts of that program that they got from you. The whole of that program has to be free software for them.

The freedoms to change and redistribute this program become inalienable rights– a concept from the Declaration of Independence. Rights that we make sure can't be taken away from you. The specific license that embodies the idea of copyleft is the GNU General Public License, a controversial license because it actually has the strength to say no to people who would be parasites on our community.

There are lots of people who don't appreciate the ideals of freedom. And they'd be very glad to take the work that we have done, and use it to get a head start in distributing a non-free program and tempting people to give up their freedom. The result would be—if we let people do that—that we would be developing these free programs, and we'd constantly have to compete with improved versions of our own programs. That's no fun.

A lot of people also feel, "I'm willing to volunteer my time to contribute to the community, but why should I volunteer my time to contribute to improving that company's proprietary program?" Some people might not even think that that's evil, but they want to get paid if they're going to do that. I, personally, would rather not do it at all.

But both of these groups of people–both the ones like me who say, "I don't want to help that non-free program to get a foothold in our community" and the ones that say, "Sure, I'd work for them, but then they'd better pay me"—both of us have a good reason to use the GNU General Public License. Because that says to that company, "You can't just take my work, and distribute it without the freedom." Whereas, the non-copyleft licenses, like the X Windows license, do permit that.

So that is the big division between the two categories of free software, license-wise. There are the programs that are copylefted so that the license defends the freedom of the software for every user. And there are the non-copylefted programs for which non-free versions are allowed. Somebody *can* take those programs and strip off the freedom. You may get that program in a non-free version.

And that problem exists today. There are still non-free versions of X Windows being used on our free operating systems. There is even hardware that is not really supported except by a non-free version of X Windows. And that's a major problem in our community. Nonetheless, I wouldn't say that X Windows is a bad thing. I'd say that the developers did not do the best possible thing that they could have done. But they *did* release a lot of software that we could all use.

There's a big difference between less than perfect, and evil. There are many gradations of good and bad. We have to resist the temptation to say, if you didn't do the absolute best possible thing, then you're no good. The people that developed X Windows made a big contribution to our community. But there's something better that they could have done. They could have copylefted parts of the program and prevented those freedom-denying versions from being distributed by others.

Now, the fact that the GNU General Public License defends your freedom, uses copyright law to defend your freedom, is, of course, why Microsoft is attacking it today. See, Microsoft would really like to be able to take all the code that we wrote and put it into proprietary programs, have somebody make some improvements. . .or even just incompatible changes is all they need. [audience laughs]

With Microsoft's marketing clout, they don't need to make it better to have their version supplant ours. They just have to make it different and incompatible. And then put it on everybody's desktop. So they really don't like the GNU GPL. Because the GNU GPL won't let them do that. It doesn't allow "embrace and extend." It says, if you want to share our code in your programs, you can. But you've got to share and share alike. The changes that you make we have to be allowed to share. So it's a two-way cooperation, which is real cooperation.

Many companies–even big companies like IBM and HP–are willing to use our software on this basis. IBM and HP contribute substantial improvements to GNU software. And they develop other free software. But Microsoft doesn't want to do that, so they give it out that businesses just can't deal with the GPL. Well, if businesses don't include IBM and HP and Sun, then maybe they're right. [audience laughs] More about that later.

I should finish the historical story. You see, we set out in 1984 not just to write some free software but to do something much more coherent: to develop an operating system that was entirely free software. So that meant we had to write piece after piece after piece. Of course, we were always looking for shortcuts. The job was so big that people said we'd never be able to finish. I thought that there was at least a chance that we'd finish it but, obviously, it's worth looking for shortcuts. So we kept looking around. Is there any program that somebody else has written that we could manage to adapt, to plug into here, and that way we won't have to write it from scratch? For instance, the X Window system. It's true it wasn't copylefted, but it was free software, so we could use it.

Now, I had wanted to put a window system into GNU from day one. I wrote a couple of window systems at MIT before I started GNU. And so even though Unix had no window system in 1984, I decided that GNU would have one. But we never ended up writing a GNU window system, because X came along. And I said: "Goody! One big job we don't have to do. We'll use X." I said, let's take X, and put it into the GNU system. And we'll make the other parts of GNU work with X, when appropriate. And we found other pieces of software that had been written by other people, like the text formatter TEX, and some library code from Berkeley. At that time there was Berkeley Unix, but it was not free software. This library code, initially, was from a different group at Berkeley, which did research on floating point. And so we fit in these pieces.

In October 1985, we founded the Free Software Foundation. So please note, the GNU Project came first. The Free Software Foundation came almost two years after the announcement of the GNU Project. And the Free Software Foundation is a tax-exempt charity that raises funds to promote the freedom to share and change software. And in the 1980's, one of the main things we did with our funds was to hire people to write parts of GNU. And essential programs, such as the shell and the C library, were written this way, as well as parts of other programs. The tar program, which is absolutely essential, although not exciting at all [audience laughs], was written this way. I believe GNU grep was written this way. And so we're approaching our goal.

By 1991, there was just one major piece missing, and that was the kernel. Now, why did I put off the kernel? Probably because it doesn't really matter what order you do the things in, at least technically it doesn't. You've got to do them all anyway. And partly because I'd hoped we'd be able to find a start at a kernel somewhere else. And we did. We found Mach, which had been developed at Carnegie Mellon. And it wasn't the whole kernel; it was the bottom half of the kernel. So we had to write the top half; things like the file system, the network code, and so on. But running on top of Mach they're running essentially as user programs, which ought to make them easier to debug. You can debug with a real source-level debugger running at the same time. I thought that way we'd be able to get these, the higher-level parts of the kernel, done in a short time. It didn't work out that way. These asynchronous, multi-threaded processes, sending messages to each other, turned out to be very hard to debug. And the Mach-based system that we were using to bootstrap with had a terrible debugging environment, and it was unreliable. It took us years and years to get the GNU kernel to work.

But, fortunately, our community did not have to wait for the GNU kernel. Because in 1991, Linus Torvalds developed another free kernel, called Linux. He used the old-fashioned monolithic design and it turns out that he got his working much faster than we got ours working. So maybe that's one of the mistakes that I made: that design decision. Anyway, at first we didn't know about Linux, because he never contacted us to talk about it, although he did know about the GNU project. But he announced it to other people and other places on the net. And so other people then did the work of combining Linux with the rest of the GNU system to make a complete free operating system. Essentially, to make the GNU plus Linux combination.

But they didn't realize that's what they were doing. You see, they said, "We have a kernel–let's look around and see what other pieces we can find to put together with the kernel." So, they looked around–and lo and behold, everything they needed was already available. What good fortune, they said. [audience laughs] It's all here. We can find everything we need. Let's just take all these different things and put it together, and have a system.

They didn't know that most of what they found was pieces of the GNU system. So they didn't realize that they were fitting Linux into the gap in the GNU system. They thought they were taking Linux and making a system out of Linux. So they called it a Linux system. [An audience member says,] "But it's more good fortune than finding the X Window System, and Mach?" [Stallman responds and continues,] Right. The difference is that the people who developed X and Mach didn't have the goal of making a complete free operating system. We're the only ones who had that. And, it was our tremendous work that made the system exist. We actually did a larger part of the system than any other project. No coincidence, because those people–they wrote useful parts of the system. But they didn't do it because they wanted the system to be finished. They had other reasons.

Now the people who developed X–they thought that designing an across-the-network window system would be a good project, and it was. And it turned out to help us make a good free operating system. But that's not what they hoped for. They didn't even think about that. It was an accident. An accidental benefit. Now, I'm not saying that what they did was bad. They did a large free software project. That's a good thing to do. But they didn't have that ultimate vision. The GNU Project is where that vision was.

And, so, we were the ones whose–every little piece that didn't get done by somebody else, we did it. Because we knew that we wouldn't have a complete system without it. And even if it was totally boring and unromantic, like tar or mv[8] [audience laughs], we did it. Or ld–you know there's nothing very exciting in ld, but I wrote one. [audience laughs] And I did make efforts to have it do a minimal amount of disk I/O so that it would be faster and handle bigger programs. I like to do a good job; I like to improve various things about the program while I'm doing

---

[8] A simple program that moves or renames files.

it. But the reason that I did it wasn't that I had brilliant ideas for a better ld. The reason I did it is that we needed one that was free. And we couldn't expect anyone else to do it. So we had to do it, or find someone to do it.

So, although at this point thousands of people and projects have contributed to this system, there is one project that is the reason that this system exists, and that's the GNU Project. It [the system] is basically the GNU System, with other things added since then.

The practice of calling the system Linux has been a great blow to the GNU Project, because we don't normally get credit for what we've done. I think Linux, the kernel, is a very useful piece of free software, and I have only good things to say about it. Well, actually, I can find a few bad things to say about it. [audience laughs] But, basically, I have good things to say about it. However, the practice of calling the GNU system "Linux" is just a mistake. I'd like to ask you please to make the small effort necessary to call the system GNU/Linux, and that way to help us get a share of the credit.

[A person in the audience yells out,] "You need a mascot! Get yourself a stuffed animal!" [Stallman responds,] We have one. [Audience member replies,] "You do?," [Stallman replies, provoking much laughter,] We have an animal–a gnu. So, yes, when you draw a penguin, draw a gnu next to it. But, let's save the questions for the end. I have more to go through.

So, why am I so concerned about this? Why do I think it is worth bothering you and perhaps lowering your opinion of me [audience laughs] to raise this issue of credit? When I do this, some people think that it's because I want my ego to be fed, right? Of course, I'm not asking you to call it "Stallmanix," right? [audience laughs] [applause]

I'm asking you to call it GNU, because I want the GNU Project to get credit. And there's a very specific reason for that, which is a lot more important than anybody getting credit, in and of itself. You see, these days, if you look around in our community most of the people talking about it and writing about it don't ever mention GNU, and they don't ever mention these goals of freedom–these political and social ideals–either. Because the place they [i.e., those] come from is GNU.

The ideas associated with Linux–the philosophy is very different. It *is* basically the apolitical philosophy of Linus Torvalds. So, when people think that the whole system is Linux, they tend to think: "Oh, it must have been all started by Linus Torvalds. His philosophy must be the one that we should look at carefully." And when they hear about the GNU philosophy, they say: "Boy, this is so idealistic, this must be awfully impractical. I'm a Linux-user, not a GNU-user." [audience laughs]

What irony! If they only knew! If they knew that the system they liked–or, in some cases, love and go wild over–is our idealistic, political philosophy made real.

They still wouldn't have to agree with us. But at least they'd see a reason to take it seriously, to think about it carefully, to give it a chance. They would see how it relates to their lives. If they realized, "I'm using the GNU system. Here's the GNU philosophy. This philosophy is why this system that I like very much exists," they'd at least consider it with a much more open mind. It doesn't mean that everybody will agree. People think different things. That's okay–people should make up their own minds. But I want this philosophy to get the benefit of the credit for the results it has achieved.

If you look around in our community, you'll find that almost everywhere, the institutions are calling the system Linux. Reporters mostly call it Linux. It's not right, but they do. The companies that package the system mostly say it [Linux]. Oh, and most of these reporters, when they write articles, they usually don't look at it as a political issue, or social issue. They're usually looking at it purely as a business question or what companies are going to succeed more or less, which is really a fairly minor question for society. And, if you look at the companies that package the GNU/Linux system for people to use, well, most of them call it Linux. And they all add non-free software to it.

See, the GNU GPL says that if you take code, and some code out of a GPL-covered program, and add some more code to make a bigger program, that whole program has to be released under the GPL. But you could put other separate programs on the same disk (hard disk or CD), and they can have other licenses. That's considered mere aggregation, and, essentially, just distributing two programs to somebody at the same time is not something we have any say over. So in fact, it is not true–sometimes I wish it were true–that if a company uses a GPL-covered program in a product, the whole product has to be free software. It's not–it doesn't go to that range–that scope. It's the whole program. If there are two separate programs that communicate with each other at arm's length–like by sending messages to each other–then they're legally separate, in general. So, these companies, by adding non-free software to the system, are giving the users, philosophically and politically, a very bad idea. They're telling the users, "It is OK to use non-free software. We're even putting it on this as a bonus."

If you look at the magazines about the use of the GNU/Linux system, most of them have a title like "Linux-something-or-other." So they're calling the system Linux most of the time. And they're filled with ads for non-free software that you could run on top of the GNU/Linux system. Now those ads have a common message. They say: "Non-free software is good for you. It's so good that you might even pay to get it." [audience laughs]

And they call these things "value-added packages," which makes a statement about their values. They're saying: Value practical convenience, not freedom. And, I don't agree with those values, so I call them "freedom-subtracted packages." [audience laughs] Because if you have installed a free operating system, then you now are living in the free world. You enjoy the benefits of liberty that we worked for so many years to give you. Those packages give you an opportunity to buckle on a chain.

And then if you look at the trade shows dedicated to the use of the GNU/Linux system, they all call themselves "Linux" shows. And they're filled with booths exhibiting non-free software, essentially putting the seal of approval on the non-free software. So, almost everywhere you look in our community, the institutions are endorsing the non-free software, totalling negating the idea of freedom that GNU was developed for. And the only place that people are likely to come across the idea of freedom is in connection with GNU, and in connection with free software, the term, free software. So this is why I ask you: Please call the system GNU/Linux. Please make people aware where the system came from and why.

Of course, just by using that name, you won't be making an explanation of the history. You can type four extra characters and write GNU/Linux; you can say two extra syllables. But GNU/Linux is fewer syllables than Windows 2000. [audience laughs] You're not telling them a lot, but you're preparing them, so that when they hear about GNU, and what it's all about, they'll see how that connects to them and their lives. And that, indirectly, makes a tremendous difference. So please help us.

You'll note that Microsoft called the GPL an "open source license." They don't want people to be thinking in terms of freedom as the issue. You'll find that they invite people to think in a narrow way, as consumers, and, of course, not even think very rationally as consumers, if they're going to choose Microsoft products. But they don't want people to think as citizens or statesmen. That's inimical to them. At least it's inimical to their current business model.

Now, how does free software. . . well, I can tell you about how free software relates to our society. A secondary topic that might be of interest to some of you is how free software relates to business.

Now, in fact, free software is *tremendously* useful for business. After all, most businesses in the advanced countries use software. Only a tiny fraction of them develop software.

And free software is tremendously advantageous for any company that uses software, because it means that you're in control. Basically, free software means the users are in control of what the program does. Either individually, if they care enough to be, or, collectively, when they care enough to be. Whoever cares enough can exert some influence. If you don't care, you don't buy. Then you use what other people prefer. But, if you do care, then you have some say. With proprietary software, you have essentially no say.

With free software, you can change what you want to change. And it doesn't matter that there are no programmers in your company; that's fine. If you wanted to move the walls in your building, you don't have to be a carpentry company. You just have to be able to go find a carpenter and say, "What will you charge to do this job?" And if you want to change around the software you use, you don't have to be a programming company. You just have to go to a programming company and say, "What will you charge to implement these features? And when will you have it done?" And if they don't do the job, you can go find somebody else.

There's a free market for support. So any business that cares about support will find a tremendous advantage in free software. With proprietary software, support is a monopoly, because one company has the source code–or maybe a small number of companies that paid a gigantic amount of money have the source code, if it's Microsoft's shared source program–but, it's very few. So there aren't very many possible sources of support for you. And that means that unless you're a real giant, they don't care about you. Your company is not important enough for them to care if they lose your business. Once you're using the program, they figure you're locked in to getting the support from them, because to switch to a different program is a gigantic job. So you end up with things like paying for the privilege of reporting a bug. [audience laughs] And once you've paid, they tell you, "Well, OK, we've noted your bug report. And in a few months, you can buy an upgrade, and you can see if we've fixed it." [audience laughs]

Support providers for free software can't get away with that. They have to please the customers. Of course, you can get a lot of good support gratis. You post your problem on the Internet. You may get an answer the next day. But that's not guaranteed, of course. If you want to be confident, you better make an arrangement with a company and pay them. And this is, of course, one of the ways that free software business works.

Another advantage of free software for businesses that use software is security and privacy. And this applies to individuals as well, but I brought it up in the context of businesses. You see, when a program is proprietary, you can't even tell what it really does.

It could have features deliberately put in that you wouldn't like if you knew about them. For example, it might have a back door to let the developer get into your machine. It might snoop on what you do and send information back. This is not unusual. Some Microsoft software did this. But it's not only Microsoft. There are other proprietary programs that snoop on the user. And you can't even tell if it does this. And, of course, even assuming that the developer's totally honest, every programmer makes mistakes. There could be bugs that affect your security that are nobody's fault. But the point is: If it's not free software, you can't find them. And you can't fix them.

Nobody has the time to check the source of every program he runs. You're not going to do that. But with free software there's a large community, and there are people in that community who are checking things. And you get the benefit of their checking, because if there's an accidental bug, there surely are, from time to time, in any program, they might find it and fix it. And people are much less likely to put in a deliberate Trojan horse, or a snooping feature, if they think they might get caught. The proprietary software developers figure they won't get caught. They'll get away with it undetected. But a free software developer has to figure that people will look at that and see it's there. In our community, we don't feel we can get away with ramming a feature down the users' throats that the users wouldn't like. We know that if the users don't like it, they'll make a modified version that doesn't have it. And then they'll all start using that version.

In fact, we can all reason enough, we can all figure this out enough steps ahead, that we probably won't put in that feature. After all, you're writing a free program; you want people to like your version; you don't want to put in a thing that a lot of people are going to hate, and have another modified version catch on instead of yours. So you just realize that the user is king in the world of free software. In the world of proprietary software, the customer is not king. Because you are only a customer. You have no say in the software you use.

In this respect, free software is a new mechanism for democracy to operate. Professor Lessig,[9] now at Stanford, noted that code functions as a kind of law. Whoever gets to write the code that just about everybody uses for all intents and purposes is writing the laws that run people's lives. With free software, these laws get written

---

[9] Lawrence Lessig wrote the introduction for this book.

in a democratic way. Not the classical form of democracy—we don't have a big election and say, "Everybody vote which way should this feature be done." [audience laughs] Instead we say, basically, those of you who want to work on implementing the feature this way, do it. And if you want to work on implementing the feature that way, do it. And, it gets done one way or the other, you know? And so, if a lot of people want it this way, it'll get done this way. In this way, everybody contributes to the social decision by simply taking steps in the direction that he wants to go.

And you're free to take as many steps, personally, as you want to take. A business is free to commission as many steps as they find useful to take. And after you add all these things up, that says which direction the software goes.

And it's often very useful to be able to take pieces out of some existing program—presumably usually large pieces, of course—and then write a certain amount of code of your own, and make a program that does exactly what you need, which would have cost you an arm and a leg to develop if you had to write it all from scratch, if you couldn't cannibalize large pieces from some existing free software package.

Another thing that results from the fact that the user is king is that we tend to be very good about compatibility and standardization. Why? Because users like that. Users are likely to reject a program that has gratuitous incompatibilities in it. Now, sometimes there's a certain group of users who actually have a need for a certain kind of incompatibility, and then they'll have it. That's OK. But when users want to follow a standard, we developers have to follow it, and we know that. And we do it. By contrast, if you look at proprietary software developers, they often find it advantageous to deliberately not follow a standard, and not because they think that they're giving the user an advantage that way, but rather because they're imposing on the user, locking the user in. And you'll even find them making changes in their file formats from time to time, just to force people to get the newest version.

Archivists[10] are finding a problem now, that files written on computers ten years ago often can't be accessed; they were written with proprietary software that's essentially lost now. If [they] were written with free software, then it could be brought up to date and run. And those records would not be lost, would not be inaccessible. They were even complaining about this on National Public Radio[11] recently in citing free software as a solution. In effect, by using a non-free program to store your own data, you are putting your head in a noose.

So, I've talked about how free software affects most business. But how does it affect that particular narrow area that is software business? Well, the answer is, mostly not at all. And the reason is that 90% of the software industry, from what I'm told, is development of custom software, software that's not meant to be released at all. For custom software, this issue, or the ethical issue of free or proprietary, doesn't arise. You see, the issue is, are you users free to change and redistribute the software? If there's only one user, and that user owns the rights, there's no problem. That user is free to do all these things. So, in effect, any custom program that was

---

[10] Many *archivists* store and share thousands of files over the Internet.

[11] National Public Radio is a private, non-profit organization that has, at the time of this speech, 620
    public radio stations that broadcast news and music daily.

developed by one company for use in-house is free software, as long as they have the sense to insist on getting the source code and all the rights.

The issue doesn't really arise for software that goes in a watch or a microwave oven or an automobile ignition system, because those are places where you don't download software to install. It's not a real computer, as far as the user is concerned, so it doesn't raise these issues enough for them to be ethically important. So, for the most part, the software industry will go along just as it's been going. And the interesting thing is that since such a large fraction of the jobs are in that part of the industry, even if there were no possibilities for free software business, the developers of free software could all get day jobs writing custom software. [audience laughs] There are so many; the ratio is so big.

But, as it happens, there is free software business. There are free software companies, and at the press conference that I'm going to have, people from a couple of them will join us. And, of course, there are also companies that are not free software businesses but do develop useful pieces of free software to release, and the free software that they produce is substantial.

Now, how do free software businesses work? Well, some of them sell copies. You're free to copy it but they can still sell thousands of copies a month. And others sell support and various kinds of services. I, personally, for the second half of the '80's, I sold free software support services. Basically I said, for $200 an hour, I'll change whatever you want me to change in GNU software that I'd written. Yes, it was a stiff rate, but if it was a program that I was the author of, people would figure that I might get the job done in a lot fewer hours. [audience laughs] And I made a living that way. In fact, I made more than I'd ever made before. I also taught classes. And I kept doing that until 1990, when I got a big prize[12] and I didn't have to do it any more.

But 1990 was when the first corporate free-software-business was formed, which was Cygnus Support. And their business was to do, essentially, the same kind of thing that I'd been doing. I certainly could have worked for them, if I had needed to do that. Since I didn't need to, I felt it was good for the movement if I remained independent of any one company. That way, I could say good and bad things about the various free software and non-free software companies, without a conflict of interest. I felt that I could serve the movement more. But if I had needed that to make a living, sure, I would have worked for them. It's an ethical business to be in. No reason I would have felt ashamed to take a job with them. And that company was profitable in its first year. It was formed with very little capital, just the money its three founders had. And it kept growing every year and being profitable every year until they got greedy and looked for outside investors, and then they messed things up. But it was several years of success, before they got greedy.

This illustrates one of the exciting things about free software. Free software demonstrates that you don't need to raise capital to develop free software. I mean, it's useful; it can help. If you do raise some capital, you can hire people and have

---

[12] The "big prize" he is referring to is the MacArthur Fellowship, also referred to by some as the "genius grant." It is a five-year grant given to individuals who show exceptional merit and promise for continued and enhanced creative work.

them write a bunch of software. But you can get a lot done with a small number of people. In fact, the tremendous efficiency of the process of developing free software is one of the reasons it's important for the world to switch to free software. And it also belies what Microsoft says, when they say the GNU GPL is bad because it makes it harder for them to raise capital to develop non-free software and take our free software and put our code into their programs that they won't share with us. Basically, we don't need to have them raising capital that way. We'll get the job done anyway. We are getting the job done.

People used to say we could never do a complete free operating system. Now we've done that and a tremendous amount more. And I would say that we're about an order of magnitude away from developing all the general purpose published software needs of the world. And this is in a world where more than 90% of the users don't use our free software yet. This is in a world where more than half of all the Web servers in the world are running on GNU/Linux with Apache as the Web server.

Question: [Inaudible] ... What did you say before, Linux?

Richard M. Stallman: I said GNU/Linux.

Question: You did?

Richard M. Stallman: Yes, if I'm talking about the kernel, I call it Linux. You know, that's it's name. The kernel was written by Linus Torvalds, and we should only call it by the name that he chose, out of respect for the author.

In general, in business most users are not using GNU/Linux. Most home users are not using our system yet. When they are, we should automatically get 10 times as many volunteers and 10 times as many customers for the free software businesses that there will be. And so that will take us that order of magnitude. So at this point, I am pretty confident that we can do the job.

And this is important, because Microsoft asks us to feel desperate. They say, "The only way you can have software to run, the only way you can have innovation, is if you give us power. Let us dominate you. Let us control what you can do with the software you're running, so that we can squeeze a lot of money out of you, and use a certain fraction of that to develop software, and take the rest as profit."

Well, you shouldn't ever feel that desperate. You shouldn't ever feel so desperate that you give up your freedom. That's very dangerous.

Another thing that Microsoft, well, not just Microsoft, people who don't support free software generally adopt a value system in which the only thing that matters is short-term practical benefits: How much money am I going to make this year? What job can I get done today? Short-term thinking and narrow thinking. Their assumption is that it is ridiculous to imagine that anybody ever might make a sacrifice for the sake of freedom.

Yesterday[13], a lot of people were making speeches about Americans who made sacrifices for the freedom of their compatriots. Some of them made great sacrifices. They even sacrificed their lives for the kinds of freedom that everyone in our country has heard about. (At least in some of the cases; I guess we have to ignore the war in Vietnam.)

---

[13] The day before was Memorial Day, a U.S. holiday on which war heroes are commemorated.

But, fortunately, to maintain our freedom in using software doesn't call for big sacrifices. Just tiny, little sacrifices are enough, like learning a command-line interface, if we don't have a Graphical User Interface (GUI) program yet. Like doing the job in this way, because we don't have a free software package to do it that way, yet. Like paying some money to a company that's going to develop a certain free software package, so that you can have it in a few years. Various little sacrifices that we can all make. And in the long run, even we will have benefited from it. You know, it is really an investment more than a sacrifice. We just have to have enough long-term view to realize it's good for us to invest in improving our society, without counting the nickels and dimes of who gets how much of the benefit from that investment.

So, at this point, I'm essentially done.

I'd like to mention that there's a new approach to free software business being proposed by Tony Stanco, which he calls "FreeDevelopers," which involves a certain business structure that hopes eventually to pay out a certain share of the profits, to all the authors of free software who have joined the organization. And they're looking at the prospects of getting some rather large government software development contracts in India now, because they're going to be using free software as the basis, having tremendous cost savings that way.

And so now I guess that I should ask for questions.

Question and Answer Session

Question: How could a company like Microsoft include a free software contract?
RMS: Well, actually, Microsoft is planning to shift a lot of its activity into services. And what they're planning to do is something dirty and dangerous, which is tie the services to the programs, one to the next, in a sort of zigzag. So that to use this service, you've got to be using this Microsoft program, which is going to mean you need to use this service, this Microsoft program...so it's all tied together. That's their plan.

Now, the interesting thing is that selling those services doesn't raise the ethical issue of free software or non-free software. It might be perfectly fine for them to have the business for those businesses selling those services over the net to exist. However, what Microsoft is planning to do is to use them to achieve an even greater lock, an even greater monopoly, on the software and the services, and this was described in an article, recently. Other people said that it is turning the net into the Microsoft Company Town.

And this is relevant because the trial court in the Microsoft antitrust trial recommended breaking up the company, Microsoft–but in a way that makes no sense, wouldn't do any good at all–into the operating system part and the applications part.

But having seen that article, I now see a useful, effective way to split up Microsoft into the services part and the software part, to require them to deal with each other only at arm's length, that the services must publish their interfaces, so that anybody can write a client to talk to those services, and, I guess, that they have to pay to get the service. Well, that's OK. That's a totally different issue.

If Microsoft is split up in this way ... services and software, they will not be able to use their software to crush competition with Microsoft services. And they won't be able to use the services to crush competition with Microsoft software. And we will be able to make the free software, and maybe you people will use it to talk to Microsoft services, and we won't mind.

Because, after all, although Microsoft is the proprietary software company that has subjugated the most people–the others have subjugated fewer people, it's not for want of trying; [audience laughs] they just haven't succeeded in subjugating as many people. So, the problem is not Microsoft and only Microsoft. Microsoft is just the biggest example of the problem we're trying to solve, which is proprietary software taking away users' freedom to cooperate and form an ethical society. So we shouldn't focus too much on Microsoft, even though they did give me the opportunity for this platform. That doesn't make them all-important. They're not the be-all and end-all.

Q: Earlier, you were discussing the philosophical differences between open source software and free software. How do you feel about the current trend of GNU/Linux distributions as they head towards supporting only Intel platforms? And the fact that it seems that less and less programmers are programming correctly, and making software that will compile anywhere? And making software that simply works on Intel systems?

RMS: I don't see an ethical issue there. Although, in fact, companies that make computers sometimes port the GNU/Linux system to it. HP apparently did this recently. And, they didn't bother paying for a port of Windows, because that would have cost too much. But getting GNU/Linux supported was, I think, five engineers for a few months. It was easily doable.

Now, of course, I encourage people to use autoconf, which is a GNU package that makes it easier to make your programs portable. I encourage them to do that. Or when somebody else fixes the bug that it didn't compile on that version of the system, and sends it to you, you should put it in. But I don't see that as an ethical issue.

Q: Two comments. One is: Recently, you spoke at MIT. I read the transcript. And someone asked about patents, and you said that "patents are a totally different issue. I have no comments on that."

RMS: Right. I actually have a lot to say about patents, but it takes an hour. [audience laughs]

Q: I wanted to say this: It seems to me that there is an issue. I mean, there is a reason that companies call both patents and copyrights things like hard property in trying to get this concept which is, if they want to use the power of the State to create a course of monopoly for themselves. And so, what's common about these things is not that they revolve around the same issues, but that motivation is not really the public service issues but the motivation of companies to get a monopoly for their private interests.

RMS: You're right that that's what they want. But there's another reason why they want to use the term intellectual property. It's that they don't want to encourage people to think carefully about copyright issues or patent issues. Because copyright law and patent law are totally different, and the effects of software copyrights and software patents are totally different.

Software patents are a restriction on programmers, prohibiting them from writing certain kinds of programs, whereas copyright doesn't do that. With copyright, at least if you wrote it yourself, you're allowed to distribute it. So, it's tremendously important to separate these issues.

They have a little bit in common, at a very low level, and everything else is different. So, please, to encourage clear thinking, discuss copyright or discuss patents. But don't discuss intellectual property. I don't have an opinion on intellectual property. I have opinions on copyrights and patents and software.

Q: You mentioned at the beginning that a functional language, like recipes, are computer programs. But there is a big cross over from food recipes to computer programs, and from English language to computer programs—the definition of "functional language" is very broad. This is causing problems in the DeCSS, DVD, case.

RMS: The issues are partly similar but partly different, for things that are not functional in nature. Part of the issue transfers but not all of it. Unfortunately, that's another hour speech. I don't have time to go into it. But I would say that all functional works ought to be free in the same sense as software. You know, textbooks, manuals, dictionaries, and recipes, and so on.

Q: I was just wondering on online music. There are similarities and differences created all through.

RMS: Right. I'd say that the minimum freedom that we should have for any kind of published information is the freedom to non-commercially redistribute it, verbatim. For functional works, we need the freedom to commercially publish a modified version, because that's tremendously useful to society. For non-functional works— things that are to entertain, or to be aesthetic, or to state a certain person's views, you know—perhaps they shouldn't be modified. And perhaps that means that it's OK to have copyright covering all commercial distribution of them.

Please remember that according to the U.S. Constitution, the purpose of copyright is to benefit the public. It is to modify the behavior of certain private parties, so that they will publish more books. And the benefit of this is that society gets to discuss issues and learn. And, you know, we have literature. We have scientific works. The purpose is to encourage that. Copyrights do not exist for the sake of authors, let alone for the sake of publishers. They exist for the sake of readers and all those who benefit from the communication of information that happens when people write and others read. And that goal I agree with.

But in the age of the computer networks, the method is no longer tenable, because it now requires draconian laws that invade everybody's privacy and terrorize everyone. Years in prison for sharing with your neighbor. It wasn't like that in the age of the printing press. Then copyright was an industrial regulation. It restricted publishers. Now it's a restriction imposed by the publishers on the public. So the power relationship is turned around 180 degrees, even if it's the same law.

Q: So you can have the same thing, but like in making music from other music?

RMS: Right. That is an interesting. . . .

Q: And unique, new works, you know, it's still a lot of cooperation.

RMS: It is. And I think that probably requires some kind of fair use concept. Certainly making a few seconds of sample and using that in making some musical work, obviously that should be fair use. Even the standard idea of fair use includes that, if you think about it. Whether courts agree, I'm not sure, but they should. That wouldn't be a real change in the system as it has existed.

Q: What do you think about publishing public information in proprietary formats?

RMS: Oh, it shouldn't be. I mean, the government should never require citizens to use a non-free program to access, to communicate with the government in any way, in either direction.

Q: I have been, what I will now say, a GNU/Linux user. . .

RMS: Thank you. [audience laughs]

Q: . . . for the past four years. The one thing that has been problematical for me and is something that is essential, I think, to all of us, is browsing the Web.

RMS: Yes.

Q: One thing that has been decidedly a weakness in using a GNU/Linux system has been browsing the Web, because the prevailing tool for that, Netscape. . .

RMS: . . . is not free software.

Let me respond to this. I want to get to the point, for the sake of getting in more. So, yes. There has been a terrible tendency for people to use Netscape Navigator on their GNU/Linux systems. In fact all the commercially packaged systems come with it. So this is an ironic situation: we worked so hard to make a free operating system, and now, if you go to the store, and you can find versions of GNU/Linux there, most of them are called Linux, and they're not free. Oh, well, part of them is. But then there's Netscape Navigator, and maybe other non-free programs as well. So it's very hard to actually find a free system, unless you know what you're doing. Or, of course, you cannot install Netscape Navigator.

Now, in fact, there have been free Web browsers for many years. There is a free Web browser that I used to use called Lynx. It's a free Web browser that is non-graphical; it's text-only. This has a tremendous advantage, in that you don't see the ads. [audience laughs] [applause]

But anyway, there is a free graphical project called Mozilla, which is now getting to the point where you can use it. And I occasionally use it.

Q: Konqueror 2.01 has been very good.

RMS: Oh, OK. So that's another free graphical browser. So, we're finally solving that problem, I guess.

Q: Can you talk to me about that philosophical/ethical division between free software and open source? Do you feel that those are irreconcilable? . . . .

[Recording switches tapes; end of question and start of answer is missing]

RMS: . . . to a freedom, and ethics. Or whether you just say, Well, I hope that you companies will decide it's more profitable to let us be allowed to do these things.

But, as I said, in a lot of practical work, it doesn't really matter what a person's politics are. When a person offers to help the GNU project, we don't say: "You have to agree with our politics." We say that in a GNU package, you've got to call the system GNU/Linux, and you've got to call it free software. What you say when you're not speaking to the GNU Project, that's up to you.

Q: The company IBM started a campaign for government agencies, to sell their big new machines, that they used Linux as selling point, and say Linux.

RMS: Yes. Of course, it's really the GNU/Linux systems. [audience laughs]

Q: That's right! Well, tell the top salesperson. He doesn't know anything for GNU.

RMS: Oh yes. The problem is that they've already carefully decided what they want to say for reasons of their advantage. And the issue of what is a more accurate, or fair, or correct way to describe it is not the primary issue that matters to a company like that. Now, some small companies, yes, there'll be a boss. And if the boss is inclined to think about things like that, he might make a decision that way. Not a giant corporation though. It's a shame.

There's another more important and more substantive issue about what IBM is doing. They're saying that they're putting a billion dollars into "Linux." But perhaps I should also put quotes around "into," as well, because some of that money is paying people to develop free software. That really is a contribution to our community. But other parts are paying people to write proprietary software, or port proprietary software to run on top of GNU/Linux, and that is not a contribution to our community. But IBM is lumping that all together into this. Some of it might be advertising, which is partly a contribution, even if it's partly wrong. So, it's a complicated situation. Some of what they're doing is contribution and some is not, and some is somewhat, but not exactly. And you can't just lump it altogether and think, "Wowee! A billion dollars from IBM." [audience laughs] That's oversimplification.

Q: Can you talk a little bit more about the thinking that went into the General Public License?

RMS: So, the thinking that went into the GNU GPL? Part of it was that I wanted to protect the freedom of the community against the phenomena that I just described with X Windows, which has happened with other free programs as well. In fact, when I was thinking about this issue, X Windows was not yet released. But I had seen this problem happen in other free programs. For instance, TeX. I wanted to make sure that the users would all have freedom. Otherwise, I realized that I might write a program, and maybe a lot of people would use the program, but they wouldn't have freedom. And what's the point of that?

But the other issue I was thinking about was, I wanted to give the community a feeling that it was not a doormat, a feeling that it was not prey to any parasite who would wander along. If you don't use copyleft, you are essentially saying: [speaking meekly] "Take my code. Do what you want. I don't say no." So anybody can come along and say: [speaking very firmly] "Ah, I want to make a non-free version of this. I'll just take it." And, then, of course, they probably make some improvements, those non-free versions might appeal to users, and replace the free versions. And then, what have you accomplished? You've only made a donation to some proprietary software project.

And when people see that that's happening, when people see, other people take what I do, and they don't ever give back, it can be demoralizing. And, this is not just speculation. I had seen that happen. That was part of what happened to wipe out the old community that I belonged to in the '70's. Some people started becoming uncooperative. And we assumed that they were profiting thereby. They certainly acted as if they thought they were profiting. And we realized that they can just take our cooperation and not give back. And there was nothing we could do about it. It was very discouraging. We, those of us who didn't like the trend, even had a discussion but we couldn't come up with any idea for how we could stop it.

The GPL is designed to stop that. It says: Yes, you are welcome to join the community and use this code. You can use it to do all sorts of jobs. But, if you release a modified version, you've got to release that to our community, as part of our community, as part of the free world.

So, in fact, there are still many ways that people can get the benefit of our work and not contribute, like you don't have to write any software. Lots of people use GNU/Linux and don't write any software. There's no requirement that you've got to do anything for us. But if you do a certain kind of thing, you've got to contribute to it. So what that means is that our community is not a doormat. And I think that that helped give people the strength to feel, Yes, we won't just be trampled underfoot by everybody. We'll stand up to this.

Q: Considering free but not copylefted software, since anybody can pick it up and make it proprietary, is it not possible also for someone to pick it up and make some changes and release the whole thing under the GPL?

RMS: Yes, it is possible.

Q: Then that would make all future copies then be GPL'ed.

RMS: From that branch. Here's why we don't generally do that. Let me explain. We could, if we wanted to, take X Windows, and make a GPL-covered copy and make changes in that. But there's a much larger group of people working on improving X Window and not GPL-ing it. So, if we did that, we would be forking from them. And that's not very nice treatment of them. And, they are a part of our community, contributing to our community.

Second, it would backfire against us, because they're doing a lot more work on X than we would be. So our version would be inferior to theirs, and people wouldn't use it, which means, why go to the trouble at all?

So when a person has written some improvement to X Windows, what I say that person should do is cooperate with the X development team. Send it to them and let them use it their way. Because they are developing a very important piece of free software. It's good for us to cooperate with them.

Q: Except, considering X, in particular, about two years ago, the X Consortium that was far into the non-free open source. . . .

RMS: Well, actually it wasn't open-source. They may have said it was. I can't remember if they said that or not. But it wasn't open source. It was restricted. You couldn't commercially distribute, I think. Or you couldn't commercially distribute a modified version, or something like that. There was a restriction that's considered unacceptable by both the Free Software movement and the Open Source movement.

And yes, that's what using a non-copyleft license leaves you open to. In fact, the X Consortium had a very rigid policy. They say: If your program is copylefted even a little bit, we won't distribute it at all. We won't put it in our distribution.

So, a lot of people were pressured in this way into not copylefting. And the result was that all of their software was wide open, later on. When the same people who had pressured a developer to be too all-permissive, then the X people later said: "All right, now we can put on restrictions," which wasn't very ethical of them.

But, given the situation, would we really want to scrape up the resources to maintain an alternate GPL-covered version of X? And it wouldn't make any sense to do that. There are so many other things we need to do. Let's do them instead. We can cooperate with the X developers.

Q: Do you have a comment, is the GNU a trademark? And is it practical to include it as part of the GNU General Public License allowing trademarks?

Richard M. Stallman: We are, actually, applying for trademark registration on GNU. But it wouldn't really have anything to do with that. It's a long story to explain why.

Q: You could require the trademark be displayed with GPL-covered programs.

RMS: No, I don't think so. The licenses cover individual programs. And when a given program is part of the GNU Project, nobody lies about that. The name of the system as a whole is a different issue. And this is an aside. It's not worth discussing more.

Q: If there was a button that you could push and force all companies to free their software, would you press it?

RMS: Well, I would only use this for published software. I think that people have the right to write a program privately and use it. And that includes companies. This is privacy issue. And it's true, there can be times when it is wrong to do that, like if it is tremendously helpful to humanity, and you are withholding it from humanity. That is a wrong but that's a different kind of wrong. It's a different issue, although it's in the same area.

But yes, I think all published software should be free software. And remember, when it's not free software, that's because of government intervention. The government is intervening to make it non-free. The government is creating special legal powers to hand out to the owners of the programs, so that they can have the police stop us from using the programs in certain ways. So I would certainly like to end that.

Ed Schonberg: Richard's presentation has generated an enormous amount of intellectual energy. I would suggest that some of it should be directed to using, and possibly writing, free software.

We should close the proceedings shortly. I want to say that Richard has injected into a profession that is known in the general public for its terminal political nerditude a level of political and moral discussion that is, I think, unprecedented in our profession. And we owe him very big for this. [Audience applause]

21 Words to Avoid

There are a number of words and phrases that we recommend avoiding, either because they are ambiguous or because they imply an opinion that we hope you may not entirely agree with.

BSD-style   The expression "BSD-style license" leads to confusion because it lumps together licenses that have important differences. For instance, the original BSD license with the advertising clause is incompatible with the GPL, but the revised BSD license is compatible with the GPL.

To avoid confusion, it is best to name the specific license in question and avoid the vague term "BSD-style."

Commercial

Please don't use "commercial" as a synonym for "non-free." That confuses two entirely different issues.

A program is commercial if it is developed as a business activity. A commercial program can be free or non-free, depending on its license. Likewise, a program developed by a school or an individual can be free or non-free, depending on its license. The two questions, what sort of entity developed the program and what freedom its users have, are independent.

In the first decade of the Free Software movement, free-software packages were almost always noncommercial; the components of the GNU/Linux operating system were developed by individuals or by nonprofit organizations such as the Free Software Foundation and universities. But in the 1990's, free commercial software started to appear.

Free commercial software is a contribution to our community, so we should encourage it. But people who think that "commercial" means "non-free" will tend to think that combination is self-contradictory, and dismiss the possibility. Let's be careful not to use the word "commercial" in that way.

Content   If you want to describe a feeling of comfort and satisfaction, by all means say "content," but using it to describe written and other works of authorship embodies a specific attitude towards those works: that they are an interchangeable commodity whose purpose is to fill a box

---

Originally written in 1996, this version is part of *Free Software, Free Society: Selected Essays of Richard M. Stallman*, 2002, GNU Press (http://www.gnupress.org); ISBN 1-882114-98-1.

and make money. In effect, it treats the works themselves with disrespect.

Those who use this term are often the publishers that push for increased copyright power in the name of the authors ("creators," as they say) of the works. The term "content" reveals what they really feel.

As long as other people use the term "content provider," political dissidents can well call themselves "malcontent providers."

Creator   The term "creator" as applied to authors implicitly compares them to a deity ("the creator"). The term is used by publishers to elevate the authors' moral stature above that of ordinary people, to justify increased copyright power that the publishers can exercise in the name of the authors.

Digital Rights Management
            "Digital Rights Management" software is actually designed to impose restrictions on computer users. The use of the word "rights" in this term is propaganda, designed to lead you unawares into seeing the issue from the viewpoint of the few that impose the restrictions, while ignoring that of the many whom the restrictions are imposed on.

Good alternatives include "Digital Restrictions Management" and "handcuffware."

For free   If you want to say that a program is free software, please don't say that it is available "for free." That term specifically means "for zero price." Free software is a matter of freedom, not price.

Free-software copies are often available for free—for example, by downloading via FTP. But free-software copies are also available for a price on CD-ROMs; meanwhile, proprietary-software copies are occasionally available for free in promotions, and some proprietary packages are normally available at no charge to certain users.

To avoid confusion, you can say that the program is available "as free software."

Freeware   Please don't use the term "freeware" as a synonym for "free software." The term "freeware" was used often in the 1980's for programs released only as executables, with source code not available. Today it has no particular agreed-on definition.

Also, if you use languages other than English, please try to avoid borrowing English words such as "free software" or "freeware." Try to use the often less ambiguous wording that your language offers. This is a list of recommended unambiguous translations for the term "free software" into various languages.

- Czech: svobodny software
- Danish: fri software OR frit programmel

- Dutch: vrije software
- Esperanto: libera softvaro
- Finnish: vapaa ohjelmisto
- French: logiciel libre
- German: freie Software
- Hungarian: szabad szoftver
- Icelandic: frjls hugbnaur
- Indonesian: perangkat lunak bebas
- Italian: software libero
- Japanese: jiyuu-na software
- Korean: ja-yu software
- Norwegian: fri programvare
- Polish: wolne oprogramowanie
- Portuguese: software livre
- Slovak: slobodny softver
- Slovenian: prosto programje
- Spanish: software libre
- Swedish: fri programvara
- Turkish: ozgur yazilim

By forming a word in your own language, you show that you are really referring to freedom and not just parroting some mysterious foreign marketing concept. The reference to freedom may at first seem strange or disturbing to your countrymen, but once they see that it means exactly what it says, they will really understand what the issue is.

Give away software

It's misleading to use the term "give away" to mean "distribute a program as free software." It has the same problem as "for free": it implies the issue is price, not freedom. One way to avoid the confusion is to say "release as free software."

Intellectual property

Publishers and lawyers like to describe copyright as "intellectual property." This term carries a hidden assumption—that the most natural way to think about the issue of copying is based on an analogy with physical objects, and our ideas of them as property.

But this analogy overlooks the crucial difference between material objects and information: information can be copied and shared almost effortlessly, while material objects can't be. Basing your thinking on this analogy is tantamount to ignoring that difference.

Even the U.S. legal system does not entirely accept this analogy, since it does not treat copyrights like physical-object property rights.

If you don't want to limit yourself to this way of thinking, it is best to avoid using the term "intellectual property" in your words and thoughts.

There is another problem with "intellectual property": it is a catch-all that lumps together several disparate legal systems, including copyright, patents, trademarks, and others, which have very little in common. These systems of law originated separately, cover different activities, operate in different ways, and raise different public policy issues. For instance, if you learn a fact about copyright law, you would do well to assume it is not true for patent law, since that is almost always true. Since these laws are so different, the term "intellectual property" is an invitation to simplistic overgeneralization. Any opinion about "intellectual property" is almost surely foolish. At that broad level, you can't even see the specific public policy issues raised by copyright law, or the different issues raised by patent law, or any of the others.

The term "intellectual property" leads people to focus on the meager common aspect of these disparate laws, which is that they establish various abstractions that can be bought and sold, and ignore the important aspect, which is the restrictions they place on the public and what good or harm those restrictions cause.

If you want to think clearly about the issues raised by patents, copyrights, and trademarks, or even learn what these laws require, the first step is to forget that you ever heard the term "intellectual property" and treat them as unrelated subjects. To give clear information and encourage clear thinking, never speak or write about "intellectual property"; instead, present the topic as copyright, patents, or whichever specific law you are discussing.

According to Professor Mark Lemley of the University of Texas Law School, the widespread use of term "intellectual property" is a recent fad, arising from the 1967 founding of the World Intellectual Property Organization[1] (WIPO). WIPO represents the interests of the holders of copyrights, patents, and trademarks, and lobbies governments to increase their power. One WIPO treaty follows the lines of the Digital Millennium Copyright Act, which has been used to censor useful free software packages in the U.S.[2]

Piracy   Publishers often refer to prohibited copying as "piracy." In this way, they imply that illegal copying is ethically equivalent to attacking ships on the high seas, kidnaping and murdering the people on them.

---

[1]   See footnote 123 in his March 1997 book review, in the *Texas Law Review*, of *Romantic Authorship and the Rhetoric of Property* by James Boyle.

[2]   See http://www.wipout.net/ for a counter-WIPO campaign.

If you don't believe that illegal copying is just like kidnaping and murder, you might prefer not to use the word "piracy" to describe it. Neutral terms such as "prohibited copying" or "unauthorized copying" are available for use instead. Some of us might even prefer to use a positive term such as "sharing information with your neighbor."

Protection   Publishers' lawyers love to use the term "protection" to describe copyright. This word carries the implication of preventing destruction or suffering; therefore, it encourages people to identify with the owner and publisher who benefit from copyright, rather than with the users who are restricted by it.

It is easy to avoid "protection" and use neutral terms instead. For example, instead of "Copyright protection lasts a very long time," you can say, "Copyright lasts a very long time."

If you want to criticize copyright instead of supporting it, you can use the term "copyright restrictions."

RAND (reasonable and non-discriminatory)

Standards bodies that promulgate patent-restricted standards that prohibit free software typically have a policy of obtaining patent licenses that require a fixed fee per copy of a conforming program. They often refer to such licenses by the term "RAND," which stands for "reasonable and non-discriminatory."

That term whitewashes a class of patent licenses that are normally neither reasonable nor non-discriminatory. It is true that these licenses do not discriminate against any specific person, but they do discriminate against the free software community, and that makes them unreasonable. Thus, half of "RAND" is deceptive and the other half is prejudiced.

Standards bodies should recognize that these licenses are discriminatory, and drop the use of the term "reasonable and non-discriminatory" or "RAND" to describe them. Until they do so, other writers who do not wish to join in the whitewashing would do well to reject that term. To accept and use it merely because patent-wielding companies have made it widespread is to let those companies dictate the views you express.

I suggest the term "uniform fee only," or "UFO" for short, as a replacement. It is accurate because the only condition in these licenses is a uniform royalty fee.

Sell software

The term "sell software" is ambiguous. Strictly speaking, exchanging a copy of a free program for a sum of money is "selling"; but people usually associate the term "sell" with proprietary restrictions on the subsequent use of the software. You can be more precise, and prevent confusion, by saying either "distributing copies of a program for a fee" or "imposing proprietary restrictions on the use of a program," depending on what you mean.

See "Selling Free Software" for more discussion of this issue.

Theft

Copyright apologists often use words like "stolen" and "theft" to describe copyright infringement. At the same time, they ask us to treat the legal system as an authority on ethics: if copying is forbidden, it must be wrong.

So it is pertinent to mention that the legal system—at least in the U.S.—rejects the idea that copyright infringement is "theft." Copyright apologists are making an appeal to authority. . .and misrepresenting what the authority says.

The idea that laws decide what is right or wrong is mistaken in general. Laws are, at their best, an attempt to achieve justice; to say that laws define justice or ethical conduct is turning things upside down.

Section Four

The Licenses

GNU General Public License

Version 2, June 1991
Copyright © 1989, 1991 Free Software Foundation, Inc.
59 Temple Place - Suite 330, Boston, MA 02111-1307, USA

Preamble

The licenses for most software are designed to take away your freedom to share
and change it. By contrast, the GNU General Public License is intended to guarantee your freedom to share and change free software—to make sure the software
is free for all its users. This General Public License applies to most of the Free
Software Foundation's software and to any other program whose authors commit
to using it. (Some other Free Software Foundation software is covered by the GNU
Library General Public License instead.) You can apply it to your programs, too.

When we speak of free software, we are referring to freedom, not price. Our
General Public Licenses are designed to make sure that you have the freedom to
distribute copies of free software (and charge for this service if you wish), that you
receive source code or can get it if you want it, that you can change the software or
use pieces of it in new free programs; and that you know you can do these things.

To protect your rights, we need to make restrictions that forbid anyone to deny
you these rights or to ask you to surrender the rights. These restrictions translate
to certain responsibilities for you if you distribute copies of the software, or if you
modify it.

For example, if you distribute copies of such a program, whether gratis or for a
fee, you must give the recipients all the rights that you have. You must make sure
that they, too, receive or can get the source code. And you must show them these
terms so they know their rights.

We protect your rights with two steps: (1) copyright the software, and (2) offer
you this license which gives you legal permission to copy, distribute and/or modify
the software.

Also, for each author's protection and ours, we want to make certain that everyone understands that there is no warranty for this free software. If the software is
modified by someone else and passed on, we want its recipients to know that what
they have is not the original, so that any problems introduced by others will not
reflect on the original authors' reputations.

Finally, any free program is threatened constantly by software patents. We wish
to avoid the danger that redistributors of a free program will individually obtain
patent licenses, in effect making the program proprietary. To prevent this, we have
made it clear that any patent must be licensed for everyone's free use or not licensed
at all.

The precise terms and conditions for copying, distribution and modification follow.

TERMS AND CONDITIONS FOR COPYING, DISTRIBUTION AND MODIFICATION

0. This License applies to any program or other work which contains a notice placed by the copyright holder saying it may be distributed under the terms of this General Public License. The "Program", below, refers to any such program or work, and a "work based on the Program" means either the Program or any derivative work under copyright law: that is to say, a work containing the Program or a portion of it, either verbatim or with modifications and/or translated into another language. (Hereinafter, translation is included without limitation in the term "modification".) Each licensee is addressed as "you".

   Activities other than copying, distribution and modification are not covered by this License; they are outside its scope. The act of running the Program is not restricted, and the output from the Program is covered only if its contents constitute a work based on the Program (independent of having been made by running the Program). Whether that is true depends on what the Program does.

1. You may copy and distribute verbatim copies of the Program's source code as you receive it, in any medium, provided that you conspicuously and appropriately publish on each copy an appropriate copyright notice and disclaimer of warranty; keep intact all the notices that refer to this License and to the absence of any warranty; and give any other recipients of the Program a copy of this License along with the Program.

   You may charge a fee for the physical act of transferring a copy, and you may at your option offer warranty protection in exchange for a fee.

2. You may modify your copy or copies of the Program or any portion of it, thus forming a work based on the Program, and copy and distribute such modifications or work under the terms of Section 1 above, provided that you also meet all of these conditions:

   a. You must cause the modified files to carry prominent notices stating that you changed the files and the date of any change.

   b. You must cause any work that you distribute or publish, that in whole or in part contains or is derived from the Program or any part thereof, to be licensed as a whole at no charge to all third parties under the terms of this License.

   c. If the modified program normally reads commands interactively when run, you must cause it, when started running for such interactive use in the most ordinary way, to print or display an announcement including an appropriate copyright notice and a notice that there is no warranty (or else, saying that you provide a warranty) and that users may redistribute the program under these conditions, and telling the user how to view a copy of this License. (Exception: if the Program itself is interactive but does not normally print such an announcement, your work based on the Program is not required to print an announcement.)

These requirements apply to the modified work as a whole. If identifiable sections of that work are not derived from the Program, and can be reasonably considered independent and separate works in themselves, then this License, and its terms, do not apply to those sections when you distribute them as separate works. But when you distribute the same sections as part of a whole which is a work based on the Program, the distribution of the whole must be on the terms of this License, whose permissions for other licensees extend to the entire whole, and thus to each and every part regardless of who wrote it.

Thus, it is not the intent of this section to claim rights or contest your rights to work written entirely by you; rather, the intent is to exercise the right to control the distribution of derivative or collective works based on the Program.

In addition, mere aggregation of another work not based on the Program with the Program (or with a work based on the Program) on a volume of a storage or distribution medium does not bring the other work under the scope of this License.

3. You may copy and distribute the Program (or a work based on it, under Section 2) in object code or executable form under the terms of Sections 1 and 2 above provided that you also do one of the following:

    a. Accompany it with the complete corresponding machine-readable source code, which must be distributed under the terms of Sections 1 and 2 above on a medium customarily used for software interchange; or,

    b. Accompany it with a written offer, valid for at least three years, to give any third party, for a charge no more than your cost of physically performing source distribution, a complete machine-readable copy of the corresponding source code, to be distributed under the terms of Sections 1 and 2 above on a medium customarily used for software interchange; or,

    c. Accompany it with the information you received as to the offer to distribute corresponding source code. (This alternative is allowed only for noncommercial distribution and only if you received the program in object code or executable form with such an offer, in accord with Subsection b above.)

The source code for a work means the preferred form of the work for making modifications to it. For an executable work, complete source code means all the source code for all modules it contains, plus any associated interface definition files, plus the scripts used to control compilation and installation of the executable. However, as a special exception, the source code distributed need not include anything that is normally distributed (in either source or binary form) with the major components (compiler, kernel, and so on) of the operating system on which the executable runs, unless that component itself accompanies the executable.

If distribution of executable or object code is made by offering access to copy from a designated place, then offering equivalent access to copy the source code from the same place counts as distribution of the source code, even though third parties are not compelled to copy the source along with the object code.

4. You may not copy, modify, sublicense, or distribute the Program except as expressly provided under this License. Any attempt otherwise to copy, modify, sublicense or distribute the Program is void, and will automatically terminate your rights under this License. However, parties who have received copies, or rights, from you under this License will not have their licenses terminated so long as such parties remain in full compliance.

5. You are not required to accept this License, since you have not signed it. However, nothing else grants you permission to modify or distribute the Program or its derivative works. These actions are prohibited by law if you do not accept this License. Therefore, by modifying or distributing the Program (or any work based on the Program), you indicate your acceptance of this License to do so, and all its terms and conditions for copying, distributing or modifying the Program or works based on it.

6. Each time you redistribute the Program (or any work based on the Program), the recipient automatically receives a license from the original licensor to copy, distribute or modify the Program subject to these terms and conditions. You may not impose any further restrictions on the recipients' exercise of the rights granted herein. You are not responsible for enforcing compliance by third parties to this License.

7. If, as a consequence of a court judgment or allegation of patent infringement or for any other reason (not limited to patent issues), conditions are imposed on you (whether by court order, agreement or otherwise) that contradict the conditions of this License, they do not excuse you from the conditions of this License. If you cannot distribute so as to satisfy simultaneously your obligations under this License and any other pertinent obligations, then as a consequence you may not distribute the Program at all. For example, if a patent license would not permit royalty-free redistribution of the Program by all those who receive copies directly or indirectly through you, then the only way you could satisfy both it and this License would be to refrain entirely from distribution of the Program.

If any portion of this section is held invalid or unenforceable under any particular circumstance, the balance of the section is intended to apply and the section as a whole is intended to apply in other circumstances.

It is not the purpose of this section to induce you to infringe any patents or other property right claims or to contest validity of any such claims; this section has the sole purpose of protecting the integrity of the free software distribution system, which is implemented by public license practices. Many people have made generous contributions to the wide range of software distributed through that system in reliance on consistent application of that system; it is up to the author/donor to decide if he or she is willing to distribute software through any other system and a licensee cannot impose that choice.

This section is intended to make thoroughly clear what is believed to be a consequence of the rest of this License.

8. If the distribution and/or use of the Program is restricted in certain countries either by patents or by copyrighted interfaces, the original copyright holder who places the Program under this License may add an explicit geographical distribution limitation excluding those countries, so that distribution is permitted only in or among countries not thus excluded. In such case, this License incorporates the limitation as if written in the body of this License.

9. The Free Software Foundation may publish revised and/or new versions of the General Public License from time to time. Such new versions will be similar in spirit to the present version, but may differ in detail to address new problems or concerns.

    Each version is given a distinguishing version number. If the Program specifies a version number of this License which applies to it and "any later version", you have the option of following the terms and conditions either of that version or of any later version published by the Free Software Foundation. If the Program does not specify a version number of this License, you may choose any version ever published by the Free Software Foundation.

10. If you wish to incorporate parts of the Program into other free programs whose distribution conditions are different, write to the author to ask for permission. For software which is copyrighted by the Free Software Foundation, write to the Free Software Foundation; we sometimes make exceptions for this. Our decision will be guided by the two goals of preserving the free status of all derivatives of our free software and of promoting the sharing and reuse of software generally.

NO WARRANTY

11. BECAUSE THE PROGRAM IS LICENSED FREE OF CHARGE, THERE IS NO WARRANTY FOR THE PROGRAM, TO THE EXTENT PERMITTED BY APPLICABLE LAW. EXCEPT WHEN OTHERWISE STATED IN WRITING THE COPYRIGHT HOLDERS AND/OR OTHER PARTIES PROVIDE THE PROGRAM "AS IS" WITHOUT WARRANTY OF ANY KIND, EITHER EXPRESSED OR IMPLIED, INCLUDING, BUT NOT LIMITED TO, THE IMPLIED WARRANTIES OF MERCHANTABILITY AND FITNESS FOR A PARTICULAR PURPOSE. THE ENTIRE RISK AS TO THE QUALITY AND PERFORMANCE OF THE PROGRAM IS WITH YOU. SHOULD THE PROGRAM PROVE DEFECTIVE, YOU ASSUME THE COST OF ALL NECESSARY SERVICING, REPAIR OR CORRECTION.

12. IN NO EVENT UNLESS REQUIRED BY APPLICABLE LAW OR AGREED TO IN WRITING WILL ANY COPYRIGHT HOLDER, OR ANY OTHER PARTY WHO MAY MODIFY AND/OR REDISTRIBUTE THE PROGRAM AS PERMITTED ABOVE, BE LIABLE TO YOU FOR DAMAGES, INCLUDING ANY GENERAL, SPECIAL, INCIDENTAL OR CONSEQUENTIAL DAMAGES ARISING OUT OF THE USE OR INABILITY TO USE THE PROGRAM (INCLUDING BUT NOT LIMITED

TO LOSS OF DATA OR DATA BEING RENDERED INACCURATE OR LOSSES SUSTAINED BY YOU OR THIRD PARTIES OR A FAILURE OF THE PROGRAM TO OPERATE WITH ANY OTHER PROGRAMS), EVEN IF SUCH HOLDER OR OTHER PARTY HAS BEEN ADVISED OF THE POSSIBILITY OF SUCH DAMAGES.

END OF TERMS AND CONDITIONS

Appendix: How to Apply These Terms to Your New Programs

If you develop a new program, and you want it to be of the greatest possible use to the public, the best way to achieve this is to make it free software which everyone can redistribute and change under these terms.

To do so, attach the following notices to the program. It is safest to attach them to the start of each source file to most effectively convey the exclusion of warranty; and each file should have at least the "copyright" line and a pointer to where the full notice is found.

    one line to give the program's name and a brief idea of what it does.
    Copyright (C) yyyy   name of author

    This program is free software; you can redistribute it and/or modify
    it under the terms of the GNU General Public License as published by
    the Free Software Foundation; either version 2 of the License, or
    (at your option) any later version.

    This program is distributed in the hope that it will be useful,
    but WITHOUT ANY WARRANTY; without even the implied warranty of
    MERCHANTABILITY or FITNESS FOR A PARTICULAR PURPOSE. See the
    GNU General Public License for more details.

    You should have received a copy of the GNU General Public License
    along with this program; if not, write to the Free Software
    Foundation, Inc.,
    59 Temple Place - Suite 330, Boston, MA 02111-1307, USA.

Also add information on how to contact you by electronic and paper mail.

If the program is interactive, make it output a short notice like this when it starts in an interactive mode:

    Gnomovision version 69, Copyright (C) 19yy name of author
    Gnomovision comes with ABSOLUTELY NO WARRANTY; for details type 'show w'.
    This is free software, and you are welcome to redistribute it
    under certain conditions; type 'show c' for details.

The hypothetical commands 'show w' and 'show c' should show the appropriate parts of the General Public License. Of course, the commands you use may be called something other than 'show w' and 'show c'; they could even be mouse-clicks or menu items—whatever suits your program.

You should also get your employer (if you work as a programmer) or your school, if any, to sign a "copyright disclaimer" for the program, if necessary. Here is a sample; alter the names:

    Yoyodyne, Inc., hereby disclaims all copyright interest in
    the program 'Gnomovision' (which makes passes at compilers)
    written by James Hacker.

signature of Ty Coon, 1 April 1989

Ty Coon, President of Vice

This General Public License does not permit incorporating your program into proprietary programs. If your program is a subroutine library, you may consider it more useful to permit linking proprietary applications with the library. If this is what you want to do, use the GNU Library General Public License instead of this License.

GNU Lesser General Public License

Version 2.1, February 1999
Copyright © 1991, 1999 Free Software Foundation, Inc.
59 Temple Place – Suite 330, Boston, MA 02111-1307, USA

Everyone is permitted to copy and distribute verbatim copies
of this license document, but changing it is not allowed.

[This is the first released version of the Lesser GPL. It also counts
as the successor of the GNU Library Public License, version 2, hence the
version number 2.1.]

Preamble

The licenses for most software are designed to take away your freedom to share
and change it. By contrast, the GNU General Public Licenses are intended to guarantee your freedom to share and change free software—to make sure the software
is free for all its users.

This license, the Lesser General Public License, applies to some specially designated software—typically libraries—of the Free Software Foundation and other
authors who decide to use it. You can use it too, but we suggest you first think
carefully about whether this license or the ordinary General Public License is the
better strategy to use in any particular case, based on the explanations below.

When we speak of free software, we are referring to freedom of use, not price.
Our General Public Licenses are designed to make sure that you have the freedom
to distribute copies of free software (and charge for this service if you wish); that
you receive source code or can get it if you want it; that you can change the software
and use pieces of it in new free programs; and that you are informed that you can
do these things.

To protect your rights, we need to make restrictions that forbid distributors to
deny you these rights or to ask you to surrender these rights. These restrictions
translate to certain responsibilities for you if you distribute copies of the library or
if you modify it.

For example, if you distribute copies of the library, whether gratis or for a fee,
you must give the recipients all the rights that we gave you. You must make sure
that they, too, receive or can get the source code. If you link other code with the
library, you must provide complete object files to the recipients, so that they can
relink them with the library after making changes to the library and recompiling it.
And you must show them these terms so they know their rights.

We protect your rights with a two-step method: (1) we copyright the library, and
(2) we offer you this license, which gives you legal permission to copy, distribute
and/or modify the library.

To protect each distributor, we want to make it very clear that there is no warranty
for the free library. Also, if the library is modified by someone else and passed
on, the recipients should know that what they have is not the original version, so

that the original author's reputation will not be affected by problems that might be introduced by others.

Finally, software patents pose a constant threat to the existence of any free program. We wish to make sure that a company cannot effectively restrict the users of a free program by obtaining a restrictive license from a patent holder. Therefore, we insist that any patent license obtained for a version of the library must be consistent with the full freedom of use specified in this license.

Most GNU software, including some libraries, is covered by the ordinary GNU General Public License. This license, the GNU Lesser General Public License, applies to certain designated libraries, and is quite different from the ordinary General Public License. We use this license for certain libraries in order to permit linking those libraries into non-free programs.

When a program is linked with a library, whether statically or using a shared library, the combination of the two is legally speaking a combined work, a derivative of the original library. The ordinary General Public License therefore permits such linking only if the entire combination fits its criteria of freedom. The Lesser General Public License permits more lax criteria for linking other code with the library.

We call this license the *Lesser* General Public License because it does *Less* to protect the user's freedom than the ordinary General Public License. It also provides other free software developers Less of an advantage over competing non-free programs. These disadvantages are the reason we use the ordinary General Public License for many libraries. However, the Lesser license provides advantages in certain special circumstances.

For example, on rare occasions, there may be a special need to encourage the widest possible use of a certain library, so that it becomes a de-facto standard. To achieve this, non-free programs must be allowed to use the library. A more frequent case is that a free library does the same job as widely used non-free libraries. In this case, there is little to gain by limiting the free library to free software only, so we use the Lesser General Public License.

In other cases, permission to use a particular library in non-free programs enables a greater number of people to use a large body of free software. For example, permission to use the GNU C Library in non-free programs enables many more people to use the whole GNU operating system, as well as its variant, the GNU/Linux operating system.

Although the Lesser General Public License is Less protective of the users' freedom, it does ensure that the user of a program that is linked with the Library has the freedom and the wherewithal to run that program using a modified version of the Library.

The precise terms and conditions for copying, distribution and modification follow. Pay close attention to the difference between a "work based on the library" and a "work that uses the library". The former contains code derived from the library, whereas the latter must be combined with the library in order to run.

TERMS AND CONDITIONS FOR COPYING, DISTRIBUTION AND MODIFICATION

0. This License Agreement applies to any software library or other program which contains a notice placed by the copyright holder or other authorized party saying it may be distributed under the terms of this Lesser General Public License (also called "this License"). Each licensee is addressed as "you".

   A "library" means a collection of software functions and/or data prepared so as to be conveniently linked with application programs (which use some of those functions and data) to form executables.

   The "Library", below, refers to any such software library or work which has been distributed under these terms. A "work based on the Library" means either the Library or any derivative work under copyright law: that is to say, a work containing the Library or a portion of it, either verbatim or with modifications and/or translated straightforwardly into another language. (Hereinafter, translation is included without limitation in the term "modification".)

   "Source code" for a work means the preferred form of the work for making modifications to it. For a library, complete source code means all the source code for all modules it contains, plus any associated interface definition files, plus the scripts used to control compilation and installation of the library.

   Activities other than copying, distribution and modification are not covered by this License; they are outside its scope. The act of running a program using the Library is not restricted, and output from such a program is covered only if its contents constitute a work based on the Library (independent of the use of the Library in a tool for writing it). Whether that is true depends on what the Library does and what the program that uses the Library does.

1. You may copy and distribute verbatim copies of the Library's complete source code as you receive it, in any medium, provided that you conspicuously and appropriately publish on each copy an appropriate copyright notice and disclaimer of warranty; keep intact all the notices that refer to this License and to the absence of any warranty; and distribute a copy of this License along with the Library.

   You may charge a fee for the physical act of transferring a copy, and you may at your option offer warranty protection in exchange for a fee.

2. You may modify your copy or copies of the Library or any portion of it, thus forming a work based on the Library, and copy and distribute such modifications or work under the terms of Section 1 above, provided that you also meet all of these conditions:

   a. The modified work must itself be a software library.

   b. You must cause the files modified to carry prominent notices stating that you changed the files and the date of any change.

   c. You must cause the whole of the work to be licensed at no charge to all third parties under the terms of this License.

d. If a facility in the modified Library refers to a function or a table of data to be supplied by an application program that uses the facility, other than as an argument passed when the facility is invoked, then you must make a good faith effort to ensure that, in the event an application does not supply such function or table, the facility still operates, and performs whatever part of its purpose remains meaningful.

(For example, a function in a library to compute square roots has a purpose that is entirely well-defined independent of the application. Therefore, Subsection 2d requires that any application-supplied function or table used by this function must be optional: if the application does not supply it, the square root function must still compute square roots.)

These requirements apply to the modified work as a whole. If identifiable sections of that work are not derived from the Library, and can be reasonably considered independent and separate works in themselves, then this License, and its terms, do not apply to those sections when you distribute them as separate works. But when you distribute the same sections as part of a whole which is a work based on the Library, the distribution of the whole must be on the terms of this License, whose permissions for other licensees extend to the entire whole, and thus to each and every part regardless of who wrote it.

Thus, it is not the intent of this section to claim rights or contest your rights to work written entirely by you; rather, the intent is to exercise the right to control the distribution of derivative or collective works based on the Library.

In addition, mere aggregation of another work not based on the Library with the Library (or with a work based on the Library) on a volume of a storage or distribution medium does not bring the other work under the scope of this License.

3. You may opt to apply the terms of the ordinary GNU General Public License instead of this License to a given copy of the Library. To do this, you must alter all the notices that refer to this License, so that they refer to the ordinary GNU General Public License, version 2, instead of to this License. (If a newer version than version 2 of the ordinary GNU General Public License has appeared, then you can specify that version instead if you wish.) Do not make any other change in these notices.

Once this change is made in a given copy, it is irreversible for that copy, so the ordinary GNU General Public License applies to all subsequent copies and derivative works made from that copy.

This option is useful when you wish to copy part of the code of the Library into a program that is not a library.

4. You may copy and distribute the Library (or a portion or derivative of it, under Section 2) in object code or executable form under the terms of Sections 1 and 2 above provided that you accompany it with the complete corresponding machine-readable source code, which must be distributed under the terms of Sections 1 and 2 above on a medium customarily used for software interchange.

If distribution of object code is made by offering access to copy from a designated place, then offering equivalent access to copy the source code from the same place satisfies the requirement to distribute the source code, even though third parties are not compelled to copy the source along with the object code.

5. A program that contains no derivative of any portion of the Library, but is designed to work with the Library by being compiled or linked with it, is called a "work that uses the Library". Such a work, in isolation, is not a derivative work of the Library, and therefore falls outside the scope of this License.

However, linking a "work that uses the Library" with the Library creates an executable that is a derivative of the Library (because it contains portions of the Library), rather than a "work that uses the library". The executable is therefore covered by this License. Section 6 states terms for distribution of such executables.

When a "work that uses the Library" uses material from a header file that is part of the Library, the object code for the work may be a derivative work of the Library even though the source code is not. Whether this is true is especially significant if the work can be linked without the Library, or if the work is itself a library. The threshold for this to be true is not precisely defined by law.

If such an object file uses only numerical parameters, data structure layouts and accessors, and small macros and small inline functions (ten lines or less in length), then the use of the object file is unrestricted, regardless of whether it is legally a derivative work. (Executables containing this object code plus portions of the Library will still fall under Section 6.)

Otherwise, if the work is a derivative of the Library, you may distribute the object code for the work under the terms of Section 6. Any executables containing that work also fall under Section 6, whether or not they are linked directly with the Library itself.

6. As an exception to the Sections above, you may also combine or link a "work that uses the Library" with the Library to produce a work containing portions of the Library, and distribute that work under terms of your choice, provided that the terms permit modification of the work for the customer's own use and reverse engineering for debugging such modifications.

You must give prominent notice with each copy of the work that the Library is used in it and that the Library and its use are covered by this License. You must supply a copy of this License. If the work during execution displays copyright notices, you must include the copyright notice for the Library among them, as well as a reference directing the user to the copy of this License. Also, you must do one of these things:

a. Accompany the work with the complete corresponding machine-readable source code for the Library including whatever changes were used in the work (which must be distributed under Sections 1 and 2 above); and, if the work is an executable linked with the Library, with the complete machine-readable "work that uses the Library", as object code and/or source code, so that the user can modify the Library and then relink to produce a modified executable containing the modified Library. (It is understood that the user who changes the contents of definitions files in the Library will not necessarily be able to recompile the application to use the modified definitions.)

b. Use a suitable shared library mechanism for linking with the Library. A suitable mechanism is one that (1) uses at run time a copy of the library already present on the user's computer system, rather than copying library functions into the executable, and (2) will operate properly with a modified version of the library, if the user installs one, as long as the modified version is interface-compatible with the version that the work was made with.

c. Accompany the work with a written offer, valid for at least three years, to give the same user the materials specified in Subsection 6a, above, for a charge no more than the cost of performing this distribution.

d. If distribution of the work is made by offering access to copy from a designated place, offer equivalent access to copy the above specified materials from the same place.

e. Verify that the user has already received a copy of these materials or that you have already sent this user a copy.

For an executable, the required form of the "work that uses the Library" must include any data and utility programs needed for reproducing the executable from it. However, as a special exception, the materials to be distributed need not include anything that is normally distributed (in either source or binary form) with the major components (compiler, kernel, and so on) of the operating system on which the executable runs, unless that component itself accompanies the executable.

It may happen that this requirement contradicts the license restrictions of other proprietary libraries that do not normally accompany the operating system. Such a contradiction means you cannot use both them and the Library together in an executable that you distribute.

7. You may place library facilities that are a work based on the Library side-by-side in a single library together with other library facilities not covered by this License, and distribute such a combined library, provided that the separate distribution of the work based on the Library and of the other library facilities is otherwise permitted, and provided that you do these two things:

a. Accompany the combined library with a copy of the same work based on the Library, uncombined with any other library facilities. This must be distributed under the terms of the Sections above.

b. Give prominent notice with the combined library of the fact that part of it is a work based on the Library, and explaining where to find the accompanying uncombined form of the same work.

8. You may not copy, modify, sublicense, link with, or distribute the Library except as expressly provided under this License. Any attempt otherwise to

copy, modify, sublicense, link with, or distribute the Library is void, and will automatically terminate your rights under this License. However, parties who have received copies, or rights, from you under this License will not have their licenses terminated so long as such parties remain in full compliance.

9. You are not required to accept this License, since you have not signed it. However, nothing else grants you permission to modify or distribute the Library or its derivative works. These actions are prohibited by law if you do not accept this License. Therefore, by modifying or distributing the Library (or any work based on the Library), you indicate your acceptance of this License to do so, and all its terms and conditions for copying, distributing or modifying the Library or works based on it.

10. Each time you redistribute the Library (or any work based on the Library), the recipient automatically receives a license from the original licensor to copy, distribute, link with or modify the Library subject to these terms and conditions. You may not impose any further restrictions on the recipients' exercise of the rights granted herein. You are not responsible for enforcing compliance by third parties with this License.

11. If, as a consequence of a court judgment or allegation of patent infringement or for any other reason (not limited to patent issues), conditions are imposed on you (whether by court order, agreement or otherwise) that contradict the conditions of this License, they do not excuse you from the conditions of this License. If you cannot distribute so as to satisfy simultaneously your obligations under this License and any other pertinent obligations, then as a consequence you may not distribute the Library at all. For example, if a patent license would not permit royalty-free redistribution of the Library by all those who receive copies directly or indirectly through you, then the only way you could satisfy both it and this License would be to refrain entirely from distribution of the Library.

If any portion of this section is held invalid or unenforceable under any particular circumstance, the balance of the section is intended to apply, and the section as a whole is intended to apply in other circumstances.

It is not the purpose of this section to induce you to infringe any patents or other property right claims or to contest validity of any such claims; this section has the sole purpose of protecting the integrity of the free software distribution system which is implemented by public license practices. Many people have made generous contributions to the wide range of software distributed through that system in reliance on consistent application of that system; it is up to the author/donor to decide if he or she is willing to distribute software through any other system and a licensee cannot impose that choice.

This section is intended to make thoroughly clear what is believed to be a consequence of the rest of this License.

12. If the distribution and/or use of the Library is restricted in certain countries either by patents or by copyrighted interfaces, the original copyright holder who places the Library under this License may add an explicit geographical

distribution limitation excluding those countries, so that distribution is permitted only in or among countries not thus excluded. In such case, this License incorporates the limitation as if written in the body of this License.

13. The Free Software Foundation may publish revised and/or new versions of the Lesser General Public License from time to time. Such new versions will be similar in spirit to the present version, but may differ in detail to address new problems or concerns.

   Each version is given a distinguishing version number. If the Library specifies a version number of this License which applies to it and "any later version", you have the option of following the terms and conditions either of that version or of any later version published by the Free Software Foundation. If the Library does not specify a license version number, you may choose any version ever published by the Free Software Foundation.

14. If you wish to incorporate parts of the Library into other free programs whose distribution conditions are incompatible with these, write to the author to ask for permission. For software which is copyrighted by the Free Software Foundation, write to the Free Software Foundation; we sometimes make exceptions for this. Our decision will be guided by the two goals of preserving the free status of all derivatives of our free software and of promoting the sharing and reuse of software generally.

NO WARRANTY

15. BECAUSE THE LIBRARY IS LICENSED FREE OF CHARGE, THERE IS NO WARRANTY FOR THE LIBRARY, TO THE EXTENT PERMITTED BY APPLICABLE LAW. EXCEPT WHEN OTHERWISE STATED IN WRITING THE COPYRIGHT HOLDERS AND/OR OTHER PARTIES PROVIDE THE LIBRARY "AS IS" WITHOUT WARRANTY OF ANY KIND, EITHER EXPRESSED OR IMPLIED, INCLUDING, BUT NOT LIMITED TO, THE IMPLIED WARRANTIES OF MERCHANTABILITY AND FITNESS FOR A PARTICULAR PURPOSE. THE ENTIRE RISK AS TO THE QUALITY AND PERFORMANCE OF THE LIBRARY IS WITH YOU. SHOULD THE LIBRARY PROVE DEFECTIVE, YOU ASSUME THE COST OF ALL NECESSARY SERVICING, REPAIR OR CORRECTION.

16. IN NO EVENT UNLESS REQUIRED BY APPLICABLE LAW OR AGREED TO IN WRITING WILL ANY COPYRIGHT HOLDER, OR ANY OTHER PARTY WHO MAY MODIFY AND/OR REDISTRIBUTE THE LIBRARY AS PERMITTED ABOVE, BE LIABLE TO YOU FOR DAMAGES, INCLUDING ANY GENERAL, SPECIAL, INCIDENTAL OR CONSEQUENTIAL DAMAGES ARISING OUT OF THE USE OR INABILITY TO USE THE LIBRARY (INCLUDING BUT NOT LIMITED TO LOSS OF DATA OR DATA BEING RENDERED INACCURATE OR LOSSES SUSTAINED BY YOU OR THIRD PARTIES OR A FAILURE OF THE LIBRARY TO OPERATE WITH ANY OTHER SOFTWARE), EVEN

IF SUCH HOLDER OR OTHER PARTY HAS BEEN ADVISED OF THE POSSIBILITY OF SUCH DAMAGES.

END OF TERMS AND CONDITIONS

How to Apply These Terms to Your New Libraries

If you develop a new library, and you want it to be of the greatest possible use to the public, we recommend making it free software that everyone can redistribute and change. You can do so by permitting redistribution under these terms (or, alternatively, under the terms of the ordinary General Public License).

To apply these terms, attach the following notices to the library. It is safest to attach them to the start of each source file to most effectively convey the exclusion of warranty; and each file should have at least the "copyright" line and a pointer to where the full notice is found.

one line to give the library's name and an idea of what it does.

```
Copyright (C) year   name of author
```

```
This library is free software; you can redistribute it and/or modify it
under the terms of the GNU Lesser General Public License as published by
the Free Software Foundation; either version 2.1 of the License, or (at
your option) any later version.
```

```
This library is distributed in the hope that it will be useful, but
WITHOUT ANY WARRANTY; without even the implied warranty of
MERCHANTABILITY or FITNESS FOR A PARTICULAR PURPOSE.  See the GNU
Lesser General Public License for more details.
```

```
You should have received a copy of the GNU Lesser General Public
License along with this library; if not, write to the Free Software
Foundation, Inc., 59 Temple Place, Suite 330, Boston, MA 02111-1307,
USA.
```

Also add information on how to contact you by electronic and paper mail.

You should also get your employer (if you work as a programmer) or your school, if any, to sign a "copyright disclaimer" for the library, if necessary. Here is a sample; alter the names:

```
Yoyodyne, Inc., hereby disclaims all copyright interest in the library
'Frob' (a library for tweaking knobs) written by James Random Hacker.
```

signature of Ty Coon, 1 April 1990

```
Ty Coon, President of Vice
```

That's all there is to it!

GNU Free Documentation License

Version 1.1, March 2000
Copyright © 2000 Free Software Foundation, Inc.
59 Temple Place, Suite 330, Boston, MA 02111-1307, USA

Everyone is permitted to copy and distribute verbatim copies
of this license document, but changing it is not allowed.

0. PREAMBLE

The purpose of this License is to make a manual, textbook, or other written
document *free* in the sense of freedom: to assure everyone the effective freedom to copy and redistribute it, with or without modifying it, either commercially or noncommercially. Secondarily, this License preserves for the author
and publisher a way to get credit for their work, while not being considered
responsible for modifications made by others.

This License is a kind of "copyleft", which means that derivative works of
the document must themselves be free in the same sense. It complements the
GNU General Public License, which is a copyleft license designed for free
software.

We have designed this License in order to use it for manuals for free software,
because free software needs free documentation: a free program should come
with manuals providing the same freedoms that the software does. But this
License is not limited to software manuals; it can be used for any textual work,
regardless of subject matter or whether it is published as a printed book. We
recommend this License principally for works whose purpose is instruction or
reference.

1. APPLICABILITY AND DEFINITIONS

This License applies to any manual or other work that contains a notice placed
by the copyright holder saying it can be distributed under the terms of this
License. The "Document", below, refers to any such manual or work. Any
member of the public is a licensee, and is addressed as "you".

A "Modified Version" of the Document means any work containing the Document or a portion of it, either copied verbatim, or with modifications and/or
translated into another language.

A "Secondary Section" is a named appendix or a front-matter section of the
Document that deals exclusively with the relationship of the publishers or authors of the Document to the Document's overall subject (or to related matters)
and contains nothing that could fall directly within that overall subject. (For
example, if the Document is in part a textbook of mathematics, a Secondary
Section may not explain any mathematics.) The relationship could be a matter
of historical connection with the subject or with related matters, or of legal,
commercial, philosophical, ethical or political position regarding them.

The "Invariant Sections" are certain Secondary Sections whose titles are designated, as being those of Invariant Sections, in the notice that says that the Document is released under this License.

The "Cover Texts" are certain short passages of text that are listed, as Front-Cover Texts or Back-Cover Texts, in the notice that says that the Document is released under this License.

A "Transparent" copy of the Document means a machine-readable copy, represented in a format whose specification is available to the general public, whose contents can be viewed and edited directly and straightforwardly with generic text editors or (for images composed of pixels) generic paint programs or (for drawings) some widely available drawing editor, and that is suitable for input to text formatters or for automatic translation to a variety of formats suitable for input to text formatters. A copy made in an otherwise Transparent file format whose markup has been designed to thwart or discourage subsequent modification by readers is not Transparent. A copy that is not "Transparent" is called "Opaque".

Examples of suitable formats for Transparent copies include plain ASCII without markup, Texinfo input format, LaTeX input format, SGML or XML using a publicly available DTD, and standard-conforming simple HTML designed for human modification. Opaque formats include PostScript, PDF, proprietary formats that can be read and edited only by proprietary word processors, SGML or XML for which the DTD and/or processing tools are not generally available, and the machine-generated HTML produced by some word processors for output purposes only.

The "Title Page" means, for a printed book, the title page itself, plus such following pages as are needed to hold, legibly, the material this License requires to appear in the title page. For works in formats which do not have any title page as such, "Title Page" means the text near the most prominent appearance of the work's title, preceding the beginning of the body of the text.

2. VERBATIM COPYING

You may copy and distribute the Document in any medium, either commercially or noncommercially, provided that this License, the copyright notices, and the license notice saying this License applies to the Document are reproduced in all copies, and that you add no other conditions whatsoever to those of this License. You may not use technical measures to obstruct or control the reading or further copying of the copies you make or distribute. However, you may accept compensation in exchange for copies. If you distribute a large enough number of copies you must also follow the conditions in section 3.

You may also lend copies, under the same conditions stated above, and you may publicly display copies.

3. COPYING IN QUANTITY

If you publish printed copies of the Document numbering more than 100, and the Document's license notice requires Cover Texts, you must enclose the copies in covers that carry, clearly and legibly, all these Cover Texts: Front-

Cover Texts on the front cover, and Back-Cover Texts on the back cover. Both covers must also clearly and legibly identify you as the publisher of these copies. The front cover must present the full title with all words of the title equally prominent and visible. You may add other material on the covers in addition. Copying with changes limited to the covers, as long as they preserve the title of the Document and satisfy these conditions, can be treated as verbatim copying in other respects.

If the required texts for either cover are too voluminous to fit legibly, you should put the first ones listed (as many as fit reasonably) on the actual cover, and continue the rest onto adjacent pages.

If you publish or distribute Opaque copies of the Document numbering more than 100, you must either include a machine-readable Transparent copy along with each Opaque copy, or state in or with each Opaque copy a publicly-accessible computer-network location containing a complete Transparent copy of the Document, free of added material, which the general network-using public has access to download anonymously at no charge using public-standard network protocols. If you use the latter option, you must take reasonably prudent steps, when you begin distribution of Opaque copies in quantity, to ensure that this Transparent copy will remain thus accessible at the stated location until at least one year after the last time you distribute an Opaque copy (directly or through your agents or retailers) of that edition to the public.

It is requested, but not required, that you contact the authors of the Document well before redistributing any large number of copies, to give them a chance to provide you with an updated version of the Document.

4. MODIFICATIONS

You may copy and distribute a Modified Version of the Document under the conditions of sections 2 and 3 above, provided that you release the Modified Version under precisely this License, with the Modified Version filling the role of the Document, thus licensing distribution and modification of the Modified Version to whoever possesses a copy of it. In addition, you must do these things in the Modified Version:

A. Use in the Title Page (and on the covers, if any) a title distinct from that of the Document, and from those of previous versions (which should, if there were any, be listed in the History section of the Document). You may use the same title as a previous version if the original publisher of that version gives permission.

B. List on the Title Page, as authors, one or more persons or entities responsible for authorship of the modifications in the Modified Version, together with at least five of the principal authors of the Document (all of its principal authors, if it has less than five).

C. State on the Title page the name of the publisher of the Modified Version, as the publisher.

D. Preserve all the copyright notices of the Document.

E. Add an appropriate copyright notice for your modifications adjacent to the other copyright notices.

F. Include, immediately after the copyright notices, a license notice giving the public permission to use the Modified Version under the terms of this License, in the form shown in the Addendum below.

G. Preserve in that license notice the full lists of Invariant Sections and required Cover Texts given in the Document's license notice.

H. Include an unaltered copy of this License.

I. Preserve the section entitled "History", and its title, and add to it an item stating at least the title, year, new authors, and publisher of the Modified Version as given on the Title Page. If there is no section entitled "History" in the Document, create one stating the title, year, authors, and publisher of the Document as given on its Title Page, then add an item describing the Modified Version as stated in the previous sentence.

J. Preserve the network location, if any, given in the Document for public access to a Transparent copy of the Document, and likewise the network locations given in the Document for previous versions it was based on. These may be placed in the "History" section. You may omit a network location for a work that was published at least four years before the Document itself, or if the original publisher of the version it refers to gives permission.

K. In any section entitled "Acknowledgments" or "Dedications", preserve the section's title, and preserve in the section all the substance and tone of each of the contributor acknowledgments and/or dedications given therein.

L. Preserve all the Invariant Sections of the Document, unaltered in their text and in their titles. Section numbers or the equivalent are not considered part of the section titles.

M. Delete any section entitled "Endorsements". Such a section may not be included in the Modified Version.

N. Do not retitle any existing section as "Endorsements" or to conflict in title with any Invariant Section.

If the Modified Version includes new front-matter sections or appendices that qualify as Secondary Sections and contain no material copied from the Document, you may at your option designate some or all of these sections as invariant. To do this, add their titles to the list of Invariant Sections in the Modified Version's license notice. These titles must be distinct from any other section titles.

You may add a section entitled "Endorsements", provided it contains nothing but endorsements of your Modified Version by various parties—for example, statements of peer review or that the text has been approved by an organization as the authoritative definition of a standard.

You may add a passage of up to five words as a Front-Cover Text, and a passage of up to 25 words as a Back-Cover Text, to the end of the list of Cover

Texts in the Modified Version. Only one passage of Front-Cover Text and one of Back-Cover Text may be added by (or through arrangements made by) any one entity. If the Document already includes a cover text for the same cover, previously added by you or by arrangement made by the same entity you are acting on behalf of, you may not add another; but you may replace the old one, on explicit permission from the previous publisher that added the old one.

The author(s) and publisher(s) of the Document do not by this License give permission to use their names for publicity for or to assert or imply endorsement of any Modified Version.

5. COMBINING DOCUMENTS

You may combine the Document with other documents released under this License, under the terms defined in section 4 above for modified versions, provided that you include in the combination all of the Invariant Sections of all of the original documents, unmodified, and list them all as Invariant Sections of your combined work in its license notice.

The combined work need only contain one copy of this License, and multiple identical Invariant Sections may be replaced with a single copy. If there are multiple Invariant Sections with the same name but different contents, make the title of each such section unique by adding at the end of it, in parentheses, the name of the original author or publisher of that section if known, or else a unique number. Make the same adjustment to the section titles in the list of Invariant Sections in the license notice of the combined work.

In the combination, you must combine any sections entitled "History" in the various original documents, forming one section entitled "History"; likewise combine any sections entitled "Acknowledgments", and any sections entitled "Dedications". You must delete all sections entitled "Endorsements."

6. COLLECTIONS OF DOCUMENTS

You may make a collection consisting of the Document and other documents released under this License, and replace the individual copies of this License in the various documents with a single copy that is included in the collection, provided that you follow the rules of this License for verbatim copying of each of the documents in all other respects.

You may extract a single document from such a collection, and distribute it individually under this License, provided you insert a copy of this License into the extracted document, and follow this License in all other respects regarding verbatim copying of that document.

7. AGGREGATION WITH INDEPENDENT WORKS

A compilation of the Document or its derivatives with other separate and independent documents or works, in or on a volume of a storage or distribution medium, does not as a whole count as a Modified Version of the Document, provided no compilation copyright is claimed for the compilation. Such a compilation is called an "aggregate", and this License does not apply to the other self-contained works thus compiled with the Document, on account of their being thus compiled, if they are not themselves derivative works of the Document.

If the Cover Text requirement of section 3 is applicable to these copies of the Document, then if the Document is less than one quarter of the entire aggregate, the Document's Cover Texts may be placed on covers that surround only the Document within the aggregate. Otherwise they must appear on covers around the whole aggregate.

8. TRANSLATION

Translation is considered a kind of modification, so you may distribute translations of the Document under the terms of section 4. Replacing Invariant Sections with translations requires special permission from their copyright holders, but you may include translations of some or all Invariant Sections in addition to the original versions of these Invariant Sections. You may include a translation of this License provided that you also include the original English version of this License. In case of a disagreement between the translation and the original English version of this License, the original English version will prevail.

9. TERMINATION

You may not copy, modify, sublicense, or distribute the Document except as expressly provided for under this License. Any other attempt to copy, modify, sublicense or distribute the Document is void, and will automatically terminate your rights under this License. However, parties who have received copies, or rights, from you under this License will not have their licenses terminated so long as such parties remain in full compliance.

10. FUTURE REVISIONS OF THIS LICENSE

The Free Software Foundation may publish new, revised versions of the GNU Free Documentation License from time to time. Such new versions will be similar in spirit to the present version, but may differ in detail to address new problems or concerns. See http://www.gnu.org/copyleft/.

Each version of the License is given a distinguishing version number. If the Document specifies that a particular numbered version of this License "or any later version" applies to it, you have the option of following the terms and conditions either of that specified version or of any later version that has been published (not as a draft) by the Free Software Foundation. If the Document does not specify a version number of this License, you may choose any version ever published (not as a draft) by the Free Software Foundation.

ADDENDUM: How to Use This License for Your Documents

To use this License in a document you have written, include a copy of the License in the document and put the following copyright and license notices just after the title page:

```
Copyright (C)  year  your name.
Permission is granted to copy, distribute and/or modify this document
under the terms of the GNU Free Documentation License, Version 1.1
or any later version published by the Free Software Foundation;
with the Invariant Sections being list their titles, with the
Front-Cover Texts being list, and with the Back-Cover Texts being list.
A copy of the license is included in the section entitled ''GNU
Free Documentation License''.
```

If you have no Invariant Sections, write "with no Invariant Sections" instead of saying which ones are invariant. If you have no Front-Cover Texts, write "no Front-Cover Texts" instead of "Front-Cover Texts being list"; likewise for Back-Cover Texts.

If your document contains nontrivial examples of program code, we recommend releasing these examples in parallel under your choice of free software license, such as the GNU General Public License, to permit their use in free software.

GNU C Language Related Manuals

GNU Make: A Program for
Directed Recompilation
by Richard M. Stallman
and Roland McGrath
1-882114-82-5, $20.00
January 2002, 196 Pages
Trade Paper, Lay Flat Binding
The GNU Make manual, written by the program's original authors, is the definitive tutorial. It also includes an introductory chapter for novice users.

The GNU C Library
Reference Manual
by S. Loosemore with Stallman, et al.
1275 Pages in Two Volumes
1-882114-54-X
$60.00 per 2-volume set
July 2001; For glibc version 2.2.x
Trade Paper, Lay Flat Binding
This manual is the canonical guide to the GNU implementation of the standard C libraries for system administrators and programmers. It covers high-and-low level interfaces, function specifications, code examples, usage recommendations.

Ninth Edition!
Debugging with GDB:
The GNU Source-Level Debugger
by Stallman, Pesch, Shebs, et al.
1-882114-88-4, $25.00
January 2002, 346 Pages
Trade Paper, Lay Flat Binding
Written for programmers by the principal author and maintainers of the GDB program. Designed so that readers can start using GDB after reading just the first chapter

Using & Porting GNU CC
by Richard M. Stallman
1-882114-38-8, $35.00
July 1999; for Ver. 2.95., 588 PagesTrade Paper, Lay Flat Binding
This thorough reference guide shows how to install, run, debug, configure and port the GNU Compiler Collection.